MLS

W9-ADU-916

PO 73590

5-14-01

Cork

Risk and Resilience

Risk and Resilience

Adults who were the children of problem drinkers

Richard Velleman and Jim Orford

harwood academic publishers

Australia • Canada • France • Germany • India • Japan
Luxembourg • Malaysia • The Netherlands • Russia • Singapore
Switzerland

Copyright © 1999 OPA (Overseas Publishers Association) N.V. Published by license under the Harwood Academic Publishers imprint, part of The Gordon and Breach Publishing Group.

First published 1999
Second printing 2000

Amsteldijk 166
1st Floor
1079 LH Amsterdam
The Netherlands

British Library Cataloguing in Publication Data

Velleman, Richard
    Risk and resilience : adults who were the children of
    problem drinkers
    1. Adult children of alcoholics – Statistics   2. Adult
    children of alcoholics – Psychology
    I. Title II. Orford, Jim
    362.2'92'3

    ISBN 90-5702-366-0

CONTENTS

LIST OF FIGURES

List of Figures

LIST OF TABLES

ACKNOWLEDGEMENTS

The research reported here was carried out under a grant from the Department of Health (UK) for whose support we are most grateful. We would like to acknowledge warmly the very considerable contribution made by the research interviewers, William Robertson, Helen Hutchinson, Cathy Austin and Laura Harris, and by Annette van Oppen who provided such able administrative support to the research team. Our greatest thanks, however, are extended to the participants in this research who gave so generously of their time to talk at length about very personal and often very painful matters.

Richard Velleman
Jim Orford

CHAPTER 1

GROWING UP WITH PARENTS WITH DRINKING PROBLEMS AND ESTABLISHING AN ADULT LIFE: FOUR ILLUSTRATIONS

This book is about young adults who grew up in families where a parent, and sometimes more than one, drank to an extent that caused problems for the families concerned. In this opening chapter four young women and men, who were participants in the research that we shall describe within this book, speak for themselves. We hope that in doing so the reader will gain an impression of the variation that is to be found amongst the recollections of childhood of people who have had parents with drinking problems, and the very varied patterns of adjustment that are displayed in young adulthood.

The four stories that follow have been selected to represent a range. They include, for example, the stories of both young women and men, of those with fathers and with mothers with drinking problems, those whose childhoods appear to have been seriously disturbed as a result and those less so, and those for whom transition to adulthood has been difficult and others for whom it has been apparently problem-free. Other than being selected to represent this range, they have been chosen at random from the project files. From our experience of interviewing over 160 young adults who had had parents with drinking problems, none of these four accounts is particularly unusual.

To preserve confidentiality the names used are fictional and many specific details have been changed. But in all essential respects these are real accounts.

ANNIE

Annie was approaching her mid-30s when she was interviewed for the project. Her father, who had died some years previously, had worked for many years as a manual worker after coming out of the armed services. He was a life-long heavy drinker and everyone knew that he drank. He went out drinking on Thursday and Friday nights and Saturday mornings and other nights too if he had the money. On Sundays he was irritable but never drank because of work the next day. On occasions when Annie and her mother would go to a pub with her father he would drink five or six pints of beer and a couple of whiskies which he said was moderate for him. In earlier years he drank much more. He was either drunk or completely sober.

When Annie was a teenager her father suffered from chronic stomach complaints and her mother made him go to the doctor. The latter never knew how much Annie's father drank and her father never admitted he had a drinking problem. The doctor advised him to stop drinking cider and prescribed tranquillisers to stop his shaking. After that her father confined his drinking to beer and barley wine for a number of years, but then went back onto cider again.

Annie's mother, who worked in a shop and also as a cleaner at a children's home, also had a drinking problem, Annie believes in retrospect, from about the time that Annie was aged 10. Her mother never admitted drinking was a problem, but Annie knows that she drank every day, getting through two litre bottles of sherry in a week. When her drinking was at its heaviest she was drinking up to a bottle every day, and would often drink at home and sometimes at work. Her mother also had bouts of depression which Annie describes as definitely being a problem. When Annie was about 15, these bouts were getting worse; by the time she was 18, her mother seemed to be drinking more and more at home and taking prescribed tablets too. At night she would take a sleeping pill and a few sherries before going to bed. At about this time her mother spent some time as a patient in a psychiatric hospital with depression.

There were financial difficulties throughout Annie's childhood and adolescence because of the money her father was spending on drink. She particularly noticed this when she went to grammar school at the age of 12. She realised that everything she had was always home-made, that she didn't have a school uniform, that she couldn't go on trips abroad, and that her parents didn't let her stay on to do 'A' levels for the same reason. She realised her family was, "different in every way".

When her father was drunk he was "disgusting" and Annie was "disgusted" with him. There were arguments between her parents several times a week. As a teenager she was aware that there was some violence; there were "a few black eyes" between her parents, on one occasion Annie was quite badly bruised herself, and on several occasions "it was pretty bad".

Despite this, Annie described her parents' relationship in mainly positive terms: "a very loving couple; very close; quite soppy over each other". Her mother had no life outside the family and "thought the world of" Annie's father when he was sober. According to Annie they made too many allowances and excuses for each other—her mother would try and get her father off to bed without an argument, and her father would encourage her mother to drink if she was depressed.

Annie herself was always very relieved if her father was not drinking and used to get terribly upset if he was. She would tell him that she hated him and wanted him to go away. She tried to get her mother to leave with her and her younger brother, but her mother said she still loved him. Annie got into arguments with her father because she was so disgusted.

Although Annie recalls her father as a man who could be very kind on occasions, and with whom there were "some very jolly" occasions on Saturday afternoons after the pub, there were too many "bad things", not much sense of a family life, few shared activities and not much closeness. But at the time of the interview, Annie described herself as having a hot temper like her father and being, like him, "conscientious, a bit of a perfectionist". She thought she was more like her father than her mother.

Annie described her mother as "a very good mother, very likeable person", and someone she had a positive relationship with until her mid-teens when her relationship with her mother appeared to have deteriorated. She was always cross and irritable and a bit soft, and Annie was never able to confide in her. Things got worse as Annie became more acutely aware of the difference between her family and others when she went to grammar school and also because her mother's depression was worsening.

Up to the age of 11, Annie described herself as having been shy but having friends including a "best friend". When she started at grammar school and became aware that her home was inferior, she developed a lack of confidence. She had no one friend in particular, and thinks that she felt "quite lonely". In her mid-teens she developed closer friendships, in particular one with a friend who lived quite near but who was "better off" and from whom Annie would conceal her father's drinking. She didn't like to bring friends home "in case", and when her best friend was round Annie would be in a "terrible state", wanting her to go before her father came home. Mostly, she didn't want friends to come round at all, or even to know where she lived.

As a teenager, Annie got more and more timid, was "always unwell", and was forever being taken to the doctor by her mother for "a bottle of tonic". She remembers getting very shaky—for example she couldn't lift a spoon easily—and at 16 she had what she describes as "a nervous break-down" and stayed in a psychiatric hospital some months. After getting over the initial shock of this she says she felt quite happy there, although it didn't get to the root of the problem and she couldn't see the sense of the treatment she was receiving. Looking back, Annie says she thinks she suf-fered from anxiety and depression from about the age of 13 until her early 30s, feeling "ill at ease, getting in a state, shaky".

At the time of the research interview, Annie was married with two young children, and was stably employed as a domestic assistant in a chil-dren's home, sometimes doing relief care work when someone else was away. She also had shorthand and typing qualifications. She left home at the age of 22 to share a flat with women friends with whom she still keeps up contact. She enjoyed her job—the place, the rest of the staff, the chil-dren and being able to help them. She said she made friends easily and currently had a lot of friends—mainly women living nearby with young children—including a number of good, close friends.

Annie's adult years had not been without their problems. In the early years of her marriage she had further periods as a psychiatric hospital in-patient and had been off work for several months with depression, once after her first child was born. Even now Annie was dissatisfied with herself, particularly with her lack of confidence and proneness to worrying and anxiety. She felt she had never been a "very open sort of person, I don't always feel at ease; but I'm working on it". At times she would find herself feeling extremely anxious and uncomfortable. Although she liked her work, she felt very self-conscious there, on her own in front of people. At one point recently she had felt she couldn't cope with work and had phoned in to give in her notice. The woman she worked for had persuaded her to change her mind which had been important to Annie—feeling that she had got over it and that someone else had thought she was important. On a checklist of recent problems, Annie checked quite a long list as 'regular' and 'major' problems, including feeling panicky, worrying and feeling depressed, anxious, shyness, lack of confidence and phobias. The interviewer noted that Annie's closest friendships were with other women who were quiet and unconfident and with whom she could talk over mutual problems of this kind.

Annie had married nearly 10 years previously and now says that her marriage was "dreadful" at first. She had had her own periods of hospitali-sation and there had been continued problems with her parents—eventu-ally her husband had not wanted anything to do with them. Over the past four or five years, however, things had gradually got much better. She thought she and her husband were now "very happy", and it was getting better all the time. They got on well together and didn't argue anymore. She confided in him about many things, discussed her feelings "from time to time", but she didn't talk to him about "silly little things like feeling awkward at work". She described her husband as "very easygoing", and this had influenced her towards the realisation that she had to live her own life—"he's got a don't care attitude, it's gradually influencing me". At the end of the interview, however, the interviewer recorded her impression that Annie and her husband were not particularly happy and that the relationship wasn't all that close.

Annie had been a moderate drinker in her teens and early 20s, but in her late 20s had had two periods of three or four months when she would buy sherry because she was depressed, and would drink two bottles a week on her own. She saw this as a problem. For the last five or six years she had returned to being a moderate drinker and felt she was now in no danger. In the week preceding the first interview she reported consuming eight units, and in the week before the second interview, 14, which she said was a bit lighter than usual. How much she drank depended she said on how relaxed she was to start with: she would drink before going to a party, for example, in order to relax herself. Her husband had not liked it when she had been drinking more heavily, and it had also given Annie a lower opinion of herself. Regarding the influence of her family background, Annie said, "I can never understand why it didn't put me off drinking. It's not something I'd really thought about. I wouldn't like to let myself in for the sort of family atmosphere I had". Her parents, she said, thought it was really marvellous to have a drink and to get quite merry. They could see no harm in it at all, in fact they encouraged it, they wanted everyone to be like them.

Annie had taken tranquillisers or anti-depressants continually from late teens to early 30s, and sleeping pills off and on during the same time. Stopping taking pills had been "very traumatic" and it had taken her a long time to adjust. By the time of the second interview Annie had taken no psychoactive drugs or medication during the previous year, but had been taking Paracetamol about every other day for headaches.

Annie said that the past had been "so terrible" that she didn't like to think back more than four or five years. But during that time things had gradually got much better and she was now happy enough with what she had in the way of family life and friends, although still dissatisfied with what she had achieved in her job. She also wished she didn't have "all these hang-ups". She thought of the future in terms of her children going to school, her having more free time, and being able to do the job she wanted to do—"I'm optimistic—I feel I've got every reason to be optimistic after having such a bad time in the past".

JOHN

In his late 20s when he took part in the research, John described his father as having drinking and emotional problems throughout his childhood, problems which John attributed to his paternal grandfather's excessive drinking and violence. The worst problems for John and his family were when his father had been both drinking and in a bad mood: he would get very irrational, and become verbally, emotionally and physically very violent. According to John he would rant and rave for hours. John described his father as paranoid, stubborn and arrogant, and inadequate.

John knew that his father nearly always drank a pint of whisky or more each day. "The drinking was constant, the central core of his social activities", and overlapping considerably with his business.

Although John recalled his parents showing some warmth and love to each other when he was young, he felt that this was more from his mother. Essentially he described his parents' relationship as "really very bad, extremely traumatic". There would be terrific rows every approximately three weeks, followed by several days of tension and not speaking. Conflicts were never resolved and their social life was all "pure performance". John believed that his parents stayed together partly because they liked the roles of persecutor and victim. His father had relationships with other women as far back as John's memory stretched. John's parents separated briefly when he was a young child, and finally separated at the time he left home to go to university.

John's father was regularly violent towards him, hitting him with sticks and canes, kicking him—a "regime of terror" as John described it. Both John and his mother had been hospitalised following attacks. When John was 16 he "lost his head" and attacked his father, which finally put a stop to his father's violence towards him. John described himself as stubborn like his father and hence resented his father getting away with unreasonable moods and "ranting on", so eventually he felt he had to try and stop him.

John would be very tense and anxious if his father was drinking heavily and in a bad mood. A sense of insecurity pervaded the family atmosphere most of the time, and John felt a great difference between his own and his friends' families, and also between the family life that they had to appear to lead, and that which in fact was occurring. Holidays were very uncomfortable, invariably involving awful scenes. John's father had no treatment for his drinking until several years after John left home, but at about the time John was starting university his father was eventually referred for treatment after threatening to kill himself.

John respected his father's intelligence, but his feelings for him were largely negative. At the age of about 14 or 15 he decided he had to try and make something of his life in spite of his father. He tried to have as little contact as possible with him and by the time John was 17 they had a very cold, formal relationship, with little closeness and confiding. John believes they had some attributes in common, including stubbornness and aggressiveness.

John describes strong loving feelings towards his mother and lots of shared activities and closeness with her as a child. But he also described her as very protective and suffocating, and said that he felt he had been indoctrinated in childhood with her view of his father as mentally ill. He felt she had played on their loyalty, made his father very jealous, and reinforced the children's feelings of guilt.

At the second interview a year later, John described his mother even more positively. Although her "emotional demands" were very great, they got on "extraordinarily well"; she was basically the symbol of security within the house, a main support which the family relied upon. He described his childhood attitudes towards his parents as, "mum was white and dad was black", but now he realised it was his views that had been polarised. Although his father "used to beat me up quite frequently", he wasn't all that bad, "a maligned character", "a very nice person on occasions".

John recalled no difficulty in making friends as a child, but did describe a definite division between home life and friends. He brought friends home with great trepidation and mainly went round to others' homes. Out of loyalty when outside the home he would not admit to anything being wrong.

Throughout childhood John said he had nervous ticks, was neurotic and emotionally disturbed, and very obsessive and anxious, but had no treatment. He failed his 'A' levels because of a big row between his parents at the time.

John now saw his life as having had three distinct phases. First, childhood which he hadn't enjoyed at all owing to the impact of his parents, but, "I don't believe in having regrets—it's all part of the learning process".

Second, university and the following years which have been "very forma-
tive, cathartic". Third, moving to another city and having good career jobs,
and a great deal of change not only involving people and places but also
"in my head".

Throughout much of his 20s John had been a smoker, a comparatively
heavy drinker reaching a maximum intake of 40 units or so a week in his
early 20s, a regular weekly user of marijuana, a regular monthly user of
'speed', and a regular weekly consumer of 'magic mushrooms' when they
were in season. He had taken cocaine more than weekly for a period of six
months in his early 20s. By the time he took part in the research he had
given up smoking, cut his drinking down to around 20 units a week, and
had stopped taking all other drugs. He had worried when he left university
that for a couple of years he was drinking a lot as an integral part of his
social life. Now he felt in no danger from drinking and enjoyed it, although
he didn't like spirits and thought he never would. Because of his father, he
felt drink was more "an issue" with him than with other people, and also
being a "nervy" type of person who tended to "go the whole hog" with
anything, he had used to drink quite a lot and also admitted to having
taken a lot of drugs in the past. He took no drugs now because it was
totally incompatible with his work and lifestyle, although he had "nothing
against them".

John was in a stable cohabiting relationship which he described as
very loving and open. His partner too was "from a broken home" and they
had a lot in common and were very well matched. He had had a previous
long-term and very "stormy" relationship with someone who was a heavy
drinker, and John was concerned that his playing the "role of rescuer" was
a theme in his relationships. At the first interview he was worried that he
might undermine his partner's independence by being too protective, but
by the time of the second interview he felt the balance of their relationship
was right. He referred also to his partner's "optimistic and light" outlook on
life balancing his rather "black" outlook.

At present, John described himself as having a hectic social life and
was able to describe close friendship relationships. He was particularly
positive about a relationship with one male friend whom he described as
having a "more female outlook" on life—John had always felt closer to
women or to men with a feminine outlook, he said.

John admitted devoting a lot of attention to his own personal development and felt that he was now reasonably satisfied, although he said he
didn't want to reach a stage of feeling "really happy in myself, not wanting
to move on", like some other people he knew. John, himself, had been "the

focal point" of any social gathering at one time, feeling resentful if others were in the limelight. But he had gone through a period of cutting himself off from people, being soliary and contemplative—"it's nice to experience different things"—and this had made him more self-critical, sensitive, quieter and shyer. He felt he was now much softer, having formally been rather, "brattish and arrogant".

John described a number of minor anxiety problems that had occurred off and on during the year that intervened between the two research interviews—worrying, feeling anxious, shyness, lack of confidence and occasionally feeling panicky. He had been to his GP several times for skin allergies. He was aware of being "a lot more anxious" than he used to be.

At the first interview he had a well-paid job as an accountant but was disillutioned with it for ethical reasons. At the second interview he had just left his former employment and started a new job that was less secure, but better paid and more challenging.

At first, the interviewer had found John nervous, voluble and difficult to pin down but he relaxed as the interview went on. The interviewer commented that John seemed to be one of those people who thrived on dissatisfaction, anxiety and challenge. She thought it interesting that what John had said about his father might well be applied to John himself—"Essentially he's a very emotionally insecure person, but he's turned that into strengths".

MARY

At the time she took part in the research, Mary was a married woman in her early 20s. She was one of the youngest of a largish family and had left the parental home when she was 17. In her opinion her father had had a drinking problem throughout her childhood, drinking perhaps the equivalent of half a bottle of spirits daily—although like many children she really could not be sure how much he drank—with 'binges' on average once a week when he might drink twice as much. The family never had drink in the house except at Christmas, but her father would drink in pubs, and in connection with his stressful work as an journalist.

When Mary was small, she often witnessed her father in what she now realised to be a drunken state. She described her father as extremely shy, finding it difficult to talk when sober, yet wanting to be highly sociable when drunk . Sometimes he would come home drunk from work. Often he would come home and go out again, sometimes leaving a note, turning up again, in a drunken state, at any time between late evening and the early hours of the next morning.

Up to the time that Mary was 10 or 11 years old, she said that she tried to ignore her father's drinking—to "not let it take up too much of my time". Throughout her childhood, her father had been a sporadic attender at Alcoholics Anonymous meetings, but it was about the time when she was 10 or 11 that her father was admitted twice, briefly, for 'drying out' in hospital. She thinks he abstained for about three months around that time. But from the time of the hospitalisations onwards, family relationships appear to have deteriorated generally, and Mary feels the problem affected her more between the ages of 10 and 15. Before the hospitalisations, her parents had always argued a lot, but they had also demonstrated tenderness and affection towards one another. From then onwards, however, Mary recalls arguments between her parents more or less every day, usually over petty things and following a recognisable pattern with her father calling her mother "neurotic". Arguments would be worse if her father was drunk and they regularly got, "a bit violent". They became serious, "once in a while", involving pushing and punching. Normally arguments between her parents would not involve Mary, although sometimes she would tell them to stop acting like children, and if she did get involved it became she and her mother, versus her father. Her father had tried to attack Mary with his fists on occasions, but Mary was never really hurt: when her father was drunk she was the more agile and usually managed to get out of the way. At times there was "a family spirit"—usually at Christmas—but generally family discussions turned into arguments. Nobody ever really listened. A meal together would rarely pass without bickering.

As a child, Mary felt she couldn't talk to her father. He was "distant", even "non-existent". She particularly remembered him promising to take her to a show and being really upset that he didn't. He was able to detach himself from the family and there was little opportunity to talk; in any case there was rarely any privacy in such a big family. But she always felt a certain amount of compassion for him, even when hating him: "At times I hated him, at times I felt sorry for him... Despite everything I love him. He cared about us—no doubt about that. He's got a heart of gold". Mary now thinks she is like her father in some ways. For example, she feels that like him she is a strong character.

Mary described her mother as, "a very good mother". They had been close but she felt their relationship had gone downhill since Mary's early teens. She had gone through phases of disliking her mother, but now said she tolerated her. She also said she was not like her mother in any way. Her mother had become very involved with Al-Anon in later years, and often went away to stay with Al-Anon friends. Mary felt that her mother had missed out a lot on life earlier and was making up for it now: her life was separate and very full. But Mary felt that this part of her mother's life was false, and she now felt sorry for her father. During Mary's childhood it was her father, "who would be away".

It was in her teens that Mary began to argue with her father and take more responsibility in the family. The interviewer noted that Mary seemed to have coped quite well. For example, when she was in her mid-teens her mother went away to visit relatives and Mary "managed" her father quite well by being firmer with him than her mother was. For example, she told him that if he got drunk she wouldn't do a thing for him, and indeed when this happened she refused to cook or wash for him. This method seemed to work and he didn't get drunk again for a whole month. Mary was critical of the way her mother waited on her father "hand and foot": "Father begged, mother forgave". Mary thinks her mother should have been less tolerant and could have done something about it by being firmer years ago.

Most of Mary's friends knew about her father's drinking. Occasionally, his drinking was an "inconvenience" but it didn't prevent her from having friends round. She said it didn't bother her much because she felt, "people should take me as I am". She felt it would have been a lot worse if she hadn't brought friends round—it would have drawn attention to the problem.

Mary was not without her problems as a teenager. In her early teens she suffered from asthma. The first occurrence was after a big row with her father and her doctor had told her it was connected with stress. It was successfully treated. She also had migraine headaches and still got them occasionally now. Her brothers and sister all had something physically wrong as well.

At the time of the research interviews Mary was employed full-time in a permanent job as a reporter. She was married to an older man whose teenage children by his first marriage were also living with them. Mary describes herself as always having been an extroverted, gregarious sort of person, never frightened of meeting people. She described close friends with whom she could be completely open, and social activities including regular sport and meals out.

At the first interview Mary said that she and her husband, "get on well", but she also described arguments and some irritation on her part. She thought he might be a bit resentful that she was so extroverted whilst he was quite shy, and he was also a worrier while she was a lot more easy going. At the second interview a year later the balance of her account was more positive. She felt she could be completely open with her husband, and she described him as, "reliable, intelligent, amusing, a fairly secure person—a good relationship, we get on well—we argue also which is good. Sometimes he is moody and unpredictable".

Mary smokes about 25 cigarettes a day, has unsuccessfully attempted to give up in the past, but thinks it is no problem, although she would prefer not to smoke and knows there are dangers attached to it. She very occasionally uses cannabis. She has never taken harder drugs, nor drunk a great deal. At the first interview she had consumed two units of alcohol in the previous week (the equivalent of a pint of beer or a double scotch) and said that this was typical. At the second interview she had consumed 14 units in the previous week and again described that as typical. Of herself she said, "I'm a sensible drinker. I don't drink for the sake of it. I like the pleasant taste. I don't drink for the effect. I don't abuse drink". About drinking in general she said, "it doesn't bother me at all—I don't mind it"; and about drunkenness, "provided they don't cause a nuisance then okay it's their life; they can get on with it". Regarding the influence of her father's drinking, she said, "It obviously has had some influence. It hasn't put me off completely, but I don't like to see people drinking excessively too regularly".

Mary said her husband does drink quite a lot. It doesn't cause any problems now but Mary feels he is in some danger. "I wouldn't say he has a problem but I do tend to worry". Mary has attempted to talk to him about it but he gets angry. She thinks worrying about her husband's drinking may have something to do with her background. Mary described herself as a fit person with no current physical or psychological problems.

Mary described several of her siblings as having mental health or criminal-legal problems or difficulties as adults.

Overall, despite some on-going difficulties over their house and her husband's children and ex-wife, Mary describes herself as very satisfied with her life in nearly all areas. She felt she had achieved a lot for her age and couldn't have done much better. She had no regrets. She had a good job, owned her own house and car, and was able to live comfortably. She was quite satisfied with her job and social life, with marriage and her relationship with her husband. She was intending to have a career and hoped to progress to a very good job; and perhaps go to college and university later. The interviewer gained the impression of a very strong character who would actually attribute this to a character building upbringing. Mary appeared as a very capable person—the dominant partner in her marriage—who, although influenced by her background, did not appear to have been adversely affected by it.

ALAN

Alan was in his late 20s when he was interviewed. He was from quite a large family, with a number of older and younger siblings. His mother, who had always worked as a cleaner or shop assistant, had a drinking problem according to Alan throughout his childhood. He remembers noticing this somewhere around the age of 6 or 8. She drank nearly every day, around the equivalent of a quarter bottle of spirits daily, often at home. Her constant drinking was only broken by two short stays in the local psychiatric hospital around the time when Alan was in his early teens. Alan described his father, who worked as a school caretaker, as a fairly heavy drinker, drinking every night of the week but never getting drunk and without problems.

When his mother was drinking, Alan's parents rowed all the time. His father had, "put up with a hell of a lot". When his mother wasn't drinking it was, "great", she was, "good as gold, lovely". The situation got worse from around the time when Alan was 8 years old. Before that, his parents would go out together, perhaps once a week, to the pub, and they would show "normal affection" to one another. From then on, Alan's mother began to show her father up and he stopped going out with her. His father would go out on his own every night and Alan understood why, as he himself had felt that he, "couldn't wait to get out", if his mother was being nasty. There was occasional violence from his father to his mother, but Alan described it as not very serious. His mother would try being violent, but was usually too drunk to do anything.

Alan and his sisters used to pour the contents of their mother's bottles down the drain. Alan would go round to friends' houses. His father and sisters used to tell Alan's mother to leave, something which Alan didn't do, although he didn't disagree with them. When they were kids, they, "just didn't count Mum, it was not a close family", and from Alan being about 8 onwards things worsened, as his mother's drinking worsened and his parents drifted apart as a result.

With his father, there were lots of shared activities, going to the pictures, helping him with cooking and housework. Unlike his mother who didn't seem to be interested in Alan at all, his father was, "happy-go-lucky, always interested, would do all he could for you at any time, you could always sit down and talk to him". With his mother on the other hand, even when she was sober she wouldn't listen, and generally she was, "jealous and possessive, nasty". Being with her was, "just miserable". Alan felt somewhat similar to his father in personality, being happy-go-lucky and liking children, and only felt similar to his mother because like her he had, "gone off the end", where drink was concerned. Alan's grandmother was an important figure throughout his childhood and "made up for Mum". He described her as a, "lovely, strong woman, very determined". When Alan was courting, it was to his grandmother that he could talk about girlfriends. In childhood he would go to his grandmother's every day to have lunch and she would take him to the pictures regularly.

Alan always had lots of good friends although these were always local kids who knew all about his mother, not school friends to whom he didn't talk about her drinking.

Alan left home at the age of 18. At the time of the interview he was married with two children, the eldest being 11 years old.

He left school without any qualifications and had a variety of different jobs, and at one time was out of work for 18 months. He felt he didn't "settle down" for a number of years, although by the time he took part in the research Alan was in stable employment as a sorter for a parcel delivery firm. However, although Alan felt he had, "bettered himself", he was dissatisfied with his job and very concerned about his and his wife's financial position. By the time of the second interview he was clearly expressing a wish to leave his employment: pay was poor, there was currently no opportunity for overtime, and he had much less opportunity to, "be his own boss", and work at his own rate than he had expected.

The other area of dissatisfaction in Alan's life was his drinking. At the age of 16 he had worked for a brewery and at age 18 in the local pub, by which stage he described himself, looking back, as a very heavy drinker. He said that he had then been a fairly heavy drinker until quite recently, when he had been going to the pub to forget his worries—mainly financial—and relax. Recently he had been going out a lot and getting drunk, perhaps four times a week. He said. "I thought I had self-control", but he found that he didn't. He admitted that when he drank he could, "be a bugger—I can get nasty like, it's not so good", and on one occasion his wife had gone home to her mother's.

There continued to be some problems with Alan's drinking between the first and second interviews. In the summer of that year, he had begun to drink cider rather than beer which made him "nasty" and also started to drink beer at home sometimes when his wife was out. Work had been very bad and they hadn't been able to make ends meet and it was this that had caused the problems. Alan's wife couldn't handle him spending money on drink, getting drunk and sometimes violent, and being deceitful about drinking at home, so she had left for two weeks and gone to her mother's. She had been particularly concerned about the children. When she came back, they had agreed that he wouldn't go out drinking alone and would tell his wife if he was going to have a drink at home. This he had done and things had been better since. Alan felt he now had "no worries" about drinking because he knew he could go for a week or two without, and felt he was, "in no danger at all", of having a problem. He said, "It makes me relax—that's good, and I wouldn't want to stay home every night". His general attitude to drinking was, "it's up to the individual—if you want to drink, drink", and towards drunkenness, "if you're enjoying yourself and having a good time it's fine, as long as there is a limit". He didn't think his family background had had any particular influence on his own drinking: his mother hadn't had much to say on the subject, and his father had simply told him to slow down, not to waste his money, although Alan knew that he didn't like him drinking.

Alan smoked around 20 cigarettes a day and also took tablets regularly for asthma and a bad chest. His doctor, whom he had seen a number of times in the year between the two interviews, told him to stop smoking because of his asthma, but Alan, "liked to have a cigarette", and stated that smoking did not worry him health-wise.

Alan's wife and children were very important to him, as were his wife's family also who lived quite near to them. Apart from Alan drinking and their financial situation, he believed that his relationship with his wife was, "great, we get on really well, nothing else goes wrong". He said they could talk about everything, could speak their minds to each other, and worked well together.

Alan felt that he got on well with other people. He had been shy in the past but now seemed okay, "chatty". Although by the second interview Alan was going out far less than previously because of his agreement with his wife that he should not go out alone, he was happy with this situation, he and his wife went out a lot together, occasionally with a big crowd of friends, and Alan had close male friends with whom he shared an interest in racing dogs. The latter was another source of enjoyment and satisfaction in his life.

In general, Alan said he wished he'd listened more to his father and to his wife when they had been first married. If he had done so he would be better off financially now. But currently he was trying to listen to his wife's good sense more than he had in the past and felt she was now influencing him. But, apart from his drinking, he still wouldn't want to change anything. He wished he could see into the future because it might help him plan things. He was neither optimistic nor pessimistic about the future, saying that they would just have to, "take it as it comes", although he did think that it might get better.

Alan's sister had married a heavy drinker, which caused problems for her and the whole family.

WHAT QUESTIONS DO THESE STORIES RAISE?

These four stories raise many of the questions that the present study was designed to answer. Amongst these are the following:

To what extent are the children of problem drinkers at risk of developing problems with their own drinking (as both Alan and Annie did for a time)?

If they do develop such problems, to what extent is that related to the problematic drinking that they observed in their own childhoods?

Is it the case that the children of problem drinkers are more likely to go on either to develop drinking problems or to have relationships with problem drinkers (as seems to have happened with John, Alan's sister, and possibly with Mary)?

Why do some children seem to be able to put behind them the often very negative experiences of childhood (as John and Mary seem to have done), whereas others seem to have quite serious problems as adults (like Annie)?

To what extent might we be justified as seeing other behaviours such as smoking (Mary, John, and Alan are or were all heavy smokers) or illicit or prescribed drug-taking (Annie, John) as being problem behaviours which are related to the parental problem drinking during childhood?

To what extent do children who have had many negative experiences with a problem-drinking parent go on to see themselves as similar to, or dissimilar from, that parent (Annie, John and Mary all say that they are like their problem drinking parent in one way or another, whereas Alan sees himself as more similar to his non-problem parent, except for his drinking)?

If it were to be the case that many of the young people whom we interviewed were relatively problem-free in adulthood, to what extent could that be because we only interviewed 'survivors'—for example, was it the case that the siblings of those we interviewed showed greater signs of having being damaged by their past experiences?

WHY ARE THESE IMPORTANT QUESTIONS?

The excessive consumption of alcoholic drinks is now recognised to be near the very top of the world league table of health and social problems.

There is much controversy over how these alcohol-related problems should be defined, what causes them, and how they should best be prevented or treated, but about their existence on a vast scale there is no dispute. In Britain one recent estimate, based on a survey of 10,000 16–64 year olds is that the point prevalence of alcohol dependence is 47 per 1,000 (Meltzer, 1994). This figure extrapolated to the whole population suggests that in the region of two to three million adults in the UK have drinking problems.

Even allowing for the fact that a relatively high proportion of such problems occur in young adults aged 16–24, it follows that the numbers of people with drink problems who are parents with children or adolescents in their care must run into at least several hundreds of thousands. It follows that such children, living with parents with drinking problems, must exist in very large numbers indeed, probably in excess of one million in Britain. In fact one estimate, widely quoted, puts the number of children in the USA, currently under the age of 18 and living with at least one parent with a drinking problem, at 6.5 million (Russell, Henderson and Blume, 1985). Russell *et al.*, further estimated that there were some 22 million adults over the age of 18 in the same country, which is one in every eight adults, who had been brought up by a parent with a drinking problem.

In a report of a Canadian study of 115 children currently living at home with at least one parent with a drinking problem—a report that remains one of the best on the subject to this day—Cork (1969) described the impact of such problems upon children's lives. The most common concern was 'parental fighting and quarrelling' into which children were often drawn as participants or peacemakers. Many of the children complained of the drinking parent's inconsistent moods, their own apprehension about the state the parent would be in when the child came home from school, or when the parent returned after drinking. Many spoke of a lack of fun and laughter at home and contrasted their own families unfavourably with those of their friends. Many had taken over responsibility for household tasks, including caring for younger siblings, and older children in particular reported a reluctance to bring friends home. As we shall see when we describe the results of our own research in Britain, these experiences are indeed common, and are amongst a wide range of stressful events and long-standing tensions and strains reported by children living with adults with drinking problems, although the extent and severity of these vary from child to child and family to family. Particularly apt, however, was the title of Cork's monograph: The Forgotten Children. It is our impression that, at the time of writing this book in the mid-1990s, these children remain surprisingly forgotten, and the particular set of circumstances they face remains oddly neglected. This has occurred, paradoxically, at a time when there is a greatly raised awareness about the rights of children, and about many of the abuses to which they are vulnerable. This neglect may be less true of the USA, where much publicity has surrounded 'children of alcoholics' in recent years, but we believe it to be true of present-day Britain and of nearly all other countries around the world.

In the present research, which we shall describe in subsequent chapters, we collected information on this subject in the form of the recollections of young adults, each aged between 16 and 35 years, who had been brought up in homes where a parent had a drinking problem. The stresses such children face is a theme to which we shall return in Chapter 2. The principal motive for this research, however, was the desire to investigate the comparatively long-term effects upon children when they grew to adulthood. We wanted to examine a range of issues connected to this adulthood adjustment, as shown by some of the questions posed earlier, at the end of the four stories. One of these issues was the phenomenon of the intergenerational transmission of alcohol problems. Reports had been coming out, principally from the USA, that alcohol problems ran in families, and that such problems must in some way be 'passed on' from one generation to the next within families, (e.g. Cotton, 1979; Goodwin, 1979). The degree of the increased risk was unknown, although there was little dispute that it existed, but some popular as well as professional writing was suggesting that the risk was many times greater for children of problem drinking parents than for children without this background. Furthermore, the view was developing in some quarters that the risk of intergenerational transmission of alcohol problems, plus an increased risk of other negative mental health and personal and social adjustment outcomes in adulthood, meant that children with parents with drinking problems were almost bound to have problems of one kind or another as adults. In the following chapter, where we critically review the research on these issues, we shall see that the evidence, although sketchy and incomplete, supports a less dramatic conclusion.

The aims were to carry out an investigation of this issue in Britain. We aimed to contribute to the growing body of research on the extent to which children of problem drinking parents were at risk, both specifically for alcohol problems and more generally for other adulthood outcomes. But we were particularly impressed by the emerging evidence, both from this area of investigation, and from writings about the effects of other childhood family stressors such as parental separation or divorce, or family economic hardship, that not all children in these groups were fated to have problems as adults. Many children appeared to 'survive', apparently unscathed or even strengthened by their experiences. Writers were beginning to emphasise the great variations to be found in adulthood outcome following stressful events and circumstances in childhood, and terms such as 'survivors', 'copers', and 'resilient children' were coming to the fore (e.g. Garmezy, 1988; Werner and Smith, 1982). We wanted to know, if some children of problem drinking parents were at risk and others were not, why this was so, and what the mechanisms might be whereby some children experience later problems, whilst others survived without.

This question of the adulthood consequences for offspring of parents with drinking problems has also, in our view, been badly neglected within British psychology, psychiatry and social science. This is nowhere better illustrated than in the comprehensive and influential review, 'Cycles of Disadvantage', carried out by Rutter and Madge in the mid-1970s. The impetus for their review was a major speech made by the then Secretary of State for Social Services, Sir Keith Joseph, in which he spoke of the intergenerational transmission of a wide variety of personal and social problems. Although he made specific reference to the importance of examining the effects of alcohol abuse, Rutter and Madge stated in their introduction, "We were guided ... by the various items noted in Sir Keith Joseph's 1972 speech—namely poverty, unemployment, poor housing, poor education attainment, crime, psychiatric disorder, inadequate parenting and problem families. He also made mention of alcoholism ... but we decided that these problems were too specific for inclusion as topics in their own right" (1976, p. 6). Not only was the area excluded as a topic in its own right; it also failed to receive a single entry in the index to a book which was, in most other ways, extremely thorough.

This is all the more surprising in the light of the findings of Cork (1969), and of other research since, that suggests that many of the features, such as parental discord, that are characteristic of the family environments where a parent has a drinking problem, are the same as those that now appear to be at the root of much of the transmission of other types of difficulty (e.g. Rutter and Madge, 1976; Emery, 1982). Not only do children of parents with drinking problems constitute a group vast in numbers, whose circumstances and outcomes deserve more attention than they have had hitherto in Britain and elsewhere, but also it seems likely that a study of this group might repay handsomely in terms of a contribution to our slowly developing understanding of normal and abnormal life development.

CHAPTER **2**

WHAT WAS ALREADY KNOWN: A REVIEW OF PREVIOUS RESEARCH

Although the four individual stories presented in the last chapter raise many issues addressed in the research reported in this book, it is important to recognise that we were not the first to have researched into the experiences of children of problem drinkers. This is important for a number of reasons, not least because no one research study on its own can hope to provide definitive answers to complex and interesting questions such as the ones posed here. Instead, it is necessary to see how the present findings complement, or alternatively contradict, the findings of others.

In this chapter the findings of previous research will be presented under five main headings: (1) research which describes the range of experiences to which a child with a problem drinking parent might be exposed; (2) the possible harms that may accrue to the offspring of parents with drinking problems whilst the offspring are still children or adolescents—the 'immediate' or 'initial' effects; (3) the longer-term or later effects upon offspring as adults; (4) the likely mechanisms or processes whereby parental problem drinking may produce the effects upon offspring that have been found to occur—the explanations that have been put forward to account for initial or later effects on offspring; (5) the wider literature on the effects on offspring of such childhood events and difficulties as parental discord, family separation, abuse of children by parents, and economic depression. The specialised subject of parental drinking problems and their effects upon children should borrow from, and contribute to, this wider literature. In looking at the latter, we shall be particularly interested in the possibility of transmission of problems in the parental generation to problems in the offspring generation, and the explanations that have been offered to account for this transmission where it has been found to occur.

In examining the literature on these questions, this chapter will draw quite heavily on material contained in various published reviews that we both have undertaken previously (Orford, 1990; Velleman, 1992a,b).

PARENTAL DRINKING PROBLEMS: THE RANGE OF EXPERIENCES TO WHICH A CHILD MIGHT BE EXPOSED

There seems no doubt that being a son or daughter living in a family where a parent has a drinking problem can be very stressful (Cork, 1969; Velleman and Orford, 1984; West and Prinz, 1987; Velleman and Orford, 1990; Orford, 1990), and several components of this stress have been identified. One of the most frequently mentioned elements is arguing between parents. Of the 115 children interviewed by Cork (1969), 98 said that 'parental fighting and quarrelling' was their main concern, whereas only one child reported 'drinking' and six 'drunkenness' as their main concern. Parental arguing in front of the child, and one parent 'saying bad things' about the other, are amongst the 'bad' stressful life events that figure in the Children of Alcoholics Life-Events Schedule (COALES) developed by Roosa *et al.* (1988). The scale was developed by consulting the opinions of a range of experts, and was able to discriminate significantly between children with and without parents with drinking problems. Many others have noted that parental conflict is a feature particularly characteristic of families where a parent has a drinking problem (e.g. Wilson and Orford, 1978; Black *et al.*, 1986; Reich *et al.*, 1988). Black *et al.* (1986) reported that adult offspring of 'alcoholics' were more likely than comparison offspring to recall frequent parental arguments, and parents arguing about 'drinking', about 'relationships with the opposite sex', and about 'everything'. There were no differences between groups in recall of parents arguing about the children, nor about the respondent him/herself specifically, although Matejcek (1981) specifically reported disunity in bringing up their children amongst 200 Czechoslovakian men with drinking problems and their wives compared to controls. From their detailed study of 11 families with parental drinking problems Wilson and Orford (1978) concluded that significant parental arguments sometimes focussed on drinking but were often about other issues such as gambling, actual or threatened infidelity, finances, or one partner's fussy behaviour.

It is also clear that family violence, although by no means inevitable in families with drinking problems, is very significantly more common where such problems exist (e.g. Black *et al.*, 1986; Jones and Houts, 1992). Jones and Houts found that both receiving and witnessing physical abuse in the family were recalled more often by students with memories of regular problem drinking within their families, and Black *et al.* (1986) found that children of 'alcoholics' reported more violence than comparisons on the part of all members of their families; most often from fathers but also from mothers, brothers, sisters, and on the part of the respondents themselves. In both studies sexual abuse was more often recalled by those who had parents with drinking problems.

Many have pointed to a relative lack of joint family activities, poor family communication, and a tense family atmosphere in families with parental drinking problems. For example, a second sub-scale of the COALES assesses 'good' life events relevant to 'children of alcoholics'. This scale, again with an ability to discriminate children with and without parents with drinking problems, contains a number of items relating to parents spending time with the child, attending school functions, getting together with relatives 'for good times', and performing household routines smoothly. Cork (1969) found that children with parents with drinking problems complained of lack of fun and laughter, and contrasted their own families unfavourably with those of their friends. She found that children felt particularly apprehensive about the mood the drinking parent would be in when the children came in from school, or the parent returned home, and Wilson and Orford (1978) also described the tension generated in the family by the anticipation of the drinking parent's moods, such as aggressiveness, irritability or depression. They further highlighted the complex ways in which excessive drinking and the associated strained atmosphere might lead to reduced communication amongst some or all members of the family. The spoiling of occasions such as family holidays, birthdays, Christmas or other family gatherings or rituals has also been specifically remarked upon by many people (e.g. Wilson and Orford, 1978; Bennett *et al.*, 1988; Roosa *et al.*, 1988).

Other research has focussed attention upon the quality of the child's relationship with his or her parents, as opposed to characteristics of the parents' relationship or the family as a whole. For example, adult children of 'alcoholics' reported to Black *et al.* (1986) that they had been less able to talk to their parents, and students who recalled regular problem drinking at home were less likely to report to Jones and Houts (1992) that they perceived positive regard towards them from their parents, and were more likely to report denial of or inattention to their feelings by their parents. Most research of this kind, however, has failed to distinguish between relationships of children with their problem drinking parents, and relationships with the non-problem drinking parents. Research has scarcely begun to do justice to the complexities involved here. Wilson and Orford (1978) found examples of close and mutually supportive 'coalitions' between some children and their non-problem drinking parents, whilst in other cases children expressed ambivalent or negative attitudes towards these parents. Regarding the problem drinking parents, children sometimes made a clear distinction between their relationships when parents were drunk and when they were sober, whilst for some children attitudes of hostility and distance and rejection towards these parents were stable feelings whether or not the parents were drinking.

Stress may extend beyond the boundaries of the family household. Roosa *et al.*'s (1988) 'bad' life events scale contains several items about such events as aunts, uncles and grandparents saying bad things about the child's parent(s), parents arguing with such relatives, and people in the neighbourhood saying bad things about their parents. A lack of close friendships and difficulty with peer group relationships is a recurrent theme. For example Cork (1969) found that older children, especially, had difficulty in making friends and were reluctant to bring friends into the home; and Black *et al.* (1986) report that children of 'alcoholics' were less able to talk to friends of the same age. Parents with drinking problems may act badly in front of children's friends (e.g. Wilson and Orford, 1978; Roosa *et al.*, 1988). Older teenagers, particularly, often feel ashamed or embarrassed to bring friends home, particularly friends of the opposite sex (Wilson and Orford, 1978).

Finally, it should be pointed out that children of parents with drinking problems have regularly been found to be at especially high risk of experiencing parental separation and/or parental death (Kammeier, 1971; Nylander, 1960; Swiecicki, 1969; Djukanobic *et al.*, 1978; Black *et al.*, 1986) and that stress experienced by children of problem drinking parents will be compounded by the stress associated with these events, and perhaps that associated with other events such as a parent's treatment and hospitalisation (Wilson and Orford, 1978).

From the above literature and our own clinical and research conversations with offspring of parents with drinking problems we know, then, that there is a wide range of negative experiences which such children may well acquire. Most obviously, the child is likely to perceive his or her drinking parent as behaving very 'oddly'. They know that their parents' behaviour is in some way different, but they may not be able to understand why. The parent may be violent to the child or to the other parent, and this can be deeply disturbing for the child. The parent may be aggressive or argumentative, or alternatively may be withdrawn. Worst of all, he or she may unpredictably be all of these at different times without the child knowing in advance what is going to happen.

The parent may get very drunk and/or behave very disruptively, not only within the family but also outside it, showing the family up. For example, the child may not only be uncertain as to whether the drinking parent is actually going to turn up to collect him or her from school, but may also not know whether, if the parent does turn up, the parent will be drunk. Embarrassment is too mild a term to describe the feeling of mortification that a child in this situation can experience. For the same reason, family occasions such as Christmas and birthdays can cause dread and foreboding in a child who does not *know* what is going to happen, but fears and imagines that he or she does. Less obviously the child may also have relationship difficulties with his or her non-problem drinking parent. Paradoxically, the child may come to view the non-drinking parent less favourably than the drinking parent, thus adding to the already considerable strain experienced by the former. The management of roles within the family may mean, for example, that it is the non-problem drinking parent who has to take over responsibility for disciplining the child, or for giving the bad news that pocket money is out of the question this week, or that there just isn't the money for new clothes or a holiday. The non-problem drinking parent's increasing preoccupation with the problem-drinking parent may mean that he or she simply has less time and energy to devote to the child. The child can therefore begin to feel abandoned by both parents. Yet another possible confusion for the child is the response of the non-problem parent who becomes increasingly hostile to the problem drinking parent. This hostility, aggression or embitterment is often due to the spouse's anger at being let down by the problem drinking partner.

PARENTAL DRINKING PROBLEMS: EARLY EFFECTS ON CHILDREN AND ADOLESCENTS

The effects on children of this kind of situation have been studied often, and in almost every study, in almost every country in which such research has been conducted, the children of problem drinking parents have been shown to have higher levels of problems than the children of non-problem drinkers. Research has examined a range of areas—academic performance, incidence of illness, self-esteem, delinquent behaviour, other behavioural difficulties—and similar findings have emerged, even when the comparison has been made with the children of parents with other sorts of problem such as physical illness or psychiatric difficulties.

We are fortunate in having a number of reviews, published over the past 20 years, of research on the association between parental alcohol problems and disturbance in their offspring whilst the latter are still children or adolescents (e.g., Warner and Rosett, 1975; El-Guebaly and Offord, 1977, 1979; Wilson, 1980, 1982; Velleman and Orford, 1984; West and Prinz, 1987; Woodside, 1988; Orford, 1990). Each of these reviews has arrived at substantially similar, and fairly clear-cut conclusions. Before summarising them, however, it is worth pointing out that these reviews also describe quite substantial methodological weaknesses in this body of research. For example, West and Prinz (1987) in their review show that, for a start, only six of the 46 studies they reviewed were longitudinal—which is the best design, although even longitudinal studies carry dangers because initial selection and subsequent attrition may limit generalisability, and because age, cohort and cultural-historical effects may be confounded (Achenbach, 1978). Three studies used a retrospective design in which respondents recalled childhood events. West and Prinz considered this to be the least adequate design because of bias introduced by forgetting, defensiveness and social desirability. Of the other studies they reviewed, 28 used parents with drinking problems as the starting point and examined their children; whilst nine started with children who were already identified as having problems, and considered the possibility of a parent having an alcohol problem. Source of information was most often the children themselves, but sometimes parents, and sometimes school, hospital or police records, were utilised.

West and Prinz list many other potential shortcomings in the body of research into the effects on children, including: the range and quality of sources of information; issues connected to the sampling—children of all ages often being studied as if they were an homogeneous group without analysing different ages separately; a general sampling bias towards parental problem drinkers who were receiving treatment which may make generalisation to the much larger total population of parents with drinking problems difficult; nearly all studies including more male than female problem drinkers and many consisting entirely of men, leading to less being known about the impact of maternal problem drinking; and sex differences being ignored, both in terms of the children, and in terms of a possible differential impact of sex of problem drinking parent on same-sex and opposite-sex children.

Possibly the biggest cause for concern with this research area is the fact that most research in this field has ignored other possibly contributing variables such as: the child's age at onset of parental problem drinking; severity of parental drinking problem; the existence of other psychological problems in either of the parents; the extent of family discord, separation, divorce and re-marriage; socio-economic status; family size; the child's relationship with both the problem drinking and the non-problem drinking parent; parental criminality; and the availability of alternative sources of support. Indeed, there is a whole host of other variables, mostly unassessed and hence remaining hidden, which could contribute in some way to effects on children.

The point about listing all these potential and actual difficulties with the existing research is to emphasise how complex the relationships might be between a parental alcohol problem, and some sort of effect on a particular child. Nor is it likely to be the case that all the factors outlined above (and there are as many which we have not listed) function in the same way. For example, some variables might *moderate* the effects on a child of having a problem drinking parent, whereas other variables might *mediate* these effects (Baron and Kenny, 1986; Sher, 1991). Factors such as the sex of the child, the child's age at onset of the parental problem, the socio-economic status of the family, the family size, or the child's relationship with the non-problem drinking parent, might operate as *moderators* of the relationship between a parental drinking problem and child outcomes. For example, boys from large families, with problem drinking fathers and poor relationships with their mothers, might be at high risk for certain harmful outcomes, whilst girls from small families with problem drinking fathers but good relationships with their mothers, might not. If a number of moderating variables were operating in anything like this complex fashion, it would be particularly difficult to identify those groups of children most at risk and the harmful effects of parental drinking problems might be obscured.

On the other hand, factors such as family discord, parental violence, parental mental ill-health, or parental separation or divorce might act as *mediators*. For example, it might be parental separation or divorce, which is known to be frequent in families where there is a drinking problem, that accounts for most of the relationship between a parental drinking problem and harmful effects on the children. Indeed, a factor such as parental separation or divorce might entirely account for the relationship, and it might be possible to show that having a parent with a drinking problem had no harmful effect unless it was associated with parental separation or divorce. It is important to point out, however, that this is not the same thing as saying that a parental drinking problem is of no importance, particularly if it could also be shown that parental drinking problems were amongst the commonest causes of parents separating or divorcing. Nevertheless, the possibility that there exist crucial mediators in the link between a parental drinking problem and childhood outcomes is a major consideration.

In particular, other reviewers (e.g. El-Guebaly and Offord, 1977, 1979; Wilson, 1982) have asked themselves whether parental conflict and family disorganisation might not provide this mediating link, and this is a crucial question to which we shall return.

Given all these methodological considerations, however, it is still possible to draw some relatively firm conclusions about the effects on children of having a parent with a drinking problem. In general the outcome of this work has been a remarkably consistent picture suggesting that parental alcohol problems put children at high risk for a wide variety of emotional and behavioural disorders.

Although the children of problem drinkers appear to have more of most sorts of problem, there are four main headings under which these problems are often categorised.

* *Anti-social behaviour, or conduct disorder*: The children of problem drinkers are consistently found to have more problems in this area: for example, aggressive behaviour, delinquency, temper tantrums, truancy. Of those studies reviewed by West and Prinz which examined this area, only one (a longitudinal study by Knop *et al.*, 1985, described below) failed to find an association between parental problem drinking and these anti-social behaviour patterns. One behaviour commonly reported alongside these anti-social behaviours is that of hyperactivity. In fact, West and Prinz argue that the evidence for this link is less convincing, since results are inconsistent and the positive results that have been found may be due to a confounding of hyperactivity with conduct disorder, particularly aggression.

* *Problems in the school environment*: The children of problem drinkers seem also to be more likely to develop problems at school including learning difficulties, reading backwardness, loss of concentration, and generally poor school performance. For example, of nine studies of IQ which West and Prinz examined, seven found significantly lower scores for children of problem drinking parents, with the other two finding no differences. Of six studies examining academic performance, five reported significantly lower performance, and one no difference. Other studies have also reported similar findings, such as a reduced rate of graduation from high school (Miller and Jang, 1977). An example of one of the better studies is the research of Knop *et al.* (1985) which took as its population all children born in Copenhagen between 1959 and 1961. These researchers found a sample of 233 boys with 'alcoholic' fathers (although no information is given about mothers' alcohol usage), and compared them with a group of 107 control boys on measures derived from school reports and

teacher ratings obtained retrospectively from the last school attended. They found that these 'high risk' children had significantly more often repeated a school year, been referred to a school psychologist, and attended a larger number of schools, and were significantly more likely to be rated by teachers as more 'impulsive-restless' (being especially high on fidgeting, restlessness, and confusion) and less 'verbally proficient' (especially on vocabulary, reading ability and oral expression). In conjunction with these studies on school performance we should note Wilson's (1982) warning that, "lack of comparison groups makes it difficult to say whether these [findings] are more common among children of 'alcoholics' than among children from other homes where there is marital conflict and family disruption" (p. 162).

* *Emotional problems*: A third area takes in emotional, psychological, and emotionally-related health difficulties. These include: a wide range of psychosomatic problems from asthma to bed-wetting; negative attitudes to parents; negative attitudes to self, with high levels of self-blame; and withdrawal, crying, and depression. For example, almost all studies which examined the association between parental drinking problems and children's emotional functioning (which has generally included anxiety, depression, low self-esteem, and perceived lack of internal control) find a strong link. Similarly, studies which examined the link between parental problem drinking and child physical health status (which includes such items as headaches, sleeping and eating problems, and rates of out-patient therapy) also find a link, although this is a less consistent finding: for example, of the five studies in this area which West and Prinz reviewed, three reported a significant relation with parental drinking problems (particularly for females), whereas the other two found no difference. West and Prinz conclude that the often asserted view that children of problem drinking parents experience interpersonal difficulties was less reliable: they could not find more than a small handful of studies, none of which used very convincing methods, which had tested this area.

These emotion-related difficulties are reported by many researchers, but again Wilson (1982) warned that, "there is an urgent need for comparative research on children in families experiencing other forms of crisis; similar patterns of family dysfunctions may operate in families disrupted by events such as unemployment, mental and physical illness or bereavement" (p. 162).

* *Problems in adolescence*: Again, studies generally support a link between parental drinking problems and conduct disorder, truancy, delinquency, and alcohol abuse in adolescence, although it is true to say that the evidence relating to the effects on adolescent children of problem drinking parents is less clear (Velleman and Orford, 1984). Although there

are some findings which suggest that the children of problem drinkers start using alcohol and other drugs somewhat earlier than do their peers, a number of studies have suggested that they do not have greatly more alcohol- or drugs-related problems than other adolescents. This could occur because difficulties specific to upbringing by a problem drinking parent are obscured by the range of difficulties which adolescents generally experience. On the other hand, these more equivocal findings in adolescence may not be unduly surprising given the findings from studies of normal adolescence (Aitken, 1979; Davies and Stacey, 1972) which show a general trend for parental influences to lessen as children grow older, and for adolescents' behaviour to become gradually more responsive to peer group pressures.

Virtually all the work examined by the reviews cited above was published in English, and nearly all of it was conducted in the USA. Working for the World Health Organization, one of us reviewed previously unpublished reports and English translations of reports published in other languages (Orford, 1990). For example, there has been a number of quite well-controlled studies reported from a range of European countries, particularly from Eastern Europe. These confirm the picture that emerges from the English-speaking reviews, that children living with parents with drinking problems are at increased risk for a range of emotional difficulties, conduct problems, and cognitive and academic difficulties. In fact if anything they suggest that the summary and conclusions outlined above may have been understated; and they certainly suggest that the harmful effects of parent excessive drinking are likely to exist on a world-wide scale. Amongst the most important non-English language research reports on this topic are the following:

From Bulgaria in the early 1980's, in a dissertation and a series of papers (Toteva, 1982, 1984, cited in Boyadjieva, undated) the findings of a study of 220 children aged between 5 and 15 years were reported. This group of children, each of whom had a parent (usually the father) who had been treated for 'alcoholism', was compared with a control group of 110 children of healthy parents. 'Neurotic' disturbances were found in 56% of the former *vs* 22.5% of the latter; antisocial behaviour was registered in 23% *vs* only 3% of the control group; and suicidal tendencies were found in a substantial minority of the former.

In the then USSR, a major study was reported by Schurygin (1978) in which 74 children (aged from less than one year to 16 years old) from 52 families where the father was suffering from chronic 'alcoholism' and had received treatment, were contrasted with an equal sized comparison group.

Schurygin reported that 'psychogenic' disorders were almost six times as frequent amongst the former group. Twenty-eight were diagnosed as suffering from one or other variant of 'patho-characteristological development'. The two commonest types were the 'inhibited' (10 children) and a 'temporary-excitable' or anti-social type (8 children).

Similarly Matejcek (1981), from Czechoslovakia, reported the results of a major investigation. Two hundred children from intact families in which the father had been registered at one of Prague's anti-alcoholic counselling centres in the years 1975 and 1976, were individually matched, on the basis of age, number of children in the family, position in the family, age of parents and education of parents, with children without 'alcoholic' parents. Teachers and parents were interviewed and the children were tested, the interviewers and examiners being blind to group membership. The children fell into three age groups: 4 to 6 years, 9 to 11 years, and 13 to 15 years. Matejcek found significant differences in intelligence in favour of the comparison group, in the oldest of the three age groups only; no difference in parents' assessments (which in many cases were felt to be unrealistic); found teachers' assessments were much closer to the formal IQ test results; and found that paediatricians' ratings of intelligence (above average, average, below average), and schoolmates' nominations of most intelligent, most gifted, and quickest children, both showed significant differences in favour of the comparison group. Children from 'alcoholic' families were also less likely to be chosen as 'best friends' on a sociometric test; and on a test of maladjustment, there were significant differences overall, and in particular for the 9–11 year-olds and (to a lesser extent) the 4–6 year-olds.

Considerable interest in the transmission of disadvantage as a result of parental drinking problems has been shown in Sweden. Nylander's monograph, published in 1960, reported a comparison of 229 children from 141 families where the fathers were 'alcoholics', with 163 control children. The groups were carefully matched and children were aged between 4 and 12 years old. Children in the former group, as in so many other studies, showed more frequent signs of mental ill-health and a wider variety of symptoms than control children: 27% of boys and 30% of girls showed 'mental insufficiency', with anxiety neuroses and depression being the commonest diagnoses, and rates being equally high amongst the three age groups (4–6, 7–9, and 10–12 years). Apart from clear psychiatric diagnoses, stress symptoms such as headaches, stomach-aches, and tiredness were very common, and children had often been investigated for physical conditions without any underlying organic reasons being confirmed. Of those children who were of school age, 48% (*vs* 10% of control children) were considered by their teachers to be problem children at school. Amongst the youngest school-age boys (7–9 years) as many as 74% with 'alcoholic' parents showed difficulty in adjusting. This sample has also been the subject of a major follow-up study, which will be referred to in the next section on adulthood outcomes.

In addition to these studies which have examined the effects on children with identified problem-drinking parents, there have been a number of studies from both Eastern and Western Europe which have looked at this question the other way on, starting with groups of children with problems of various kinds and examining the rates of parental problem drinking to be found amongst them. High rates have been reported amongst delinquent children, those with learning difficulties, and children who have attempted suicide, although lack of control groups makes it difficult to interpret the results of some of these studies (Orford, 1990).

In summary, then, it seems clear from a wide range of studies and reviews, conducted in many countries, that having a parent with a drinking problem raises the risk of a child developing one or more of a large number of problems, difficulties and disorders during their childhood years. These difficulties are often summarised in terms of anti-social behaviour, emotional and psychological difficulties, and poorer school performance, although they are not confined to these areas alone.

Two things, however, are not clear. The first is *why* having a parent with an alcohol problem should lead to the development of these difficulties—what mechanism is responsible? Are there important mediating, causal variables to be identified? For example, El-Guebaly and Offord (1977) point out that a core issue in the studies of offspring of problem drinkers is whether the most significant contribution to risk is the parental drinking problem itself or the social and familial disorganisation often associated with both poverty and alcohol problems. This issue of mechanisms will be returned to later in this chapter.

The second thing which is not clear is what the *long-term* effects are of having had a parent with a drinking problem. It is often assumed that disturbance in childhood automatically leads to disturbance in adulthood, and the evidence reviewed above coupled with the evidence to be presented in the next section from retrospective reports of current problem drinkers is often taken to imply that such long-term effects do occur. Yet a major problem with the research literature is that it generally looks at the adjustment problems of offspring when they were children, with very little follow-through to determine whether these disturbed children become maladjusted adults. Often the results of studies of offspring as children are projected forward to suggest that these children are generally at risk. Yet as Heller, Sher and Benson (1982) argued in their paper on 'Problems associated with risk over-prediction in studies of offspring of alcoholics', "While it can be granted that growing up in the home of an alcoholic parent can produce problems for the child, it would seem that the most crucial question is whether there are any residual effects associated with these earlier difficult years. Given the disequilibrium and inconsistency likely to be present in the home of a parent with a drinking problem, it would not be surprising to discover negative effects on offspring as children. More crucial is information which might indicate whether problems noted early in development persevere into adulthood" (p. 190).

Although we do not agree with the implication that childhood problems that do not persist are unimportant, it is true to say that the studies of the effects on children do not in themselves show whether or not these problems continue into adulthood, and if they do, how they manifest themselves. It is this issue that we will now examine.

PARENTAL DRINKING PROBLEMS: EFFECTS ON OFFSPRING AS ADULTS

One possibility that must be considered is that the stressful circumstances associated with having a parent with a drinking problem only have an impact on offspring in the form of various harmful outcomes in the short-term (and perhaps only whilst the stresses operate), but not in the longer term. This has certainly been noted by those who have studied children or adolescents whilst they are still young enough to be living at home. For example, Schurygin (1978) in his study of children of problem drinking parents in the then USSR, followed up, over a period of two years or more, children who displayed either 'inhibited' or 'temporary excitable' disorders that were traced to origins in families with 'alcoholic' fathers. Where stress had been resolved by death, departure or 'cure' of the father, a reversal in the child's behaviour problems was observed, with the inhibited children becoming more active, lively, tender and accessible, and the 'temporary-excitable' children becoming more balanced in mood.

Roosa *et al.* (1990) tested adolescents of high school age twice with an interval of three months between occasions, using the 'good' and 'bad' sub-scales of the COALES and measures of anxiety and depression. The latter were correlated with both types of life event in the expected directions. The statistical procedure known as structural equation modelling showed a satisfactory fit of the data to a model which supposed that a parental drinking problem was influential on symptoms only indirectly via positive and negative life events. After three months symptoms were somewhat worse if stress had worsened, but there was very little evidence of an independent influence of circumstances three months earlier.

Work by both Moos (Moos and Billings, 1982; Moos, Finney and Cronkite, 1990) and by Callan and Jackson (1986) has found that the personal functioning of adolescent children of 'recovered alcoholics' is indistinguishable from that of matched control adolescents who have never had parents with drinking problems, and that both are significantly better in personal functioning than matched groups of adolescents with still-drinking parents with drinking problems. Moos *et al.* (1990) conclude: "The stress-related influence of parental alcoholism seems to diminish or disappear when the parent succeeds in controlling his or her alcohol abuse" (p. 183). It should be noted in passing that Moos *et al.*, although they have not directly concerned themselves with the longer-term transmission of problems into adulthood, have put forward a detailed, contextual model of the influences that bear upon the functioning of children with problem drinking parents. As well as aspects of family atmosphere such as family arguments and lack of family cohesion, they have found evidence for the importance of levels of anxiety and depression in the problem drinking parent, levels of depression in the non-problem drinking parent, and avoidant styles of coping used by either parent.

Although these findings imply that the longer-term risk to the children of problem drinkers may be less striking than might be supposed, it is the case that a considerable amount of research effort has been invested in examining longer-term effects. Indeed, it is reasonable to hypothesize that growing up in an environment where one (or both) parent(s) had a drinking problem might affect all sorts of areas of adult adjustment. Unfortunately, however, the study of the possible long-term effects of having had a parent with a drinking problem has been dominated by the search for evidence of intergenerational transmission of alcohol problems themselves. In other words, the main adulthood outcome which has been studied in the offspring generation is excessive drinking and other outcomes have tended to be neglected.

Drinking Outcomes

There have been many studies in which adults who are currently defined as having a drinking problem are asked whether one or both of their parents had such a problem. Cotton (1979) in her major review of the area examined 36 such studies. These all showed that excessive drinkers were more likely to report having had a parent who had a problem with drinking than would be expected from the general population figures. For example, when estimated rates of 'alcoholism' in the general population have been compared with those in the families of 'alcoholics' (as has been done for example by Winokur *et al.*, 1970; Reich *et al.*, 1975; and McKenna and Pickens, 1981), it is found that male 'alcoholics' are 2.2 times as likely as males in the general population to report having had an 'alcoholic' father, and 1.6 times as likely to report having had an 'alcoholic' mother, and female 'alcoholics' are 3.3 times as likely to report having had an 'alcoholic' father and 2.4 times as likely to report having had an 'alcoholic' mother. A study typical of many others is that by McKenna and Pickens (1981). This study examined 1,930 patients (1,520 men and 410 women) categorized as 'chronic alcoholics'. 21% of the men and 27% of the women reported 'alcoholism' in one or both parents, and 3.2% of the men and 6.6% of the women reported that both parents were 'alcoholic'. This study then went on to relate the number of 'alcoholic parents' (0, 1, or 2) to a series of other measures, finding that the children of two 'alcoholic parents' were more likely than the children of one 'alcoholic' (who were more likely than the children of non-'alcoholics') to have been younger when first intoxicated, to have had more pre-treatment behavioural problems, and to have proceeded more rapidly from first intoxication to alcoholism treatment.

The finding that problem drinkers report high levels of parental problem drinking is not confined to research from English-speaking countries (Orford, 1990): similar results were shown by research from Chile (Kattan *et al.*, 1973), USSR (Paschenkov, 1976), Iceland (Helgason and Asmundsson, 1975), and Hungary (Laszlo, 1970).

For example, in the Icelandic study (Helgason and Asmundsson, 1975), 70 men under 30 years of age who had been convicted for public drunkenness at least twice within one month, and who lived in Reykjavik or vicinity, were matched for age, school attended, examination successes and intelligence with 70 controls. Each young man was asked about family background and a number of mothers were contacted to check on the answers. Significantly more fathers of the 'alcohol abusers' than of the controls were reported to have been 'excessive drinkers' (37% *vs* 13%) and significantly fewer abstainers (17% *vs* 34%). The authors also commented that their data suggested more psychiatric symptoms amongst mothers although the latter had not been recognised as ill (the rate of excessive drinking amongst mothers was negligible). Significantly more 'abusers' had experienced changes in family structure during childhood, mostly as a consequence of divorce which was often related to the father's excessive drinking (53% *vs* 23% at least one such change; 21% *vs* 9% two or more changes; 12% *vs* 3% three or more changes).

There is consistent evidence, then, that when people with current or previous alcohol problems are asked about their family backgrounds, they are more likely to report a parent with a drinking problem than are people in the general population.

It also seems reasonable to expect that there might be gender differences. It is the case that the majority of the work which has been conducted in this area has been with men—both as the problem drinkers in the first generation, and as the offspring in the second generation. Research which has been carried out with more of a focus on women, though, suggests that when alcohol problems do occur in women a positive family history is more often found than is the case for men with drinking problems. Evidence for this suggestion has come from a retrospective study (Latcham, 1985) and a US population survey (Midanik, 1983), as well as from the review articles cited above which showed that the likelihood of having either or both of an 'alcoholic' mother or father was 50% greater for female 'alcoholics' than it was for male 'alcoholics'. It could be the case that a more severe family history of problematic drinking is a necessary condition for women to manifest drinking problems themselves. Alternatively, women might be more influenced by the home environment than men. It is possible, also, that women might be more sensitive to drinking in the family, might use a less restrictive definition of problem or excessive drinking, and might therefore be more likely to report a positive family history (Midanik, 1983).

Irrespective of any gender differences, however, there are major difficulties with this type of retrospective research conducted on samples who already have alcohol problems. These difficulties are due primarily to the respondents' treatment status. First, it is not known how representative problem drinkers are who are hospitalized or in treatment as compared with problem drinkers in the community at large. It is known from general population surveys (e.g. Cahalan, 1970) that the majority of problem drinkers are never treated professionally, and it is possible that the greater representation of parental drinking problems among treated problem drinkers simply reflects the latter's greater propensity to seek treatment rather than their greater risk of developing problems.

Second, by only examining offspring who are casualties, no information is made available about the percentage of offspring who do well *despite* parental drinking status. Even if one accepts that having a parental drinking problem does raise the risk of offspring problem drinking, investigating only the casualites of this upbringing does not allow for an accurate assessment of the real degree of risk. The danger of over-predicting the future risk for people thought to be in a high risk group on account of events or difficulties in earlier life which are presumed to be harmful, has been pointed out in relation to the children of problem drinkers specifically (Heller *et al.*, 1982) and in the field of psychology and prevention more generally (Orford, 1992).

There are relatively fewer reports of research which has either examined respondents drawn from the community or which has utilized a longitudinal, prospective design. Among the more important prospective studies are those by Rydelius (1981), Nylander and Rydelius (1982), Miller and Jang (1977), and Beardslee *et al.* (1986), and among the very few community studies are those by Clair and Genest (1987) and Benson and Heller (1987).

Prospective Studies

Longitudinal research is a highly difficult area, replete with pitfalls (Baekeland *et al.*, 1975; Baltes, 1968; Wall and Williams, 1970). Some of these are: that measures taken at the outset often become irrelevant (or at least less than wholly satisfactory) a generation later; the distorting effects of selective sampling (e.g. studying only child guidance clinic referrals, see Robins, 1966, below) and selective attrition; and the effects upon respondents of being repeatedly tested. Besides these problems, the fact is that longitudinal studies are extremely costly and time consuming, and they require a long-term commitment from both funding agencies and researchers since, as Heller *et al.* (1982) argue, few researchers, "would be prepared to wait, as at-risk children matured, for a period of time which could correspond to their productive lives as researchers!" (p. 195).

Nevertheless, two sorts of prospective study of relevance to our interests have been performed. The first concerns follow-ups of samples of children drawn from child guidance clinics or other similar sources; and the second concerns follow-ups of samples of the children of problem drinkers.

The Cambridge-Somerville Youth Study started in 1935 as an experiment in delinquency prevention. The group of youths was made up of 650 boys (average age 9 years), "referred by schools, welfare agencies, police, and churches" (McCord and McCord, 1960, p. 6). Half of these boys

(N = 325) were 'normal' and half (N = 325) 'predelinquent' (p. 6). These terms are not rigourously defined, delinquency prognosis being assigned on an 11-point scale by a committee of judges who, "considered the boy's likelihood of becoming delinquent" (p. 7). Half of each group received a 5-year counselling programme. It was also found that some of both the 'predelinquent' and the control boys had alcohol-misusing parents (defined as, "...repeated drinking [which] at some time prior to 1945 had interfered with their interpersonal relations or their social or economic functioning", McCord and McCord, 1962, p. 415). The fact that some of both groups had 'alcoholic fathers' enabled the issue of intergenerational transmission to be investigated. These authors followed up 255 out of the 325 'treated' participants and found that 29 of their sample had so far developed alcohol problems. The existence of such a problem was based on four criteria: "Any of the subjects who had been members of Alcoholics Anonymous, who had been referred to a hospital in Massachusetts for alcoholism, who were known as alcoholics by the Boston Committee on Alcoholism or by other social agencies, or who had been convicted by the courts for public drunkenness at least twice were considered alcoholic" (McCord and McCord, 1962, p. 414). When they examined the status of the parents of these 29 alcohol misusers, they found that 22% of the sons of 51 alcohol-misusing fathers had become alcohol misusers themselves, as compared to 12% of the sons of 126 non-alcohol misusers, a difference which seems large but which is not statistically significant. They also found that 31% of the sons of 26 criminal fathers as compared to 12% of the sons of 151 non-criminal fathers had become alcohol misusers, a statistically significant result. There are numerous problems with this study—the McCords did not reinterview their participants, taking all their information from records and public agencies; a disproportionate number of their alcohol-misusing offspring came from the 'predelinquent' group, confusing the issue of parental alcohol-misuse status with the fact that the child was already designated 'at-risk' at the start of the study; the authors never separated out the effect of parental alcohol misuse from that of parental conflict and family disharmony; and the study was only conducted with males. These problems imply that one should interpret the Cambridge-Somerville results with some caution, but this should not detract from the fact that the research is one of the few major longitudinal studies which has attempted to examine the intergenerational effects of alcohol misuse.

Robins (1966) followed up 382 boys who were admitted at approximately age 13 to a child guidance clinic some 30 years previously, collecting reliable information on 286 of these men. Robins found that so far 78

(27%) of the sample had developed an alcohol problem at some point in their lives, but that, "fathers reported to drink excessively were no more likely to produce alcoholic children than fathers who were arrested, were erratic workers, had deserted, were guilty of sexual misbehaviour, or beat their wives or children. Apparently the presence of an antisocial father in the home predisposes a child to excessive drinking whether or not the father sets an example of drinking" (Robins *et al.*, 1962, p. 407). On the other hand, Robins found that the type of referral to the child guidance clinic in the first place was important in predicting those who would later misuse alcohol. "Patients referred for antisocial behaviour had a very high rate of excess alcohol intake as adults as compared with other patients or control subjects...almost half the men who had been antisocial referrals had some social problems with alcohol, and one-fifth were still having problems at time of follow-up" (Robins, 1966, p. 61). Again problems exist with this study—most of the child guidance referrals were for antisocial behaviour, creating a biased and more at-risk population; and due to this, large numbers of the sample went on to develop what Robins terms 'sociopathy' as well as alcohol problems, creating problems in separating out clearly distinctive antecedents of alcohol misuse from those of 'sociopathy'.

Nylander (1979) reported a similar study. A total of 2,164 child guidance attenders were followed up 20 years later. Of this number, 123 (99 men and 24 women) had developed problems with their alcohol or drug use to the extent of being described as 'chronic addicts'. The average age of the children at the time they made contact with the child guidance clinic was 9 years. Nylander's data show that, "a remarkably large proportion of those who became chronic addicts came from home environments that were very badly disturbed; 42% of the boys and 38% of the girls had fathers who were alcoholics or who were mentally sick, 29% of the boys and 38% of the girls had mothers who were alcoholics or who were mentally sick, and 60% of the boys and 58% of the girls had parents who were divorced. In the majority of cases, 92% of the boys and 83% of the girls, the symptoms registered (on referral) were of the 'acting-out' type, and at the time of their contact with the clinic 57% of the boys and 33% of the girls were already exhibiting antisocial symptoms (pilfering, theft, absconding, etc.)" (pp. 25–26). Unluckily, Nylander does not allow the reader to separate out the influence of 'alcoholism' versus 'mental sickness', nor these from the influence of divorce. Berry (1967; Ricks and Berry, 1970) reported the results of a similar study that reached very similar conclusions. In agreement with the previously cited studies, Berry found that boys who later developed alcohol problems were more often referred in the first place for problems concerning 'acting out' or aggressive delinquency, and came from homes which were characterized by chaos and disorganization.

These studies, however, all suffer from the problem that their results were derived from samples of people who had already exhibited a dispro-portionate amount of antisocial behaviour prior to the development of any alcohol or other drug problems. The second group of studies involves following up the children of problem drinkers irrespective of whether the offspring had problems themselves as children, although this is a group already shown in the first part of this chapter to be at greatly increased risk of developing problems during childhood. Rydelius (1981) conducted a 20-year follow up, using public records, of the children who were the subjects of the study by Nylander (1960) that was reviewed earlier in this chapter. These children showed a relatively poor adulthood adjustment when compared with a matched control group. The data Rydelius presented show that the sons of 'alcoholic' fathers were more likely to have been registered as having alcohol and criminal problems, to have needed social services assistance, to have had more days of sickness, to have made more use of both physical and psychiatric clinics and hospitals, and during their visits to the physical hospitals to have been noted more frequently as showing signs of alcohol misuse and drunkenness. The evidence for poor outcome for daughters is less clear, but they too were more likely to have needed social services assistance, had more days of sickness, made more visits to psychiatric hospitals or clinics for problems with alcohol or drugs, made more visits to physical hospitals and clinics, and during their visits to these physical hospitals to have been noted more frequently as showing signs of alcohol misuse. Daughters were also more likely to have had more children, and sons more changes of domicile. Rydelius reports that the factors in childhood which best correlated with poor adulthood adjustment were symptoms of aggression in the child and signs of neglect in the child such as poor dental status. Certainly the former factor accords with the studies following up child guidance populations, suggesting that childhood antisocial behaviour is strongly linked to later adulthood alcohol misuse.

A problem with the above study, noted by the author, is that the chil-dren originally recruited by Nylander were predominantly from lower social status groups, raising the possibility that these findings are not generalizable to other populations with a different social status. In order to examine this possibility further, Nylander and Rydelius (1982) performed a second study utilizing a follow-back design. They selected all the male 'alcoholics' who had attended a local alcoholism clinic between 1962 and 1967 who

(a) had children and (b) belonged to either the highest or the lowest social strata. This selection exercise created a sample of 90 treated alcoholics, 50 men from the lowest and 40 men from the highest social classes, who between them had 185 children, 85 from the high class families and 100 from the low. These children ranged in age from 5 to 48. They then searched official records for evidence of problematic outcome. Their conclusion was that if the father is a 'chronic alcoholic', coming from a higher social class family of origin does not improve outcome. "Despite a better social and economic background they get into financial trouble just as often, they are responsible for as many acts of juvenile asocial behaviour, and they become criminals and addicts to the same degree as the children with a far worse social and economic background" (p. 813).

Again, both these studies suffer from the fact that the sampling might well be biased—the same issue as was discussed earlier while reviewing the effects on offspring while they are still children. The children were selected because their parents were in treatment for their alcohol problems, and as Heller *et al.* (1982) argue, "the point is that we simply do not know how representative alcoholics who are hospitalized or in treatment are compared with alcoholics, problem, or heavy drinkers in the community at large. Similarly, we do not know the extent of the risk to offspring when parental drinking is untreated" (p. 188).

Three other prospective studies have not been confined to the offspring of treated problem drinkers. Miller and Jang (1977) followed up 259 children reared in lower-class, poor, multi-problem urban families, 20 years after their initial selection for the study. 147 of these children had an 'alcoholic parent' and 112 of them were controls with no official record of alcoholism but with a "similar multiplicity of problems" (p. 24). The criteria for categorizing parents as 'alcoholics' were not, however, reported. All the respondents were interviewed. Miller and Jang found that 36% of the offspring group as opposed to 16% of the control group drank heavily (defined as drinking five or more drinks per occasion), and that those offspring with 'alcoholic' parents fared less well in terms of mental health problems, marital difficulties of their own, employment, and financial stability.

The most important prospective study in this category is that by Vaillant (1983; Beardslee *et al.*, 1986; Drake and Vaillant, 1988). They report on a 40-year prospective study of working-class families in which 170 men with one or more 'alcoholic' parents were compared with 230 men without an 'alcoholic' parent. They found that the degree of exposure to 'alcoholism' in childhood (as assessed on a 15-point scale created by including all material collected originally on the child and his family until age 17—direct interview material, family interviews, school records, psychological tests) was significantly correlated with later life alcohol use (r = 0.22), alcoholism (r = 0.21), sociopathy (r = 0.17), and death by the time of the 40-year follow-up (r = 0.18). However, they also found that most of this impairment occurred in those offspring who actually developed alcoholism; when they were eliminated from the analysis, there were no significant differences between the two groups. This finding led the authors to conclude that there existed, "considerable resiliency in terms of overall functioning, in children of alcoholics who do not develop alcohol misuse" (p. 589). The authors also report that degree of exposure to parental alcoholism was unrelated to later life rates of unemployment, poor physical health, or measures of 'adult ego functioning'.

Finally, Knop *et al.* (1985) are following up the cohort of 233 sons of alcoholic fathers born in Copenhagen in 1959–1961, which was described earlier, comparing them with 107 control children. The group of children were 19–20 at the time of the research reported in 1985. Data are presented examining these young people's alcohol consumption in the previous week. There were no differences between the two groups, with average consumption equalling 17 and 18 units of alcohol (1 unit = 1/4 oz absolute alcohol) in the offspring and control groups, respectively (which is a similar amount to Danish norms for that group), and with 36 and 34%, respectively, consuming more than 20 units of alcohol in the preceding week.

Community Samples

Considering the problems inherent in conducting longitudinal research outlined above, it is not surprising that so few studies of this type have been carried out. What is surprising is that, given the theoretical and practical interest in this area, so few studies using community samples have been performed.

Nevertheless, there have now been a number of studies reported in which young adults, with and without family histories of 'alcoholism', have been asked about their own drinking and drinking problems. From our point of view, however, there are a number of difficulties in interpreting the results of these studies. For one thing, some of them are more concerned with a positive family history of 'alcoholism' than with having had a parent at home with a drinking problem. Hence they include in the 'family history positive' group, those with first degree relatives other than parents who have drinking problems (e.g. Schuckit and Sweeney, 1987, counted siblings with drinking problems although it appears that most of the family history positive group had at least one parent with a drinking problem) or even second degree relatives (e.g. Pandina and Johnson, 1990, counted both sib-lings and grandparents). A second problem is that samples have mostly been confined to college or university students in the USA. Furthermore, in terms of age the participants have almost all been in a transitional stage of the life cycle, most in their late teens or very early 20s. Most are therefore still very close to the experiences of childhood; indeed some are presum-ably still living with parents although the proportion still living at home is usually not stated. In fact, it is sometimes left unspecified whether a crucial variable, such as whether the young adult considers that s/he has (or has had) a drinking problem, refers only to a recent period of time (such as the last 12 months) or to the whole of the person's life time up to the present (e.g. Pandina and Johnson, 1990). Furthermore, the youthfulness of these samples means that many who will as adults develop drinking problems have yet to do so. All in all, these studies are rather limited as investigations of the long-term adulthood consequences of having been brought up in a home where one or both parents had drinking problems.

Notwithstanding these limitations, however, a pattern is beginning to emerge from these studies. The first, perhaps surprising finding is an absence of substantial differences in recent alcohol consumption between those with and without parents (and sometimes siblings and grandparents) with alcohol problems (Schuckit and Sweeney, 1987; Alterman, Searles and Hall, 1989; Engs, 1990; Pandina and Johnson, 1990). So, for example, Engs reported that there was no association between family history of alco-hol abuse and the mean amount of alcohol consumed per week, and fur-ther that there was no difference in terms of drinking patterns between those with a family history, and those with a negative family background without such a family history. There are some small differences which are reported. For example, Schuckit and Sweeney found that, amongst male university students and non-academic staff, those with both first and sec-ond degree 'alcoholic' relatives reported the highest mean number of drinking days per month and the earliest age of onset of drinking. Another study (Alterman *et al.*), of male college students, found those with 'alcoholic' fathers reported on average more days drinking per month, more drinks consumed per day, and more days intoxicated monthly than those with only second degree 'alcoholic' relatives, or those with no such relatives. Yet these were trends only, and the differences were small and statistically insignificant. These results showing a lack of substantial differences could be partly due to the academic high achievement of the samples, but Pandina and Johnson also found no differences between groups on a combined alcohol quantity/frequency/frequency-of-intoxication measure in a random community sample.

Differences do sometimes emerge, however, when the outcome of interest has been alcohol-related problems, as opposed to alcohol-consumption measures, and particularly when participants have been asked for global assessments of whether they have drinking problems themselves. Schuckit and Sweeney (1987) found group differences for a number of self-reported alcohol-related problems (e.g. experience of morning shakes, black-outs, drunk and disorderly offences, persistent problems with alcohol) and in terms of a number of indices of drug use and drug problems (e.g. used hallucinogens, used amphetamines, used cocaine, drug-related hospital visit). In most instances it was the group with both first *and* second degree 'alcoholic' relatives that stood out from the others. Pandina and Johnson (1990) found no group differences in scores on standard scales of harmful consequences of alcohol consumption and of marijuana consumption, but did find substantial differences in the numbers of respondents stating that they had an alcohol or drug problem, or that they had been in treatment for such (12% of those with parents or grandparents with drinking problems versus 6% of those without). Most of the problems reported were alcohol-related but the difference was equally great and significant in the case of drug problems. Most of this difference, however, was attributable to a four-fivefold contrast for the female members of the sample. Claydon (1987) also found significantly higher proportions of first year university students with 'alcoholic' parents (based on a global Yes/Not Sure/No statement plus answers to a standard 30-item Children of Alcoholics Screening Test developed by Pilat and Jones, 1982) reporting having drinking problems (9.8% *vs* 2.5% of those without 'alcoholic' parents), drug problems (4.9% *vs* 1.5%) and eating problems (13.1% *vs* 5.8%). Male students were significantly more likely than females to have drinking and drug problems, but female 'children of alcoholics' were *proportionally* more likely than males to have such problems. On the other hand, female students were overall more likely to have eating problems, but male 'children of alcoholics' were *proportionally* more likely to have such problems than females. It is also interesting to note that for each type of problem the positive group includes a majority who were 'not sure' whether they had the problem. It seems very likely that children of parents with drinking problems may be more than usually sensitive to the possibility of developing such problems themselves.

Of special note is the study carried out by Benson (1980; Barnes *et al.*, 1978; Benson and Heller, 1987). She screened women employed by a U.S. university and 1,145 women enrolled in undergraduate psychology classes in the same university. From this she created a sample of 129 daughters of 'alcoholic' fathers, and a sample of 111 daughters of non-alcoholic fathers to act as a control group, split into a group of 30 with 'psychiatrically disturbed fathers' and a group of 81 with fathers with neither alcohol nor psychiatric problems. She compared these three groups and found that there were no differences in alcohol consumption, but that daughters of both the 'problem parent' groups showed a higher level of 'neurotic symptomatology' and 'acting out' than did the comparison group. She further found that very little of the variance in outcome was related to the existence of a parent with a drinking problem *per se*, finding instead that family climate and social support were more important influences on daughters' adjustment than was a father's history of alcohol problems or psychiatric difficulties. There were problems with this study, however: Benson utilized only women (although this is a refreshing difference from the usual sex bias to males), and only college level respondents, and so it is unclear how her results might generalize to the wider population. There is also the possibility, raised by the author herself, that this sample, by having attained a college level of education, "may have already succeeded to some extent in overcoming the effects of parental alcoholism. Thus [the] sample may be more representative of a subgroup of less vulnerable daughters or 'coping successes' than of all daughters of alcoholic fathers" (Barnes *et al.*, 1978, p. 220).

A study using a community sample which does not suffer from some of the problems outlined above is that by Parker and Harford (1987). They used data from an interview study of a representative sample of over 1,100 employed men and women aged over 18 who lived in metropolitan Detroit. They divided their sample into five categories of drinker and found that 17% (N = 13 out of 76) of the men with heavier drinking parents were dependent drinkers with drink-related problems—i.e. the most serious category—whereas only 6% (N = 22 out of 373) of the men with lighter drinking parents were in this category. The figures for women show that 9% (N = 9 out of 103) with heavier drinking parents were dependent drinkers with drink-related problems, whereas only 2% (8 out of 414) with lighter drinking parents were in this category. It may be thought that this result contradicts Benson's findings, reviewed above, but this is not the case. Benson reported that there were no differences in levels of alcohol consumption on the basis of father's drinking category, whereas Parker and Harford reported on their respondents' drink-related problems and their symptoms of dependence; consumption was not reported.

There are problems with this study as well—the percentages in all the categories are very low (other than for male "dependent drinkers with drink-related problems" who had heavy drinking parents); the methods of ascertaining parental drinking status are extremely loose and were not subject to any checks or clarifications; the timespans during which the parent might have been a heavy drinker were not specified; the relationship between 'heavy' drinking in this study and 'problem drinking' or 'alcoholism' in other studies is not explicated; and no other measures of adulthood adjustment were included besides drink-related problems. On the other hand, this is a study utilizing a large sample; it examines both men and women; it does not study selected populations of students; and it does include socio-economic status variables in its analyses.

A further study using a community sample is also reported by Parker and Harford (1988). In this study the authors reanalyzed data from a national survey of the drinking practices of adults in the United States. The sample consisted of 1,772 adults (762 men and 1,010 women) with a mean age of 45 for the men and 44 for the women. Parker and Harford show that, once socio-demographic characteristics are controlled for, having an alcohol-misusing parent places sons at risk for dependent problem drinking (13% of men with alcohol-misusing parents are classified as dependent problem drinkers *vs* 4% of men without such parents), both sons and daughters are at risk for divorce or separation (11% of men with alcohol-misusing parents are classified as having disrupted marriages *vs* 6% of men without such parenting, and 15% of women with alcohol-misusing parents *vs* 8% of women without such parenting), and daughters are at risk for depressive symptomatology (28% of women having alcohol-misusing parents score 16 or more on the Centre for Epidemiological Studies Depression Scale *vs* 17% of women without such parenting). When a regression analysis is performed on these variables, controlling for age, education, family income, and race, all the above results reach statistical significance at the $p < 0.05$ level. As with the previous Parker and Harford paper reviewed above, alcohol consumption was not reported in this paper.

A final study to be reviewed in this section is of a representative sample of adults living in the USA (a household survey carried out in one county in New York State, Russell *et al.*, 1990) which produced comparable findings. Russell (1990) has reviewed the results of this study and those of the national drinking practices survey described above. When she computed the relative odds of having any alcohol-related problems in the past year, for those adults with 'father-only-alcoholic' versus 'neither-parent-alcoholic' (these being the largest categories), and did the same for the relative odds of having any alcohol-dependence symptoms in the past year, the relative odds ratios were found to be comparatively modest. For men these lay between 1.4 : 1 and 1.7 : 1, and for women between 0.9 : 1 and 3.0 : 1. As she says, these results, "...seem to indicate that past clinical studies may overestimate the prevalence of alcoholism among children of alcoholics in the general population" (p. 35).

She warns, however, that there may be great variability in the magnitude of risk for different sub-groups in the population. For example, an analysis of the New York State data by race and age produced some interesting results. For young whites (aged 19–34 years) and for older blacks (aged 55 years or more), the relative odds ratio for those with a positive family history of alcohol problems was modest and not significantly different from zero. For older whites (particularly those aged 55 or more) and for younger blacks, however, there was a significant three-fold or greater increased risk of alcohol abuse or dependence. Furthermore, it is clear from other results presented by Russell (1990) that the two sets of data she reviewed both suggest that women who report that *both* their parents have drinking problems are particularly at risk, although the numbers are very small. She also expresses concern that the judgements of offspring about the alcohol problems of their parents may not always be reliable—although she points out that there is evidence that such judgements often contain false negatives, but very rarely false positives (Thompson *et al.*, 1982)—and that the types of population survey that she reviewed are rarely sufficiently fine-grained to differentiate between types of 'alcoholism' which may have different aetiologies and run different courses across the life-span.

Before passing on to look at adulthood outcome variables other than drinking, it is important to note the suggestion that has been made that many offspring of the heaviest drinking parents may show a definite pattern of reaction against, or non-imitation of, their parents' heavy drinking. For example, Harburg *et al.* (1990) claimed to find evidence of this from a longitudinal community survey carried out in the USA. It was possible to compare the self-reports of drinking of the second generation as adults (aged 34 years on average, but ranging from late teens to 70s) with parallel reports given by their parents 17 years earlier. Their data certainly show that the biggest discrepancies between parent and offspring drinking—with offspring drinking relatively less than parents—occurs for those groups with the heaviest drinking parents. One explanation for this is in terms of a statistical artefact, namely 'regression to the mean', whereby those families towards the extremes of a distribution in the first generation are most likely to move towards the population mean in the second generation.

Harburg *et al.* argue, however, that this is not the case, since the same effect is not found at the other end of the distribution: their data show that offspring with abstinent or very light drinking parents are also particularly likely to be abstemious themselves as adults, whereas the 'regression to the mean' effect would predict that these offspring would be heavier drinkers in adulthood. Furthermore, there are some patterns in the data that suggest that non-imitation of very heavy drinking parents may really be occurring for some groups. In fact, this was most often the case for women with heavy drinking fathers, where the father displayed any signs of problem drinking while the daughter was growing up. In contrast, those women with heavy drinking fathers where the father showed no such signs were significantly less likely to report being abstainers or light drinkers themselves, and more likely to report being heavy drinkers. Harburg *et al.* are not the first to have made the observation that heavy or parental problem drinking may lead to abstention or very light drinking in the offspring (e.g. Vaillant, 1983; Hughes, Stewart and Barraclough, 1985).

In summary, then, although there exists extensive evidence demonstrating negative outcomes for the children of problem drinkers while they are still children, the evidence of negative outcomes once they reach adulthood, at least in terms of their drinking, is far less clear. The data from retrospective studies of current problem drinkers, and from prospective studies of children selected due to their problem status as children (such as the Robins study cited earlier) certainly suggest that there are strong inter-generational continuities at work. Yet the evidence from community samples and from prospective studies following-up problem-free children suggests that this risk may be greatly exaggerated.

In fact, it seems that, in terms of the adulthood adjustment of the children of problem drinkers, the outcome depends to a great extent upon the sampling and the exact nature of the outcome criteria. Adults with alcohol problems report problematic childhoods and a greater likelihood of having a problem-drinking parent; and problem children with alcohol-misusing parents are more likely to develop adulthood problems involving alcohol misuse. Yet adults with alcohol-misusing parents recruited from community samples, and children with problem drinking parents but without obvious problems as children, when followed up into adulthood, although reporting difficult childhoods, have not been found to report very different drinking outcomes than comparison respondents, at least when the outcome criterion is alcohol consumption. When the criterion has been alcohol-related problems or alcohol dependence, a moderately increased risk has most often been the finding.

Other Adulthood Outcomes

As we have outlined previously, most research on the adulthood outcomes for children of parents with drinking problems has been motivated by the search for specific transmission of drinking problems from one generation to the next. Depending upon one's beliefs about the ways in which transmission between the generations occurs—and theories about mechanisms of transmission will be the subject of the following section—this focus on drinking outcomes may or may not be thought unfortunate. It is certainly the case that there has been far less research devoted to possible outcomes in adulthood other than heavy or problematic drinking itself. What little work there has been is fragmentary and inconclusive but does at least suggest hypotheses for further testing.

For example, in Rydelius' (1981) 20-year follow-up of the children included in Nylander's (1960) Swedish study, referred to earlier, sons of fathers with drinking problems were more likely than controls to have had five or more changes of domicile as adults, to have had records with the social service assistance register, to have had notifications on the criminal offences register, to have had more days of sickness, and more visits to general hospitals. Of course, part of the difference might be the result of the development of problematic drinking in a relatively high proportion of the sons of problem drinking fathers, but this is probably not the whole explanation. There is much evidence, for example, that the origins of alcohol problems and of criminality, or what many psychiatrists call 'anti-social personality', are closely interlinked in complex ways (Pulkkinen, 1983). The existence of one may raise the risk of the other occurring later, both within the lifetime of a single individual as well as across generations.

Rydelius' study raises another issue which can very easily become submerged but which we wish to keep close to the surface of discussion throughout this book. This is the issue of gender differences in processes of transmission between the generations. There were some interesting sex differences in Rydelius' findings. For one thing results were less clear for daughters of problem drinking fathers. For example, they were not significantly more likely than control women to have had many changes of domicile or to have had notifications on the criminal offences register. They had more days of sickness, however, and more visits to general hospitals. One significant difference emerged for daughters that was not present for sons: daughters of fathers with drinking problems had had more children themselves by the time the study was carried out. We shall return, towards the end of this chapter, to consider this latter finding and others like it.

There is psychiatric research, also, that suggests that the risks for daughters of problem drinking parents may be rather different than those for sons. Several retrospective family studies of psychiatric populations have shown that for women patients, compared to men, there may be a relatively strong link between a family history of drinking problems and outcomes such as 'anti-social personality', 'borderline personality disorder', eating disorder of the bulimic type, and depression (Winokur, 1972; Lewis *et al.*, 1983; Collins *et al.*, 1985; Loranger and Tulis, 1985). These findings are supported by community surveys. For example, the study cited earlier by Parker and Harford (1988) of a national survey of drinking practices by adults in the United States showed that daughters (but not sons) are at increased risk for depressive symptoms.

Many researchers have been more interested in effects upon adulthood personality than upon psychiatric disorder. In fact, although it has often been assumed that a parental drinking problem will leave its mark on the adulthood personality of the offspring, there is remarkably little sound evidence for this. Windle (1990) reviewed 27 studies of the personalities of offspring of problem drinking parents. Between them these studies appear to have produced next to nothing of note, with far more negative results than positive. For example, three out of four studies of anxiety or 'neuroticism' found no significant differences between 'children of alcoholics' and controls, and five studies of positive attributes such as self-esteem and outgoingness, produced no differences. It is possible, however, that weaknesses in the research might be responsible. Study populations varied greatly in age of offspring and were often unrepresentative—a number only included university students for example (something which we have already noted above concerning many of the community samples). Furthermore, most studies relied upon a rather simple, and probably outdated, notion of personality which views this in terms of a collection of traits which remain relatively stable throughout adult life. Windle was critical of the research on these grounds, and also stressed the need to acknowledge that the developmental pathways through life may be different for men and women. For example, if women do develop drinking problems in adulthood, Windle argues that this is very likely to follow depression or marital dissatisfaction, whereas for men depression and marital problems are more likely to *follow* the development of drinking problems (Dahlgren, 1979; Helzer and Pryzbeck, 1988, cited by Windle, 1990).

There is now a great deal of interest in this subject, particularly in the USA, and new research findings are coming out all the time. These may clarify the position eventually, but to date they are not fully convincing. For example Rearden and Markwell (1989) did find lower scores on a standard scale of self-esteem for college students who were identified as 'children of alcoholics', but this sample was of course still comparatively youthful (average age 19 years) and the difference in self-esteem scores of 'children of alcoholics' *vs* controls was a small one. In a college sample of the same age, Jarmas and Kazak (1992) found 'children of alcoholics' to score significantly higher than controls on a sub-scale of a Depressive Experiences Questionnaire designed to assess self-criticism. This finding is in fact more interesting than most because it was predicted on the basis of the researchers' theory about the family circumstances of children of problem drinking parents and how those might affect adulthood personality. It was just this kind of self-criticism or what they called 'introjective depression'— rather than other kinds of depressive experiences which were measured but which showed no differences between groups—which they expected would follow from the inconsistent and ambivalent images of parental figures that were likely to pertain for children of problem drinking parents.

Black (e.g. 1979) has been one of the most consistent advocates in the USA for the position that all children of problem drinking parents are affected even in the long term and even when appearances are to the contrary. She and her colleagues (Black *et al.*, 1986) compared 409 children of problem drinking parents with 179 controls, all adults aged 28 years or more, in terms of problems in a number of areas of personality. Large percentages of the former group admitted to problems such as problems trusting people (60%), problems identifying feelings (58%) and problems putting self first (65%). There were, however, a number of difficulties with the methods used in this research. Participants were recruited via notices in a number of specialist magazines and journals and would hence have had some professional or personal interest in alcohol problems: indeed no less than 37% of the 'children of alcoholics' described themselves as 'alcoholic' and 21% considered themselves to be married to an 'alcoholic'. The method used was a self-completed, postal questionnaire, and there is no indication that the personality problems were defined at all carefully. Quite apart from these problems of method, it is interesting to note that members of the control group also reported these personality problems in quite large numbers (35%, 35% and 50%, respectively, considered they had the three problems mentioned above).

Another approach to the question of effects on adulthood personality which has been suggested by Black (e.g. 1979) and taken up by others, is that of defensive role patterns developed in the family of origin as a means of coping with a parental drinking problem. For example, Rhodes and

Blackham (1987) developed a Children of Alcoholics Family Role Instrument (CAFRI) on the basis of Black's ideas, to assess four roles: responsible child, adjuster, placator, and acting-out child. They found higher scores on acting-out role for a small group of high school students with parents with drinking problems compared to controls, with borderline differences for adjuster and placator. The groups were almost identical on the responsible child scale although this is one of the roles that children of problem drinking parents are often said to adopt. The main problem with this small study from our point of view is the age of the participants (mid to late teens). There is no evidence from this study that these roles have become rigid nor that they will necessarily be dysfunctional in the long term, as Black's theory suggests. Nevertheless, this work has the advantage of being derived from a theory of what happens to offspring of parents with drinking problems and how they develop.

The discussion about both Black's work (and research derived from her writings) and that of Jarmas and Kazak has implied that we should take their research somewhat more seriously because both stemmed from relatively clear theoretical notions. This is worth making explicit. Too much of the research into this area has been of the 'trawl' kind, where researchers have realised that the area is of interest, and then investigated it in a seemingly atheoretical way. It is our belief that sufficient is known about child and adult development, about the genesis of psychological problems, and about the impact of early life experiences on later adult adjustment, for research to proceed in a far more theory-driven way, where researchers would make testable predictions as to what they would expect to find given their theoretical position. Making the theory explicit enables an informed and far more interesting, in-depth, and critical debate to take place.

Despite its undoubted theoretical interest, Black's work has been much criticised. For example, Burk and Sher (1988) are amongst those who have been highly critical of the assumption made by Black and others that all 'children of alcoholics' (or COAs as they are often referred to in the literature from the USA) either display clear signs of maladjustment as adults, or have carried into adulthood dysfunctional, defensively adoptive roles. They argue that it is possible to identify perfectly well-adjusted young adults who have had parents with drinking problems (they cite Werner's 1986 report on 'resilient offspring of alcoholics', as well as Burk's, 1985, own unpublished work) and they suggest that there is a real danger of over-predicting adulthood risk or even of *creating* some additional harm by a process of labelling people as 'children of alcoholics' who would not otherwise be at risk.

Burk and Sher (1988) point out that we need to know far more about the variables associated with long-term risk before we can be confident about identifying high risk groups and offering preventive interventions. There are signs that work is beginning on identifying these variables but it is at an early stage. For example, Clair and Genest (1987) compared 30 young adults (aged between 18–23 years) who had 'alcoholic' fathers and who were recruited from a range of sources, with 40 university students without parents with drinking problems. The former group were just significantly higher on a scale of depression-proneness but there were no differences on a measure of self-esteem. Within the former group, however, depression-proneness and low self-esteem were significantly correlated with the participants' reports of lack of family-of-origin cohesion and emotional expressiveness as well as with less informational and emotional support received and problem-focussed coping used at home between the ages of 13 and 18. The sample size for this study was small and the methodology weak in a number of respects, but this is at least one study that goes beyond a simple comparison of those with and without a history of drinking problems, seeking to find those factors that might put people particularly at risk.

Another recent study, with larger numbers but again confined to students, which is also suggestive of the directions in which one might look for leads on this question of risk, asked young adults with and without problem drinking parents to fill in a lengthy inventory about their own verbal and non-verbal social skills (Jones and Houts, 1992). Having a problem drinking parent was only directly related to one of seven social skills scales (emotional sensitivity was reported to be less for those young people with parents with drinking problems) but most of the significant effects involving parental problem drinking were interaction effects involving aspects of the rated family environment. For example, non-verbal emotional expression (the ability to be animated and display emotions, especially sadness and anger) and verbal social expression (the ability to express oneself verbally and enjoy socialising with others) were both low when the young person reported both parental problem drinking and parental criticism. In fact the results of the Jones and Houts study show that gender effects were considerably stronger than either the direct or interaction effects of having had a parent with a drinking problem, with women reporting higher scores for scales such as emotional expression, emotional sensitivity and social expression, and with men reporting higher scores on emotional control and social manipulation.

Berkowitz and Perkins (1988) report interaction effects between gender and having had a parent with a drinking problem amongst their sample of several hundred college students (mostly aged between 18–20 years). Although they found that offspring of problem drinking parents were similar to others on most of the personality measures they used, the former were higher on a scale of self-depreciation (a measure of depression and low self-esteem). The difference was significant for women alone but not for men. One other measure—independence-autonomy—was significantly higher for male offspring of parents with drinking problems but not for females.

Although many of these studies suggest possible long-term effects on the offspring of problem drinkers, they are very limited in a number of ways. They are mostly purely cross-sectional in design, involving retrospective accounts of family life, and having no follow-up. Almost all are based on University samples of very young adults who have only recently left home. Such studies can tell us nothing about the longer-term adulthood consequences of having been brought up in a family where a parent had a drinking problem. These studies of possible moderating factors and interaction effects, however, do begin to take us into a discussion of the mechanisms whereby transmission of alcohol problems in one generation to problems in the next generation might occur.

Before moving on to examine possible mechanisms of transmission in greater detail, mention should be made of a particular form of transmission (if indeed that is the right word in this case) that has been supposed to affect daughters in particular. The idea has long been held that offspring of parents with drinking problems—particularly women with fathers with such problems—are more likely as adults to marry people with drinking problems. Indeed, there exists some tentative evidence to substantiate such a claim: for example, James and Goldman (1971) and MacDonald (1956) found that 22% and 28%, respectively, of wives of men with drinking problems were also daughters of men with such problems. In the literature of the 1950's there was a strong tendency to interpret these observations and findings in terms of conscious or unconscious mate 'choice' on the part of women who, it was claimed, were attracted to men who were already heavy drinkers, or who had personality characteristics which predisposed them to develop drinking problems. The mechanisms thought to be involved varied, but they included the idea that such a marriage represented a displaced, unconscious attempt to cure the father's alcohol problems (e.g. Kubie, 1956). Although such ideas are unattractive to more recent writers who adopt a general structural approach, or a more specific feminist approach to family issues (e.g. Dobash and Dobash, 1987), and despite the fact that they run the risk of perpetuating negative stereotypes of family members (Orford, 1987), these models for understanding the wives and daughters of problem drinkers are still strongly held by some. They have recently enjoyed a renaissance owing to the rise of the 'co-dependency' model (e.g. Haaken, 1990), which suggests again that people, particularly women, seek and remain in relationships with problem drinkers because they themselves are dependent upon being in such relationships.

One of the few studies which employed a control group to examine whether in fact the daughters of problem drinkers were more likely to be married to problem drinkers was that reported by Nici (1979). She compared the questionnaire responses of 28 wives of men with alcohol problems with those of 25 wives of hospitalised and 33 wives of non-hospitalised men without such problems. Five (18%) of the first group had had at least one parent described as having an alcohol problem (although it is not stated how many of these were fathers) compared to none in either comparison group—a statistically significant finding. Studies such as this, of course, suffer from the same problems of sampling as do the studies of problem drinkers in treatment that were reviewed at the beginning of this chapter. Simply knowing how many problem drinkers (or wives of problem drinkers as in these cases) report parents with drinking problems as compared to the general population or to specific comparison groups gives us no information about the percentage of offspring who do well *despite* their parental drink problem. Nevertheless, these studies do imply that daughters of male problem drinkers might be at particular risk of marrying someone with an alcohol problem, and this possibility needs further investigation, and further theoretical development, to enable us to better understand why this particular form of transmission might be taking place.

Finally, the possibility should be raised that some of the long-term effects of having been brought up in a home where a parent had a drinking problem might be seen as positive and adaptive rather than negative and harmful. For example, if increased independence or autonomy occurs in male offspring as Berkowitz and Perkins' (1988) findings suggest, these qualities may be useful in adult life. Some intriguing findings were pro-duced in a study in which a large number of close relatives of men treated for 'alcoholism' at the mental hospital in Iceland between 1881 and 1940 were traced through national archives. For sons, it was found that their risk of also having been admitted for the treatment of 'alcohol addiction' was five to six times that for the general population. What was additionally dis-covered, however, was that the close relatives of hospitalised 'alcoholics' were also more likely to be cited in Iceland's Who's Who and to have found employment in occupations requiring communication or social skills—such as professors, lawyers, clergymen, and parliamentarians (Karlsson, 1985). It was thought that the common factor in such successes might be, "…a drive to get things done, to make one's influence felt, or to convert others to one's opinion" (pp. 187–8).

In summary, then, very much less research has been conducted examining outcomes in the next generation which are not alcohol-related. What work that has been carried out is fragmentary and inconclusive, and often the theoretical base is not made explicit. There are some indications, however, that there might be gender differences in outcomes, with daughters possibly being more at risk for depression, for eating disorders, for various psychiatric 'personality disorders', and for marrying a problem drinker. There are also some indications that for both genders, there might be negative effects on self-esteem, particular types of depression, and interpersonal skills; and there has additionally been the suggestion that there might also be positive effects on offspring. Such an idea links in with the growing research area of 'resilience' which we will discuss later in this chapter.

POSSIBLE MECHANISMS OF TRANSMISSION

In order to establish beyond doubt that transmission does occur from one generation to the next, and certainly to be able to understand the process of transmission sufficiently to be confident about intervening preventively, we need to understand why certain characteristics of parents or conditions of childhood family life influence the next generation as adults. There are a number of possible mechanisms whereby alcohol problems in one generation might have effects on the next. For the sake of simplicity these will be dealt with under three subheadings: (1) Genetic-biological mechanisms, (2) Alcohol-specific environmental mechanisms (e.g. offspring learn to drink excessively by modelling themselves upon heavy drinking parents), and (3) General environmental mechanisms (e.g. offspring are affected by the family discord associated with a parental drinking problem).

Genetic-Biological Mechanisms

Twenty five years ago it might have been possible to write this summary of the possible mechanisms of intergenerational transmission with only a passing reference to genetics, or perhaps without any mention of it at all.

The assumption was widely held that sociological, peer group, family and other environmental factors could completely explain both the origins of drinking problems and the fact that they ran in families. Besides these factors genetics was thought to be of trivial importance. Since then there has been a resurgence of interest in genetic mechanisms generally in medicine (with the phenomenal growth of molecular genetics (Rowe, 1990)), and this has been true in the alcohol field as well. A number of twin, adoption and other studies have been conducted to establish whether and to what extent alcohol problems may be hereditary.

One of the most detailed and fair reviews of the role of genetics in the aetiology of drinking problems is that written by Searles (1988). His review focussed particularly upon those studies using the adoption methods since other methods used in behaviour genetics, such as family or consanguinity studies and studies of half siblings, cannot easily separate the effects of genetic and environmental similarities between family members. Twin studies appear to be able to make this separation by comparing monozygotic (MZ) and dizygotic (DZ) twins, but even then the possibility cannot be completely ruled out that monozygotic twins share more similar environments than do dizygotic twins. The two best twin studies according to Searles each found a substantial genetic influence. Hrubek and Omenn (1981) found a heritability for 'alcoholism' of 0.57 after examining the medical histories of a large number of male twin pairs who were aged 51–61 at the time of the study. Loehlin and Nichols (1976) studied a very large number of twins who were still attending high school and found heritability estimates ranging from 0.30 to 0.68 for various indices of alcohol abuse for males, but on the whole much lower heritability estimates for women. Cadoret (1990) reviewed those and eleven other twin studies from Sweden, Finland, the USA, Italy, Japan, Australia and the U.K. All found higher concordance rates for alcohol consumption, heavy drinking, or alcohol problems, amongst MZ than amongst DZ twin pairs, with the exception of the one British study (Gurling *et al.*, 1984) which found a small difference in the other direction.

The two major adoption studies reviewed by Searles were carried out in Scandinavian countries where extensive medical, criminal and personal records on the whole population were available. The first was that carried out by Goodwin and his colleagues in Denmark (Goodwin *et al.*, 1973, 1974, 1977). They found a significantly higher rate of 'alcoholism' (18% versus 5%) and higher rates of hospitalisation and symptoms associated with alcohol abuse amongst sons of parents hospitalised for 'alcoholism' (85% were fathers) than amongst sons of 'non-alcoholics' although all had been adopted away from these biological parents within the first six weeks of life. Rates for the sons of 'alcoholics' were just as high as rates for brothers who remained to be reared by their natural parents. The same results did not apply to daughters.

These results not only suggest that the genetic influence is strong, but also that environmental influence is negligible, and the results of this study have become quite widely known. Searles expressed surprise that this study had not been subject to more critical scrutiny than had been the case, and was inclined to attribute this to the apparently rather complex statistical methods used by modern behaviour geneticists, plus the neglect of genetics by social scientists who believe geneticists to be biased and their results as offering pseudo-scientific support for racist and oppressive policies. In fact, according to Searles and to other reviewers such as Peele (1986), the conclusions of the Danish studies can be questioned on a number of grounds. These include the relatively small sample sizes used (55 sons of alcoholics, 30 brothers, and 78 sons of non-alcoholics); the rather low threshold used to define 'alcoholism' amongst adoptees; the fact that the control group included individuals with parents who had been hospitalised with some other psychiatric diagnosis; that there was an unusually high rate of psychopathology amongst foster parents; and that sons of 'alcoholics' had a high divorce rate which in some cases could have been a cause of drinking problems. It is also the case that there were potentially very serious arithmetic inconsistencies in the original paper.

The second adoption study, carried out in Sweden, had a much larger sample size (Bohman *et al.*, 1981; Cloninger *et al.*, 1981). It also concluded that genetic influence was important and that the picture was different for men and women. It concluded in addition, however, that there were two types of alcohol abuse. One type was much more strongly genetically influenced—the 'male limited' type with an estimated heritability of 0.90—but it was much less prevalent (24%) amongst the adoptees, was confined to males, and was associated with severe alcohol abuse, extensive treatment, and severe criminality in the biological fathers. The more prevalent type—'milieu limited'—was found to have both genetic and environmental causes. Daughters of 'alcoholic' mothers were found to be particularly susceptible regardless of the presence of alcohol abuse in the fathers.

Once again Searles expressed surprise at the lack of critical comment on this study. He pointed out that: the rate of 'alcoholism' in biological parents was unusually high, which may indicate the use of a loose criterion for alcohol abuse or the possibility that the sample may have been unrepresentative of the general population because alcohol abuse was a factor influencing adoption; the study included no non-adopted control group; results for women were based upon very small numbers who showed any alcohol abuse; no account was taken of possible intrauterine effects; and alcohol problems in adoptees were measured only by the very crude index of appearance in Temperance Board and treatment records which may explain the absence of an expected increase in risk with age (which ranged from 23–43 years). All these factors may have affected the results. Although this study has usually been cited in support of genetic influence, Searles re-tabulated the results for male adoptees to show that only a minority (37.7%) of those with any alcohol abuse were positive for genetic influence (as opposed to 30.4% who were positive for environmental influence although this was based on very limited data), and that 45.0% were without genetic or measured environmental influence. This suggested to Searles that, "... environmental pressures, particularly ones that had not been identified, are substantially more important in determining alcohol abuse than are genetic factors" (p. 161). He also concluded that the apparent discovery of two types of alcohol problem should be considered at best preliminary and at worst unfounded.

Also relevant to the debate about genetic influence are the many studies that have now examined individuals, usually young men, with a family history of alcohol problems (so called 'high risk' or 'family history positive' individuals) to see whether they differ from those without a family history in ways that might suggest a mechanism for genetic transmission. No such mechanisms have yet been clearly established but there are a number of promising leads. A number of studies from the USA and from Denmark have suggested, for example, that young men with positive family histories of serious alcohol problems are less affected than those without such histories by moderate doses of alcohol. For example, the former rated themselves as less intoxicated and demonstrated less body sway (Schuckit, 1987). One study found that young men with a strong family history of drinking problems (father, paternal grandfather, and at least one other male on the father's side of the family) showed high cardiovascular reactivity (measured by changes in heart rate and changes in amplitude of digital blood volume) to an aversive stimulus (an electric shock) without alcohol, but showed less reaction than other groups after consuming alcohol (Finn and Pihl, 1987). These studies are at least consistent with the hypothesis that some men may inherit a vulnerability to developing drinking problems by virtue of their psychobiological responses to alcohol. Alcohol may for them be comparatively less aversive and/or more positively rewarding than for others.

It should be borne in mind, however, that the numbers of participants in these studies has often been quite small. The pattern of results has not always been consistent from study to study and the results need replicating. Furthermore, although in these studies groups are carefully matched for details of the participants' own drinking habits, the possibility cannot be completely ruled out that differences may be due to family influences transmitted by some environmental rather than genetic route.

Other possible biological 'markers' of vulnerability that have been investigated include brain-wave activity and the presence or absence of certain liver enzymes (Schuckit, 1987). Particular interest has focussed on the possibility that the absence of a particular form of the enzyme aldehyde dehydrogenase might protect people from drinking problems since its absence results in particularly high levels of blood acid aldehyde after drinking, leading to facial flushing, palpitations and nausea. It has been suggested that this 'flushing' response to small doses of alcohol might explain the comparatively low rate of alcohol problems amongst Chinese and other Oriental groups who are particularly likely to have inherited the lack of this enzyme. It is difficult to explain on this basis, however, why other groups with a high rate of this abnormality, such as Eskimos and North American Indians, should have comparatively high rates of drinking problems (Peele, 1986); nor is it clear whether these findings have relevance to differences in risk in other ethnic groups (Schuckit, 1987).

In fact the way behaviour geneticists now think about genetic influence has come a long way from the days when the debate was polarised in terms of 'nature' versus 'nurture' or even from the time when a single heritability estimate could be taken as providing a definitive answer to the question of how important genetics is in influencing a particular trait. For one thing, it is now generally accepted even by those whose primary scientific interest is in genetic-biological mechanisms that, "The final development of this disorder [i.e. 'alcoholism'] probably depends on the interaction between biological and environmental factors" (Schuckit, 1987, p. 307). It is also generally believed that any genetic influence is likely to depend upon the operation of many genes acting together (i.e. polygenetic inheritance) and that different sets of genes may contribute to different outcome variables. For example, Murray and Stabenau (1982) state, "It is ... unwise to assume that the same genetic factors contribute to an individual's likelihood of becoming dependent on alcohol as influence, for example, the same individual's chances of committing a crime while drunk" (p. 143).

To add to the complexity, it is accepted now that genetic and environmental influence may well be correlated. Three ways in which this may happen have been outlined (Plomin *et al.*, 1977; Searles, 1988). The correlation may be 'passive' i.e. children are exposed to environments that are not independent of their inherited genes. Or it may be 'reactive/evocative' i.e. other people respond differently to children with different genotypes. Or it may be 'active/niche seeking' i.e. individuals themselves may actively seek environments that suit their genotypes. Searles made the point that the implications of gene-environment correlations for the aetiology of alcohol problems had scarcely begun to be considered. He also pointed out that some such correlations of relevance for alcohol problems might actually be negative e.g. the existence of positive genetic influence might lead to a seeking of environments that *reduce* risk, and hence serve to compensate for the positive genotype. For example, the non-problem drinking parent may make special efforts to create such an environment, as may at-risk offspring themselves. Passive forms of gene-environment correlation might be particularly common in the early years of life, with the more active forms becoming more common later and continuing throughout life.

One thing is clear: behaviour genetics and the search for markers of genetically transmitted vulnerability are highly complex undertakings fraught with many of the same difficulties and uncertainties faced by those of us who have focussed our attention more upon environmental factors. Behaviour genetics relies upon 'quasi-experiments' or natural experiments such as twin births and adoption, rather than upon neat, controlled experiments. Multivariate statistics are used to test the goodness of fit to the data provided by certain models which inevitably have to make a number of simplifying assumptions e.g. that MZ twins are no more likely than other siblings to share environments, or that genetic and environmental influences are uncorrelated. In the case of the transmission of alcohol problems from one generation to the next, the weight of evidence currently implies that a genetic contribution of some degree should not be ignored, at least for some kinds of drinking problems amongst men. Much of the research has been confined to men, however, and there is as yet no convincing evidence of the importance of genetic influence for women. Even for men, genetic influence appears to be complex, partial and still mysterious, and much, perhaps most, of the variation in adulthood outcome may be explicable in environmental terms.

Alcohol-Specific Environmental Mechanisms

When it comes to exploring possible ways in which having a parent with a drinking problem might influence the future course of one's life, numerous possibilities present themselves. Amongst these are a number, based broadly upon social learning theory, that suggest a specific link between the way parents drink and the way their offspring learn to think, feel and act in relation to alcohol. Because these are specific hypotheses they are of course of little help in explaining other adulthood outcomes besides those related to the consumption of alcohol itself. Nevertheless, they are powerful contenders for explaining the one adulthood outcome for children of problem drinking parents that has captured most attention, namely the oft-claimed increased risk of repeating the pattern of excessive drinking in the next generation.

The specific theory that is most commonly put forward to explain a link between problem drinking in one generation and the next is that of behavioural modelling. Humans, like other animals, are strongly influenced by observing the actions of those around them, and tend to pick up their behaviour. The parent-child relationship provides the ideal conditions for the imitation or copying of behaviour (Bandura, 1971), since children are usually exposed to their parents as models over lengthy periods of time, parents are in a position of relatively high social power in relation to the child, and the parent is often held in high esteem by the child. Nor is the means of passing on drinking habits from parent to child limited to observational learning. Parents actively encourage certain offspring behaviours and discourage others by a variety of means. More subtle and difficult to resist, perhaps, is the influence parents may wield simply by making drinking in various ways and degrees more or less available at home. It is, after all, at home where the large majority of young adults report that they are first introduced to alcohol (Hawker, 1978; Barnes, 1990; Ellickson and Hayes, 1991; Foxcroft and Lowe, 1991). By a variety of means, therefore, we might reasonably expect that the drinking habits of parents would 'rub off' on their children. Indeed, surveys of adolescent and young adult populations have repeatedly shown the existence of significant positive correlations between the extent of parent and offspring drinking (Jessor and Jessor, 1977; Orford, 1985). The same is true for a number of health-related lifestyle behaviours including smoking (e.g. Bauman *et al.*, 1990). Although some of the surveys of drinking have focussed upon special groups such as students or have relied upon the young adult informants for data on parental drinking, others have employed more representative samples and separate interviews with parents and offspring (e.g. Barnes *et al.*, 1986) and still found the same results.

Cross-sectional surveys almost always find that the drinking habits of close friends are much more highly correlated with young people's drinking than is the drinking of parents. Since friends' and parents' drinking are usually themselves correlated, the latter is often swamped by the former in multivariate statistical analysis (e.g. Orford *et al.*, 1974). It may be wrong, however, to draw the conclusion that parental influence is unimportant besides the influence of a peer group. For one thing parental influence can be presumed to start operating at an earlier age and indeed may be amongst the factors influencing choice of friends and the drinking habits of friendship groups once formed, as has been suggested by Kandel and Andrews (1987) and Foxcroft and Lowe (1991).

It may also be the case that parental drinking may have delayed effects and/or may affect the drinking of offspring in ways that are more crucial in terms of risk for future problem drinking, than is the case for the influence of the drinking of friends. A number of studies of the use of illicit drugs have shown that different factors may be differentially predictive at different stages of the process of developing problems (e.g. Robins *et al.*, 1977; Kandel, 1978). Since many studies of young people's drinking have been carried out at or before the peak age for drinking and heavy drinking (which is late teens to early 20s, at least for young men), it is not inconceivable that the most telling factors with regard to problem drinking in the next generation may have their greatest impact at a somewhat later age when the normative pattern is for drinking to settle down to more moderate adult levels.

At whatever age and stage parental problem drinking is of influence, there are a number of contending theories about how it has its influence and none of these are mutually incompatible. It has been suggested, for example, that adolescents with parents with drinking problems acquire more of an expectation that alcohol will enhance cognitive and motor functioning, perhaps as a result of hearing a parent report such effects or observing the effect of alcohol in reducing a parent's withdrawal symptoms (Brown *et al.*, 1987; Sher, 1991). Parental influence might be more important than that of peers with respect to non-social expectations such as these. A similar suggestion is that a family history of alcohol use could serve to model the use of alcohol as a way of coping with stress (Chassin *et al.*, 1988). Yet another suggestion, for which some experimental evidence has been found (Chipperfield and Vogel-Sprott, 1988), is that young adults with positive family histories of drinking problems are more influenced in their levels of drinking by the levels of drinking of a companion. This heightened susceptibility to drinking modelling effects might be explained in terms of an ambivalent attitude towards drinking at home or ambiguous or contradictory parental drinking models. Indeed this notion that children brought up in homes where a parent has a serious drinking problem lack a stable, clear and unambiguous idea of what constitutes normal or appropriate drinking, is one that has often been put forward to explain the link between problem drinking in one generation and the next.

Following on from this, there have been a number of quite specific hypotheses which have drawn upon social-learning models in their generation. Some of these include:

—that modelling will be along *same-gender* lines (boys will tend to model themselves on heavy drinking fathers; girls, on heavy drinking mothers);
—that modelling will depend on the *degree of positive relationship* with parents (the more positive the relationship with problem drinking parents, the more likely it is that the offspring will adopt their behaviour); and
—that modelling will interact with the *availability of the role model* (that greater exposure to the problem drinking of the parent, or exposure to the problem drinking over a greater number of years, or exposure to more than one problem drinking role model, will increase the risk of problem drinking in the offspring).

All of these hypotheses were examined in the research described in later chapters.

Non-specific Environmental Mechanisms

A larger number of writers have taken an alternative view, supposing that harmful outcomes are caused by negative features of the family environment that are associated with having a parent with a drinking problem. These features might include the stress of living in such a family environment, inconsistent and confusing interactions between problem drinking parents and child, alternating love and fear experienced by children towards their parents, and reversal of parent and child roles within the family (Burk and Sher, 1988). Factors such as these are of course not confined to families with alcohol problems, and if they are responsible for negative outcomes for the offspring then we should expect these outcomes to be just as common amongst offspring who experience such negative features in the *absence* of parental problem drinking.

The stresses inherent in being brought up in a family where one or both parents has a drinking problem have been reviewed at the start of this chapter. In summary, it can safely be said that being a child of a parent with a drinking problem can be a highly stressful experience—although the degree of stress is very variable and it would be wrong to assume that the experiences of all such children are identical. When such a family upbringing is stressful, however, there is a large measure of agreement about what some of the main components of this stress actually are. It is quite another matter, though, to argue that stress in childhood provides proof of the cause of transmission of problems from one generation to the next, or that by identifying sources of stress we have understood the mechanisms of transmission. To throw more light on these issues we need to turn to research that has attempted to correlate certain kinds of childhood experience, amongst the children of problem drinking parents, with outcomes for those children.

In her study of University women in the USA referred to earlier Benson (1980; Benson and Heller, 1987) found, amongst daughters of problem drinking parents, that those with 'neurotic' or 'acting out' symptoms were more likely to report coming from homes with higher levels of parental conflict and having had poorer, more inconsistent relationships with both mothers and fathers. It is interesting to note in passing that parental conflict was reported to be much greater, and that relationships with mothers and fathers much poorer, in the group of 15 daughters for whom *both* parents were described as having alcohol problems.

In a study of similar design—although with much weaker methodology in terms of sample size and selection—Clair and Genest (1987) found depression-proneness in young adult children of problem drinking parents to be significantly negatively correlated with certain dimensions of recalled family atmosphere as measured by the much-used Family Environment Scale (FES: Moos and Moos, 1981). The key dimensions were family cohesion (Cohesion), the degree to which the family atmosphere encouraged free expression of feelings and attitudes (Expressiveness), and the degree to which independence and autonomy of the child were encouraged (Independence). The degree to which open conflict occurred in the family (Conflict) was not significantly correlated with depression-proneness although it had been predicted that it would be.

Although they reported no analyses of differences within the group of children of problem drinking parents, Jarmas and Kazak (1992) found that their University student group of children of problem drinking parents as a whole reported less family Cohesion and Expressiveness and more Conflict on the FES. They also reported significantly lower scores on a Communication Scale designed to assess clarity and directness of verbal messages in the family, and higher scores on a Parental Inconsistency of Love Scale. The findings about lower levels of cohesion and expressiveness were in line with these researchers' predictions that children of problem drinking parents would be prone to self-criticism ('introjective depression' as they termed it) as a result of difficulty in resolving fragmented and ambivalent internalised parental images arising from parental inconsistency and poor communication. Jones and Houts (1992) have also highlighted the importance of family communication patterns in their study of the self-reported social skills of University students. Their findings suggested that young people who recalled regular problem drinking at home plus either parental criticism of the child or denial of the expression of feelings in the family were most likely to report poor ability to display non-verbal and verbal emotions, a heightened sense of control over one's own emotions, and a greater sensitivity to emotional cues of others.

In addition to searching for family factors that might provide the starting point for a mechanism of transmission of problems from one generation to the next, Clair and Genest (1987) examined possible moderating factors such as social support available in adolescence and the ways adolescents attempted to cope with stress. Using the well known Ways of Coping Questionnaire (Folkman and Lazarus, 1980) they found that children of problem drinking parents reported using more emotion-focussed ways of coping in their teens. In particular, they reported tending to use more wishful thinking as well as avoidant strategies such as smoking, drinking and eating. Clair and Genest suggested that, since such coping patterns were modelled by the problem drinking parent, this might be a basis for the intra-familial transmission of alcohol problems. This suggests that children of problem drinking parents might be in double jeopardy, exposed to stress and the need to cope with it and to a model of heavy drinking as a means of coping. In their study, however, it was the relative underuse of problem-focussed coping strategies (taking action to deal with the source of stress rather than finding ways of dealing with the emotions caused by it) that was correlated with depression-proneness. The latter was also correlated with reports of having received lesser amounts of both informational and emotional support as adolescents. Possible compensatory factors that have been identified for individual families include engagement in peer group activities and support from family, friends and neighbours (Wilson and Orford, 1978). Other possibly important factors that have scarcely even been considered include the influence of siblings on environmental transmission mechanisms (Rowe, 1990).

The authors of each of the above mentioned research reports subscribe, on the whole, to a non-specific environmental view of transmission, and would tend to agree with Benson and Heller's (1987) statement that it may not be a parental drinking problem *per se* that is most closely linked to negative offspring effects, "...but rather the social and family conditions that are the frequent concomitants of parental disturbances" (p. 310). Although these studies suggest some of the directions in which we might look to discover such mechanisms, they are very limited in a number of ways, not least because they rarely specify the mechanisms that might exist which could turn the experiences of childhood into the effects in adulthood.

The research so far reviewed in this section presents a passive and one-way picture, whereby parental behaviour exerts a blanket and deterministic effect on the offspring. Moos *et al.* (1990) suggest that temperamental characteristics of the children are also important in influencing outcomes. Whilst there has been very little research addressing this question, the report by Werner (1986) is relevant even though the sample of children studied had at that time only reached the age of 18. The report concerned 49 offspring of parents with drinking problems who were part of a much larger longitudinal study of Hawaiian children examined at birth and followed at ages 1, 2, 10 and 18. By the latter age 41% had developed 'serious coping problems', either with records of repeated or serious delinquencies or with serious mental health problems. Werner was interested in the factors that differentiated these children from the majority who appeared to have been remarkably resilient despite the parental alcohol problems in their families and the fact that most had been reared in conditions of chronic poverty. Of the factors that significantly differentiated resilient children from those who had developed problems by the age of 18, a number were already preset at birth or by age two years. These included: maternal 'alcoholism' and especially maternal drinking during pregnancy; not being described as 'cuddly and affectionate' during the first year of life; the birth of another sibling within the first two years of life; and conflict between parents during the same period of time. It is important to bear in mind that most studies of the long-term effects of parental drinking problems on the next generation, including the study to be reported upon later in this book, are quite unable because of their design to assess the importance of these early operating factors. It is intended to follow up the group studied by Werner (1986) to age 30, but these findings from the sample at age 18 already raise some extremely interesting issues concerning the theoretical models that we might utilise to enable us to better understand how these factors present from birth or during very early childhood might account for resilient versus problematic development. These issues, and wider ones relating to deterministic versus interactive theories of transmission, will be returned to later.

Amongst the most interesting work of recent years on the possible environmental mechanisms at work in the transmission of alcohol problems from one generation to the next has been that of Bennett and her colleagues. Their work has focussed upon family rituals—especially family dinner-times and holidays—because: "As highly patterned, symbolic, rule-governed activities, rituals provide a sociocultural context within which family members assume roles that they repetitively re-enact over time" (Bennett *et al.*, 1987, p. 112). In an early study they obtained evidence suggesting that the maintenance of 'distinct' family rituals despite a parent's drinking problem might be a factor that protected offspring against developing similar problems themselves as adults (Wolin *et al.*, 1980). The number of families was small (25), however, and it was necessary to exclude families intermediate or unclear in terms of ritual distinctiveness or transmission in order to obtain significant findings. In a later study they attempted to replicate this finding, including also a study of the offspring's spouses (Bennett *et al.*, 1987).

The sample used in this later study is interesting, being recruited both from treatment agencies and through newspaper advertisements. Their sample was unusual also because it included only those families of origin (30 in number, all of which had remained intact) from each of which at least two married offspring and their spouses were available for study (a total of 68 such 'new' families). Offspring were of average age 33 years at the time of the study and had been married for an average of 11 years. All the offspring had at least one parent who was a 'problem drinker' or 'definitely alcoholic' and the same was true of 20% of the spouses.

Offspring and spouse were separately interviewed using a semi-structured interview focussing upon family life as a child (interviews took approximately 1½ hours) and offspring and spouse were interviewed together using a second semi-structured interview that focussed upon present family life (also taking approximately 1½ hours). The main variables to do with family of origin rituals, their maintenance in the face of parental drinking problems and their transmission into the life of the new families were coded according to a detailed instruction manual. Bennett *et al.* hypothesised that some of these variables would be 'risk factors' which might increase the likelihood of the transmission of drinking problems, and that some would be 'protective factors' which might work in the opposite direction. Inter-rater reliability was tested on data from a sub-sample of 18 couples. Although all the reliability coefficients are significant, some are modest (in the range 0.4 to 0.6) and only significant at the 0.05 or 0.01 probability level.

The dependent variable was whether the new family was a 'transmitter' or 'non-transmitter' family. To qualify for the former group, either offspring or spouse had to be judged to be or to have been a 'problem drinker' or 'alcoholic'. Of the total of 27 transmitter couples, five were so classified solely on the basis of the spouse's problem drinking. All five spouses were husbands of daughters of 'alcoholic' fathers. It is important to note, therefore, that 'transmission' as Bennett *et al.* were defining it includes both direct transmission to the new family in the form of a drinking problem in the offspring, and indirect transmission via marriage.

Results were analysed in terms of hierarchical multiple regression, and they examined both groups of variables, and particular individual variables. Their findings showed that the most important group of variables contained those that between them identified which family of origin the offspring came from; with the next most important group being a set principally concerned with use of rituals in the families of origin. When variables were examined individually, four of them were significantly related to the dependent variable. The most significant (a risk factor) was whether the offspring was a son of an alcoholic father. The remaining three were protective factors, and they included whether the offspring's family dinner-ritual remained 'distinctive' (i.e. was minimally altered) during the parent's heaviest drinking years ($p<0.05$); whether the spouse's family of origin observed dinner-rituals at a high level ($p<0.02$); and whether there had been a high level of 'planfulness' or 'deliberateness' on the part of offspring and spouse in choosing to follow the family rituals of one or other family of origin ($p<0.006$).

Elsewhere Bennett and Wolin (1990) provide more detail about what they mean by 'deliberateness'. They state:

Highly deliberate couples plan early in marriage how they wish to be similar to or different from their families of origin and are able to follow through on those ideas. Low deliberate couples either never develop such a plan and instead take a fatalistic view of their future together, or they do have a plan that simply does not work out (pp. 203–4).

From this quotation and from the illustrations they provide, it does seem possible that this research group may be picking up characteristics of family functioning which are more general than their specific theory supposes. It seems possible that high deliberate families are generally maritally satisfied or competent in their decision-making. Indeed, the transmission of drinking problems and deliberateness may be confounded, since couples may be rated as low on deliberateness either because they lack clear plans, or because their plans do not work out. Similarly, in the 'old' families, the specific 'failure to keep rituals distinct in the face of parental heavy drinking' may be picking up a more general family discord and disorganisation. Nevertheless, the results are undoubtedly intriguing, and the authors discussed their results in terms of an underlying theme of 'selective disengagement and re-engagement' as a means of 'survival' amongst children of problem drinking parents. Components of this common theme are, according to Bennett *et al.*, the ability of the family of origin to separate itself from the potentially disruptive behaviour of the problem drinking family member (preserving distinct family rituals is one way of doing this), the child's efforts to disengage from disruptive elements of family life and to engage with others outside the family, the process of selecting a partner and forming a new family, and the new couple's attempt to select a heritage that may emphasise positive rather than negative aspects of their respective families of origin.

In summary, then, there is a wide variety of possible mechanisms which have been put forward to explain the link between parental problem drinking and any long-term deleterious effects on the offspring. We have concluded above that the weight of evidence currently implies that a genetic contribution of some degree should not be ignored, at least for some kinds of drinking problems amongst men; although even for men, genetic influence appears to be complex, partial and still unclear. We also conclude that there are strong possibilities that an alcohol-specific, environmental, behavioural modelling mechanism (e.g. offspring learning to drink excessively by modelling themselves upon heavy drinking parents) might be at work. We have suggested a number of general and specific hypotheses which such a mechanism might present, including that adolescents with parents with drinking problems acquire more of an expectation that alcohol will enhance cognitive and motor functioning; that parental alcohol use could serve to model the use of alcohol as a way of coping with stress; that modelling might be along gender specific lines; that modelling might depend on the degree of positive relationship with either parent; and that modelling might interact with the availability of the role model.

Finally, it has been concluded that the majority of writers have taken a third view, suggesting that general environmental mechanisms (e.g. offspring are affected by the family discord associated with a parental drinking problem) are the ways that effects are passed from one generation to the next. Again a number of specific and general hypotheses are possible regarding the features of the family lives of problem drinkers which might lead to problematic outcomes, including the stress of living in such a family environment, inconsistent and confusing interactions between problem drinking parents and child, alternating love and fear experienced by children towards their parents, and reversal of parent and child roles within the family. It was also suggested that the characteristics of the child him- or her-self might also affect outcomes. Finally it was suggested that issues such as deliberateness, competency in decision making, the ability of the family of origin to separate itself from the potentially disruptive behaviour of the problem drinking family member, the child's efforts to dis-engage from disruptive elements of family life and to engage with others outside the family, the process of selecting a partner and forming a new family, and the new couple's attempt to select a heritage that may empha-sise positive rather than negative aspects of their respective families of ori-gin, all might throw light on the non-specific mechanisms which might be responsible for the production of negative outcomes in the adult offspring of problem drinkers.

WHAT CAN WE LEARN FROM THE WIDER LITERATURE?

Although a quite extensive body of literature has been reviewed in the pre-ceding sections, much of it has been performed by a relatively small num-ber of workers who have specialised in the study of alcohol problems. It is the case that there has been a neglect of the children of problem drinkers, and especially of an examination of their adulthood adjustment, on the part of researchers who investigate more general psychological and psychi-atric phenomena. On the other side of the same coin is the failure of spe-cialised alcohol researchers and clinicians to borrow ideas from the far wider literature on families, intergenerational continuity, and life-span development. One of us has pointed out before the dangers, in the study of excessive drinking and marriage, of reinventing the wheel and of failing to keep up with new ideas in the wider literature (Orford, 1975), and the same is true in relation to the subject of the present book. In the following section we shall draw selectively—since the potentially relevant literature is enormous—upon recent work on the effects upon offspring development of such family-related circumstances as parental separation and divorce, inter-parent violence and discord, parental psychiatric disorder, child physi-cal and sexual abuse, and family economic hardship. We shall concentrate upon ideas that are emerging about processes and mechanisms of intergen-erational influence, and ideas about the ways in which these are best studied. We shall focus in this section exclusively upon environmental transmission although the likely contribution, to some degree, of genetic mechanisms of influence should never be forgotten.

The general conclusion that emerges from the wider literature is that there are few simple generalisations that can be made about intergenerational continuity, that mechanisms of transmission are complex, and that moderating and mediating variables are many. The picture that emerges is one of great complexity and many previously held assumptions now look woefully over-simple.

Violence

This is even true of the effects upon offspring of parental violence towards children, where it has often been uncritically assumed that there is a 'cycle of violence' wherein violence in one generation 'begets violence' in the next. Widom (1989) critically examined the research literature bearing upon this assumption. Although she found consistent evidence that abused children manifest more aggressive and problematic behaviour as young children, methodological shortcomings made it difficult to draw confident conclusions about longer-term effects in terms of outcomes such as abusive parenting, delinquency or violent crime. What was clear, however, was that long-term negative outcomes are by no means as predictable as simple notions of transmission might suppose. Studies of abusive parenting, for example, suggest that the majority of parents who report a history of child abuse probably do not abuse their own children (Hunter and Kilstrom, 1979; Hereenkohl et al., 1983, both cited by Widom, 1989). Widom concluded:

... Being abused as a child may increase one's risk for becoming an abusive parent, a delinquent, or an adult violent criminal. However, on the basis of the findings from the existing literature, it cannot be said that the pathway is straight or certain. It is likely that our conceptualization of the relationship between child abuse and violence has been overly simplistic...

Finally, it is important to draw attention to the persistent transmission of confident conclusions in this literature with little regard to data or lack thereof. Unqualified repetitions of the 'cycle of violence' then persist, despite the recognition of serious shortcomings in these studies. In support of the cycle of violence hypothesis, citations are often made of reports that present no data at all (1989, p. 24).

Nevertheless, it has to be admitted that despite all the research that has been carried out on different aspects of this subject, because of the methodological weaknesses of much of the research, and particularly because reliance is usually placed upon retrospective reports of child abuse and/or upon self-reports of adulthood violence, it is still impossible to know whether reported relationships of violence across generations represent an accurate picture, over-estimates of the relationship, or under-estimates (Widom, 1989). Furthermore, as with research on children of problem drinking parents, most of the research on the long-term consequences of family violence has focussed on transmission of the same behaviours or characteristics, in this case subsequent abusive behaviour and aggression, largely overlooking the possibility that abuse may lead to other, sometimes less overt, negative outcomes such as severe anxiety, withdrawal, depression, or self-destructive behaviour (Widom, 1989).

Childhood Sexual Abuse

Browne and Finkelhor (1986) reviewed research evidence specifically on the impact of child sexual abuse. This is now recognised to be, like parental drinking problems, of common occurrence and very often occurring over a prolonged period of time during childhood. Regarding initial effects (i.e. occurring within two years of the termination of abuse—they prefer the term 'initial' rather than 'short-term' since the latter may appear to make the assumption that reactions do not persist) the research evidence was sketchy but it supported the view that children who were sexually abused were more likely than other children to experience both 'internalised' effects (particularly fear) and 'externalised' effects (particularly anger and hostility). In addition, it is interesting to note the finding from one study that a higher proportion of incest victims than comparisons had tried to run away from home as adolescents (33% *vs* 5%—Herman, 1981, cited by Browne and Finkelhor) and from another study that a higher percentage of incest victims than comparisons had actually left home before the age of 18 (50% *vs* 20%). Younger children had often gone to relatives whereas older daughters had run away or eloped, sometimes making early marriages in order to escape the abuse (Meiselman, 1978, cited by Browne and Finkelhor).

Regarding long-term effects (5–25 years later) there was, according to Browne and Finkelhor, consistent evidence from a variety of studies, including both studies of clinical populations and those employing random, community samples, that children who were sexually abused are significantly more likely than others to experience depression, anxiety, low self-esteem, distrust and hostility towards others (more particularly towards their mothers and women in general than towards their fathers and men in general), and are more likely to attempt suicide. There was also evidence that, as adults, people who were abused as children are more likely to be the victims of rape and other forms of abuse from partners and others, and are more likely to abuse alcohol or other substances. Browne and Finkelhor make the point, however, that much of the adulthood disturbance reported is moderate and that under one fifth of victims show serious disturbance as adults (at least as measured by the procedures used in the research reported). If this is correct, it follows that the majority show moderate or no psychological difficulty as adults which, "…give(s) reassurance to victims that extreme long-term effects are not inevitable" (p. 72). They are critical, nevertheless, of the 'adulto-centric' bias towards assessing the seriousness of childhood stressors only in terms of the existence of long-term effects.

The research reviewed by Browne and Finkelhor failed to find evidence that child sexual abuse has greater impact (initial or long-term) when it occurs at different ages, nor depending upon the length of time in childhood over which it lasts. On the other hand, Browne and Finkelhor did find tentative evidence, from a very small number of studies, that abuse by fathers or stepfathers, abuse involving genital contact, abuse involving force, and abuse followed by unsupportive family reactions and/or the child being removed from home, may have more negative impact.

Browne and Finkelhor reach a similar conclusion to the one we reached earlier when discussing the issue of parental drinking problems: it is extremely difficult to disentangle all the different factors involved in such a way that simple cause and effect relationships can be exposed, or simple modelling versus general family environment theories proven. Pre-existing family factors such as family conflict or emotional neglect, the nature of the sexual abuse itself, and the subsequent reactions of others, both family and the wider network of friends and professional agencies, all interlink to create a highly complex interplay of influences.

As with ideas about transmission in the alcohol field, there is now a great deal of support in the wider literature for non-specific environmental mechanisms which stress the importance of the quality of the family care-taking environment or the quality of parent-child relationships rather than specific events or circumstances of abuse, parental psychiatric disorder, or parental separation or divorce. As an example, Harter *et al.* (1988), in the case of child sexual abuse, found that characteristics of the family of upbringing (adaptability and cohesion) reported by college women in a southern state of the USA were more strongly associated with measures of social adjustment than was the fact of childhood sexual abuse itself.

Psychiatric Problems

Those who have studied the possible intergenerational transmission of psychiatric problems have come to a similar conclusion. Quinton, Rutter and Gulliver (1990) have reported the ongoing follow-up of 115 offspring (and their spouses) of psychiatric patients, who were first studied in 1965 and 1971. Amongst their principal conclusions was the importance of psychological disorder in childhood and adolescence for predicting later adult disorder. Incidentally, they were surprised to find that emotional disorders of childhood (sometimes referred to as 'internalised') were just as predictive as conduct disorders ('externalised')—it had been assumed on the basis of previous research that the latter carried a much worse prognosis (Robins *et al.*, 1971; Robins, 1972). Not only do these researchers find continuity of disorder from childhood to adulthood, but they conclude that family disturbance, particularly in the form of persistent family discord, in the family of origin, is one of the most important mediators of problems at later times. Such family disturbance seems to be more important than the fact of having a parent with a psychiatric condition (Rutter, 1988; Quinton *et al.*, 1990).

Indeed Rutter and Madge (1976) had reached this conclusion some years previously:

... It has been shown that family discord and marital disharmony are considerably more common when one parent has a psychiatric condition and that *within* a group of families in all of which one parent is a psychiatric patient, marital disharmony is strongly associated with conduct disorders in the children ... At least so far as boys are concerned, parental mental disorder seems to lead to psychiatric problems in the children, partly because of the family discord and marital disharmony with which it is associated (p. 210 their emphasis).

Marital or Family Disturbance

Parental divorce and separation constitutes another set of family-related childhood circumstances which has been widely researched. Again a similar conclusion has emerged: the quality of family life before, during and after separation may be as important as, if not more important than, the fact of separation and divorce itself. For example, with respect to the link between parental separation and offspring problems of conduct and delinquency, Rutter and Madge (1976) concluded:

... discordant and disturbed intrafamilial relationships may ... lead to disorders of conduct or to recidivist delinquency, and perhaps to problems in parenting.

Separation experiences are often part of this process, but the evidence suggests that it is not the separation *per se* which matters but rather the family disharmony which preceded and led to the separation (pp. 317–18).

Similarly, studies of the effects upon offspring of family economic hardship during the 'great depression' years of the late 1920s and early 1930s in the USA, using data from cohorts of children followed over time, have supported the idea that when adverse effects result, these are mediated by effects upon the quality of family life. These important analyses, which link the macro conditions of the economy with the micro social world of the family and the psychology of the individual family member, as very few studies do, have been carried out by Elder, Caspi and their colleagues (e.g. Liker and Elder, 1983; Elder and Caspi, 1988). Depending upon a number of factors, such as offspring gender and age at the time of family economic loss, hardship had an adverse effect on the mental health of some children and upon their subsequent education. But these researchers favour a non-specific mechanism:

The adverse consequences of stressful economic times do not necessarily have direct effects. They are more often produced indirectly through their disorganizing effects on family relationships...

To the extent that economic stress increases unstable behaviour, marital discord, and rates and levels of unpredictable, hostile exchanges, children are at risk. On the other hand, as long as unstable behaviour is kept in check, as long as marital conflicts are resolved as usual, and as long as discipline remains consistently applied, children should be protected from the psychological costs of environmental stressors...

With panel data over an eight-year period (1930–1938), our research has shown that the influence of family income loss on the problem behaviour of children is indirect. Drastic income loss increased the prospect of children's problem behaviour, but only by increasing aversive interactions within the family (1988, pp. 35, 36, 39).

There have been a number of important reviews of the link between marital or family disturbance and the adjustment of offspring when the latter are still children or adolescents. Although the conclusions of these reviews appear not to bear so directly upon our main interest, which is the longer-term effects on offspring as adults, they are of course important if it is the case that many childhood psychological problems persist in one form or another into adulthood. Furthermore, these reviews examine likely mechanisms linking family and child problems, and these ideas are invaluable to us in building a picture of how parental drinking problems might affect children in the short and longer-term.

The first of these reviews was carried out by Emery (1982) who reviewed the results of some of the best studies then available on the subject of the psychological disturbances experienced by children of discordant or divorced parents—he used the term 'family turmoil' to refer collectively to discord in marriage, marital separation or divorce. He concluded that, although many studies were weak in sampling, design or methods, the best studies did confirm that, "... the relation between marital and child problems ... is nevertheless a real and important one" (p. 312).

Emery went on to explore what dimensions of marital turmoil might be particularly important for child disturbance and what theories might account for the link. He concluded that the available evidence supported the view that it was marital conflict that was largely responsible for the association between divorce and child disturbance, and also between individual parental psychopathology and problems amongst children. In particular, there was reason to believe that conflict that was openly hostile, as well as conflict that lasted for a longer period of time, had the greatest effect.

Grych and Fincham (1990) have provided a more recent review of the link between marital problems and children's adjustment. Their review concentrated, however, on overt marital conflict which is not necessarily the same as marital dissatisfaction with which they believed it had been confused in the past. They reviewed a total of 19 studies examining the link between marital conflict and children's adjustment, 15 of which produced significant findings (this was the case for seven of eight studies examining children from separated or divorced families, and in eight of 11 studies of children from intact families). Several studies indicated that conflict predicted child problems over and above marital satisfaction. They concluded that research, "... documents a modest but consistent relationship between interparental conflict and children's adjustment ..." (p. 269). Negative child outcomes included both externalising and internalising problems, but also lack of social competence, cognitive competence and academic school achievement: a range of problems parallel to those associated with parental alcohol problems, as reviewed at the start of this chapter. Nevertheless, they urge that more attention should be paid to other, perhaps less obvious but equally harmful, negative outcomes such as low self-esteem and poor peer relations.

From the studies of childhood problems that they reviewed, plus experimental studies examining children's immediate responses to angry and aggressive exchanges between adults carried out by Cummings and colleagues (e.g. Cummings *et al.*, 1984), Grych and Fincham concluded that both more intense forms of marital conflict (e.g. involving physical aggression), and a higher frequency of conflict, are more upsetting to children than less intense and less frequent conflict, and are more strongly related to childhood problems. Furthermore, there was evidence that the cessation of conflict is associated with a reduction of problem behaviours (e.g. Hetherington *et al.*, 1982; Long *et al.*, 1988). They pointed out that there had been comparatively little study of factors such as the content of parental conflicts or the resolution of such conflicts.

Mechanisms

But how exactly does marital family disturbance or conflict put the offspring at risk? In order to understand the relevance of this wider literature for children of problem drinking parents, and in order to fully appreciate the risks that such children run, and hence to have some hope of preventing harmful outcomes, we need to have a much closer understanding of the processes at work. Regarding theories about how marital turmoil and child disturbance might be linked, Emery (1982) concluded that the evidence he reviewed and other work supported both modelling and discipline theories i.e. conflict might lead to parents becoming poorer models (e.g. modelling aggression) or might lead to rejection of parents as models, and turmoil might lead to changes in discipline particularly in the direction of more inconsistent discipline. Other theories with some attraction were 'stress'—marital problems can be thought of as a stressor to which children, as well as adults, are differentially exposed—and 'taking on the symptom'—one child might become the focus of larger family conflicts, for example in serving the function of distracting parents from their own conflicts.

Grych and Fincham (1990) concluded that our understanding of the link between marital conflict and children's problems was still very limited. Evidence was certainly consistent with modelling (they pointed out that modelling does not consist simply of the mimicking of adult behaviour e.g. children may learn that aggression is an appropriate response but inhibit it in the presence of adults) or with marital conflict as a stressor, but there had been no very direct tests of these hypotheses. They also concluded, however, that less direct mechanisms could not be ruled out. For example, marital conflict might have its effect via a worsening of parent-child relationships (one study found that the quality of parent-child relationships accounted for the link between marital conflict and child problems, but another found that the link remained even after adjusting for parent-child relationships) or via intra-parent or inter-parent inconsistency in discipline.

Modelling

Modelling remains a popular choice of mechanism for explaining continuities between the behaviours of one generation and the next. For example, Belsky and Pensky (1988), who summarised evidence on the intergenerational continuity of child maltreatment, spouse abuse, marital divorce and separation, the quality of early parent-child relationships, and marital happiness, treated modelling as a leading possibility. They concluded that there is evidence for intergenerational continuity in the cases of the topics they examined. Although they often seemed to fall into the common error of stating results without indicating the strength of effects, in summary Belsky and Pensky did state clearly that most of the research they examined had produced relatively low levels of association between problems in successive generations.

Like Grych and Fincham (1990), Belsky and Pensky were critical of a simple social learning theory that relied entirely on imitation. They also cited Cummings *et al.*'s experimental work with infants (1981, 1985, cited by Belsky and Pensky) which showed that infants responded to naturally occurring and simulated anger with distress (unlike their pleasurable responses to expressions of affection), but they seldom responded by exactly mimicking others' expressions of anger. A contagion of affect response was more common, and although aggression towards peers did increase this did not conform to strict modelling.

Modelling as a basis for intergenerational transmission has been much discussed in the context of family violence, and here again the suggestion is that the processes at work are more complicated than the simple term 'imitation' would seem to imply. For example, using a large, representative sample of adults in the USA, although having to rely upon self-report and retrospective recall, Kalmuss (1984) obtained results suggesting that exposure to both marital and parent-to-child 'hitting' in adolescence contributed to severe adulthood marital aggression, but it was recall of parent-to-parent hitting that exerted the stronger effect. Contrary to predictions that would be made by some theories of modelling, however, the effects appeared not to be sex specific. Observing father hitting mother, for example, increased the likelihood that sons would be victims as well as perpetrators of marital violence, and also that daughters would be perpetrators as well as victims. This supported the finding of some other researchers (e.g. Gelles, 1976, cited by Kalmuss) that women who witnessed spouse abuse in their families of origin were more likely to be victims of it in their own marriages, although other research has not found this effect (e.g. Pagelow, 1981, cited by Kalmuss, 1984; Rosenbaum and O'Leary, 1981).

Kalmuss herself favoured a role-specific theory of modelling: what was carried forward into the next generation was a propensity to behave aggressively when occupying the same role (in this case that of spouse) as that occupied by the aggressive model. In support of this idea, are results from an impressive study reported by Huesmann *et al.* (1984). They studied the aggression of eight year old children and their parents and, 22 years later, the aggression of the offspring, now aged 30, and their children many of whom were of the same age as their parents had been on the first occasion, 22 years earlier. They found that the role-specific links in aggression were just as strong, in fact very slightly stronger, across a span of 22 years, than the contemporaneous links between parent and child aggression. In other words, in terms of aggression, offspring at age 30 tended to be like their parents at the same age, and their children aged about eight years tended to be like their fathers had been at that age. These links were if anything slightly stronger than those between parental and child aggression at either time.

Inconsistency

The notion of inconsistent or arbitrary parental discipline, and its harmful effects for children, remains very popular. Elder and Caspi (1988) gave it a central place in the model they developed to explain why economic hardship might be harmful for some children:

> ... the master link between environmental stress and children's problem behaviour was inconsistent and arbitrary parenting. Arbitrary behaviour (rated by the Institute staff on the basis of maternal interviews) refers to inconsistent discipline that expresses the parental mood rather than a response to the child's behaviour; its result is that the child never knows what to expect. Inconsistent parenting has been repeatedly implicated in the development of externalizing problems..., and our findings suggest that economic change may well increase the probability of arbitrary behaviours by fathers. As long as discipline is consistently applied, children seem to be highly resilient under a wide range of parental styles ... (p. 39).

Their full model views arbitrary paternal discipline as the result of a combination of personal characteristics of the father (which they refer to as 'instability') and adverse circumstances to which the father is exposed (in this case economic hardship and resulting family conflict). Personal instability is again a key concept for these same authors in their work on intergenerational continuity across several generations. For example,

Caspi and Elder (1988) reported on their analysis of data from women in four generations of families included in the Berkeley Guidance Study. This study was initiated in 1928 with every third birth in the city of Berkeley over an 18 month period and involved a direct study of parents and children, and later the grandchildren, plus reports by parents of the grandparent generation. Their analyses suggested continuities in problem behaviour and problem relationships across the four generations. Furthermore, they believed their evidence supported a particular model of continuity, namely that personal instability (e.g. ill-tempered, irritable, under-controlled) leads to marital conflict and non-optimal parenting (e.g. hostility and arbitrary discipline), and that it is the latter that leads to personal instability in the next generation, hence maintaining the cycle. Their analysis of data from the second and third generations also suggested that it was the childhood problem behaviours thus created in the next generation (e.g. quarrelsome, negativistic, irritable) that linked the aversive socialisation environment that these children experienced with the behavioural difficulties that they subsequently showed in adulthood. They could find no evidence of a direct link between parental behaviour and adulthood behaviour in the next generation once childhood problem behaviour in the new generation was controlled.

There are two major problems with this often-cited work however. One is that measures of the same construct (e.g. personal instability) were not always the same from one generation to the next. This particularly concerned the first generation who were never actually seen. The second problem involves the familiar temptation to summarise findings in a way that suggests far more continuity than has actually been demonstrated. Multiplying the path coefficients (in their path analysis diagrams) suggests comparatively low indices of transmission from one generation to the next and virtually zero transmission across more than two generations. Caspi and Elder's summary of their findings, on the other hand, implies a much greater degree of continuity. Once again, however, we cannot tell whether the many difficulties involved in doing this kind of research have led to an overestimate or an underestimate of the extent of continuity.

More Complex Models

Grych and Fincham themselves put forward a model that pointed to the importance of such contextual and cognitive factors as the child's memory of past instances of conflict, expectations of conflict and its outcome in the present, child temperament and mood, attributions, blame, and coping behaviours. Many of these factors change with child development e.g. children at a particular age are likely to blame themselves for parental conflict or parental divorce, whereas children at an older age are less likely to do so; older children have more options for ways of coping that are independent of their parents. Studies of the marital conflict/childhood problems link, however, show no consistent effect of the child's age, which may indicate that different developmental factors are cancelling each other out. Incidentally, the hypothetical example which Grych and Fincham gave to illustrate their model of a child overhearing a parental quarrel from the next room, has many features which are reminiscent of situations that arise regularly in the family lives of children with problem drinking parents. Features of this example include: an intense argument (loud and emotional), carrying on for some time, without resolution of the conflict, reminiscent of previous inter-parental conflicts witnessed by the child, and involving content which refers to the child (Mother accusing Father of not spending enough time with him).

Of course, witnessing inter-parental violence is likely to have many, complex effects as Martin *et al.* (1987) demonstrated in their study of 15 year olds. Those adolescents who reported parental violence reported feeling that differences in the family were less well resolved, feeling angry about the unfair way they were treated by parents, feeling confused about the things parents said or did, feeling it was more difficult to sincerely say they were sorry to their parents following disagreements, and feeling less satisfied with the parents' relationship and with their own relationship with parents and with siblings. It made comparatively little difference whether maternal violence was verbal or physical (much the most significant difference being between non-violence and violence of any kind), but in the case of fathers there was an additional effect of physical violence though again the difference between non-violence and verbal-only violence was much the more significant. These results suggest not only that modelling is likely to be quite complicated but also that it may be impossible in practice to clearly separate out processes such as modelling, inconsistent parenting, stress, and fear.

Resilience

It is notable that most of the leading theories about continuity are couched in negative, even pathological, terms. Occasionally, key variables are phrased in the positive, however, as in Coombs and Landsverk's (1988) study linking 'positive father sentiment' (closeness to father, wanting to be like father, perceiving father trust, perceiving father encouragement and praise, talking with father about personal problems) and 'positive mother sentiment' to lack of involvement in drug use on the part of Californian adolescents. Another example is the study reported by Lobdell and Perlman (1986) which found a significant correlation between mothers' and daughters' self-reported loneliness, and correlations between lack of loneliness on the part of daughters and their feelings of positive involvement with parents, closeness to parents, and the feelings of reliability and trust in parents.

A variant of this more positive theme is the hypothesis that the maintenance of a good relationship with one parent can protect a child against the adverse effects of marital or family discord (Emery, 1982; Rutter, 1985) or economic hardship (Elder and Caspi, 1988). Whether or not the security of one good relationship with a parent exerts a protective effect by directly impinging upon the child, for example by bolstering the child's self-esteem, or whether the effect is indirect via the efforts of the one parent to ensure that the child is out of the way of major family discord, is not clear (Elder and Caspi, 1988).

Interactions

So far our discussion of the wider literature has tended to proceed on the assumption that there are recordable events occurring in childhood, or measurable qualities of family life or relationships, which have a more or less direct effect, via one or at most a very small number of discrete and understandable mechanisms, upon measurable outcomes for the offspring later in life. It is this rather deterministic model that has guided most of the work in the wider field in the past and which continues to guide most of the work in the more specialised field concerned with children of problem drinking parents. Those who are working at the forefront of the wider field are beginning to develop, slowly but surely, more complex and dynamic ways of understanding continuity, and these are making older ways of viewing the subject look decidedly old-fashioned.

For a start there is now widespread recognition of the likelihood of interaction effects. There is nothing particularly new about this, but in quantitative research in the social sciences it takes careful and costly research to demonstrate the existence of such effects.

Some good examples of interaction effects are to be found in the results of work by Hetherington and her colleagues on the effects of divorce upon children (e.g. 1982, 1988), and of Brown G. and his colleagues on the family antecedents of depression in women (e.g. 1978, 1987). Although Hetherington's work concerns effects of divorce in childhood or adolescence, it does provide an excellent demonstration of the likely complexity of the effects of family events and circumstances. Her initial report (e.g. Hetherington, Cox and Cox, 1982) dealt with effects in the first year or two after parental divorce, at which time many of the children and their continuing caretakers (mostly their mothers) were experiencing disorganisation and distress to some degree or another. By six years after divorce, when the children in her sample were aged 10 years (e.g. Hetherington, 1988), the picture was much more varied and it appeared to depend upon the complex interaction of different factors. For one thing, many of the children's caretakers had now re-married which made an assessment of the factors involved in the children's adjustment even more complicated:

Attempts to assess the long-term effects of divorce on parents and children, and the factors that mediate these outcomes, face the difficulty that family members encounter widely varying sequences of family reorganizations and family experiences following divorce. For most parents and children divorce is only one in a series of family transitions that follow separation (Hetherington, 1988, p. 313).

Some of the complex interaction effects which resulted were such that variables even had opposite effects depending upon other circumstances. For example, whereas marital satisfaction was related to positive family relationships in non-divorced families, in divorced families where the caretaking parent had re-married, satisfaction in the new marriage was related to increased family conflict and behaviour problems, especially in stepdaughters. Another example concerned authoritative parenting. Whereas this was related to fewer behaviour problems in children in homes where divorced mothers had not re-married, in new step-families attempts at authoritative parenting by the step-father were associated with rejection of him by the children and with children's problem behaviour.

In 1988 Brown reported on the results of two studies of London women. One was a study of 139 women living in Walthamstow who had experienced loss of their mothers either by death or by separation of at least 12 months before the age of 17. The second was a study of 353 women living in Islington, all caring for children at home. The first study showed that loss related to a considerably increased risk of depression in adult life, and that 'lack of care' on the part of key caretakers in the women's childhoods—marked rejection or indifference or marked lack of control—was a critical link. The Islington study confirmed the importance of this variable of 'lack of care', although in this study the relationship with depression was not at all strong.

The method of statistical analysis of data used by Brown—analysis of contingency tables using log-linear analysis—is, he claimed, capable of revealing interaction effects that would be missed by other methods—e.g. path analysis—popular with some researchers. In particular, he claimed to find evidence of a number of 'chain' effects whereby the impact of a factor in a woman's history was potentiated by an event or circumstance occurring later in life. Some of these potentiating factors were very recent e.g. 'lack of care' in childhood plus a very recent stressful event or set of circumstances was associated with a high risk of depression. These he referred to as 'late interactive chains'. In other instances the potentiating factor had occurred in the past (an 'early interactive chain') e.g. 'lack of care' was only related to a raised risk of depression in middle class women when they had married early.

There were in fact a number of complex interactions involving socio-economic status in these results. For example, failure to cope adequately with pre-marital pregnancy was associated with subsequent working-class status, and hence eventual increased risk of depression, but in addition pre-marital pregnancy was associated with increased risk for working-class women irrespective of coping. For middle-class women, lack of care was associated with risk of depression irrespective of pre-marital pregnancy: in fact those who successfully coped with the latter tended more often to rise in class status compared with their fathers.

Socio-economic status is one variable that would be expected to be involved in interaction effects in studies of life-span development and inter-generational continuity, and yet it goes unexamined in most of the research reports. Sex of offspring is another that we shall look at in some detail below. Ethnicity is another largely neglected variable. An indication of how important the latter might be is provided by Mechanic and Hansell's (1989) study of the relative effects of family conflict and divorce on the well-being of adolescents. The study was carried out in the USA and included sizeable sub-groups of Asian and Hispanic adolescents, and there were some interesting differences along ethnic lines. Overall, they found 'conflict in intact families' to be associated with poorer well-being than 'divorce with low conflict', although the worst outcome was in those adolescents experiencing both. Asian adolescents from recently *divorced* families, however, reported significantly more depressed mood, anxiety and physical symptoms over time than did other adolescents. Amongst Hispanic adolescents, on the other hand, it was those who reported *family conflict* who showed more of these negative outcomes over time than other adolescents. The authors speculate that divorce may be particularly devastating for Asian families, whilst relatively large extended Hispanic families may provide much support provided they remain non-conflictual.

Sex Differences

Sex differences, although they are sometimes ignored, have much more often been examined, and the results appear to form a discernible pattern. There appear to be three recurring themes.

The first is that the nature of boys' and girls' relationships with parents, under conditions of adversity or change, may be different. There is evidence of this both in the work on divorce and that on economic hardship. Six years after divorce, 10 year old boys and their divorced, non-re-married mothers were often still having problems (Hetherington, 1988). Boys in these families were more often still having problems, were more often engaged in anti-social behaviour that their mothers did not know about, and there were more problems between siblings. Divorced, non-re-married mothers and their daughters, on the other hand, mostly expressed considerable satisfaction with their relationship; these girls were thought to have 'grown up faster' (Hetherington, 1988). Similarly, boys who were in their early childhoods when their families were adversely affected by the economic depression, were more adversely affected than girls, and Elder traced this difference to the fact that boys lost more in terms of closeness to their fathers without compensation in their relationship with mothers, whereas girls lost less in their relationships with their fathers and developed stronger ties with their mothers (cited by Bronfenbrenner, 1979, p. 279).

Another recurring theme relates to the types of psychological problems that female and male offspring are likely to show. In his review of the effects of marital turmoil on children, Emery (1982) concluded that there was considerable evidence that marital turmoil had a greater effect on boys than on girls. This was confounded, however, by the fact that it also seemed to be the case that parental conflict was more strongly related to children's problems of under-control (e.g. aggression, conduct disorders) than to the other broad and well-accepted dimension of child disturbance, problems of over-control (e.g. anxiety, withdrawal); and problems of under-control seemed far more likely to be apparent in boys than in girls. Emery therefore argued that effects on girls might be masked because they might respond with less noticeable problems such as anxiety and withdrawal or even by becoming particularly well-behaved. It is interesting to note that by the time Grych and Fincham (1990) published their updated review they were able to find more evidence that marital problems were associated with children's problems of over-control (or 'internalising' problems) as well as problems of under-control ('externalising'); and this finding then meant that there appeared to be no overall indication that girls were less affected by their parents' problems than were boys.

An additional important point to note is that continuity in difficulties may occur over a substantial number of years during the life course, although the nature of those difficulties may change along sex lines. For example, Quinton, Rutter and Gulliver (1990) in reporting their follow-up into adulthood of offspring of former psychiatric patients, noted a switch from 'conduct disorder' in girls during childhood or adolescence to emotional disorders in adulthood, a switch that was much less likely to occur for males. An apparent switch in the opposite direction has been documented by Block, Gjerde and Block (1991). They were interested in whether depressive tendencies at age 18 could be predicted from personality ratings made by psychologists of children when aged 11. The answer was positive, but what interests us here is the fact that different ratings were predictive for girls and boys:

…both concurrently and prospectively, depressive symptoms in boys tended to be associated with an unsocialised, aggressive, self-aggrandizing undercontrol…but in girls, depressive symptoms were associated with an oversocialized, intropunitive, overcontrol… (p. 733).

All these various sex differences suggest the possibility that boys and girls respond quite differently to various stresses, and that these differences might occur on sex-typed lines.

A third, and related, theme that recurs in the wider literature is the greater risk of early pregnancy, early marriage, and unhappy marriage, run by young women who have experienced adverse family circumstances, than is the case for young men. For example, Maughan and Pickles (1990) were interested in the fate of children in the National Child Development Study (all British children who were born in one week in March 1958) who were either legitimately-born, adopted, or illegitimately-born but remaining with their natural mothers. For women there was a significant difference in the rate of teenage motherhood: 32% for the illegitimately-born, 13% for those adopted, and 9% for those legitimately born; but there were no differences in rates of paternity for men. (In fact for men there was a significant difference in terms of average job length, which was significantly greater for the legitimately-born group than for the other two groups.)

Rutter, Quinton and Hill (1990) compared the results of two follow-up studies, one of girls, the other of boys, of children who were brought up in the care of children's homes. In each case outcome was compared with that of a general population sample of the same age, never admitted into care, living with their families in the same general area. Nearly 20% of ex-care women (but none of their controls) had children ever taken into care themselves, but this was true of scarcely any of the ex-care men. It was also the case that ex-care men were much less likely than women from a similar background to be disadvantaged in their choice of spouse: of those ever married or cohabiting, 52% of ex-care women versus 19% of controls married 'deviant' men, but the equivalent was only true of 27% versus 17% for men marrying 'deviant' women. Rutter *et al.* concluded that this was because men are less likely than women to seek escape from unhappy family circumstances through parenthood or marriage. Rates of teenage parenthood were 41% versus 5% for women, and 9% versus 2% for men. Figures for cohabitation at age 18 or younger were 40% versus 5% in women and 18% versus 12% in men. Marriage for negative reasons was 36% versus 0% in women and 12% versus 2% in men. All these differences were significant for women, and none significant for men.

Similarly, in their follow-up study of the offspring of former psychiatric patients, Quinton *et al.* (1990) found that women offspring were significantly more likely to have had broken cohabitations and to have become pregnant by age 19, in comparison to control women, with non-existent or much reduced effects for men.

Transactions

So far we have presented a complex picture of issues concerned with inter-generational continuities. But the picture of continuity that is developing in this wider literature—of transmission from parents and family to offspring as children, and thence to offspring as adults—is more complicated still. It is one, not just made up of interactions, but of transactions over time. Furthermore, the transactions that are of interest may, as already noted, involve factors operating on levels as widely varied as the state of the national economy and an individual's feelings of self-esteem. This is, of course, nowhere better illustrated than in Elder's work on economic adversity. The consequences for family life and for children's adjustment depended, amongst other things, upon financial loss for the family, the personal stability of the father, whether the marital bond was strong prior to financial loss, how old the child was at the time and what the child's sex was (Liker and Elder, 1983; Elder and Caspi, 1988).

But there are other demonstrations of this same point from research on offending and on mental health. Kolvin *et al.*'s (1988) family deprivation index, assessed when children in the Newcastle County Thousand Family Study were five years old, and which was strongly predictive of later offending, including factors as varied as overcrowded housing, dependence of the family upon state or community subsistence, and marital instability and 'poor mothering' ('ineffective' father was amongst additional stress factors for those families low in terms of deprivation). In the Cambridge Study in Delinquent Development, offending career was affected not only by family and individual factors, but was also favourably affected by moving out of London, by marriage, especially if a man married an unconvicted woman, and by avoiding unemployment (Farrington, 1988).

Quinton and Rutter and their colleagues have found that the re-creation of disturbed family relationships in early adulthood, amongst institution-reared girls, could not all be attributed to personality functioning. Those from disrupted homes were more likely to return to them after being in care, more likely to leave home early because of this, and more likely to become pregnant before age 19, regardless of whether they showed disorder in their teens or not (Quinton, 1988). Brown G. and his colleagues, too, in their work on depression in women, have been developing a complex model that has two mutually influential strands, one more to do with circumstances (a 'conveyor belt', although not inevitable, of loss of mother, circumstances surrounding leaving home, pre-marital pregnancy, and severe life events connected with marriage or motherhood), the other more to do with internal characteristics, particularly attitudes about self and her world, and styles of attachment (Brown, 1988).

Many writers warn against the assumption that cause and effect runs in one direction, from parental characteristics or marital or family quality to child behaviour and development. It should not be assumed, for example, that maternal over-protection is the cause rather than the effect of adolescent drug use (Blechman, 1982), that parental irritable discipline is necessarily the cause rather than the effect of antisocial behaviour in offspring (Patterson and Dishion, 1988), or that strained family relationships and isolation of the child from family activities are causes rather than effects of juvenile delinquency (Silbereisen and Walper, 1988). This warning was forcefully made by Bell (1968) a number of years ago but often goes unheeded.

The picture is yet more complicated if one accepts Brown's (1988) point that the two strands in development—the person and her or his circumstances—are themselves not independent. Choice of friends and of partner are not accidental and tend to follow a rule of 'homophily' i.e. like chooses like (Kandel, Davies and Bayder, 1990). Even extreme adversity is unlikely to be purely accidental. Robins (1988), reporting on two natural

experiments—combat in Vietnam and the effects of suffering flood dam-
age—makes the interesting point that much of the excess symptomatology
shown by people with such experiences may be due to selection factors.
For example, the soldiers in Vietnam who saw a great deal of combat had
on average more behaviour problems and fewer occupational skills before
Vietnam, reflecting the fact that they were younger, and that many had
enlisted as high school drop-outs, and presumably had fewer occupational
skills that might have kept them behind the lines. Similarly, those who lived
in flooded areas were poorer and less well educated than those who lived
on higher, and therefore more expensive land. In both cases controlling for
social class and school achievement virtually erased the initial correlation
between experience and symptoms.

As already mentioned, Caspi and Elder (1988) concluded that continuity of interpersonal style from childhood to adulthood was one of the links
making for continuity in problem behaviour and problem relationships
across two or more generations. Caspi, Elder and Herbener (1990) describe
data from the Berkeley Guidance Study that bear directly on this point.
They believe that three interactional styles are particularly important and
show continuity over the life course: ill-temperedness, shyness, and depen-
dency. Twenty years after they were first assessed, the ill-tempered boys
were described as under-controlled, irritable and moody; shy boys as both-
ered by demands, withdrawing when frustrated, and showing reluctance to
act; and dependent boys as calm, warm, giving, arousing nurturance, and
turned to for advice. Furthermore, ill-temperedness predicted low educational attainment and low status at first job independently of class origins,
as well as divorce or separation. Shyness predicted late marriage and
parenthood and late first entering of stable career (a functionally related
job held for at least six years), even after controlling for class origins and
a number of other background factors. Shyness then had an indirect influence on low occupational achievement and stability via late entry into a
stable career. Dependent boys, on the other hand, tended to be 'on time' in
their domestic and work careers, had an orderly passage from youth to
adulthood in terms of completing school before assuming a career or getting married. They were more likely than others to remain married and to
have wives who were more satisfied with their marriages. Caspi *et al.*
believed that interactional styles might persist across time:

...because they directly provoke the environment to respond to the individual in
characteristic ways, thereby setting up reciprocal person-environment interactions
that may be replicated in new situations.

Moreover, because individuals selectively seek out situations that are compatible with their disposition, they may thereby construct skewed environments that sustain and support their orientation to the world (p. 32).

Others who have studied child, or child-to-adult development have similarly pointed out the complexities involved. Hinde (1988) is one such writer. Amongst the several complexities that he points to is the way in which continuities may have a fragile dependence upon consistency in the environment, or may depend on changes in the environment e.g. a review of the effects of early life enrichment programmes (Maughan, 1988, cited by Hinde, 1988) shows that long-term effects may be dependent upon such social factors as continued parental support for education, positive personality characteristics and supportive teachers. Perhaps we should be looking not for strict continuity, he suggests, but for what Sroufe *et al.* (1985, cited by Hinde, 1988) have called 'coherence across transformations' i.e. causal connections between experiences at one age and subsequent psychological behavioural outcomes that may depend upon complex person × situation interaction effects.

SUMMARY AND CONCLUSION

All this has taken us a long way from the simple proposition that there is some single readily understood environmental mechanism whereby parental problems, such as excessive drinking, are translated with inevitable regularity into harmful outcomes when the offspring are grown to adults. Regarding continuity within individuals from childhood to adulthood, Hinde (1988) concluded:

Individuals are neither infinitely malleable, hostages of whatever winds of fortune they may encounter, nor are they rigidly consistent, maintaining an identical psychological structure as they pass through life's successive stages. The contrast between continuity and discontinuity is useful only as a descriptive tool that opens the way to questions about process ... (p. 367).

When it comes to intergenerational transmission, which involves both an impact on offspring whilst in contact with caregiving parents plus continuity into adulthood, such are the complexities involved that it is scarcely surprising that harmful outcomes are not inevitable and that many offspring who have faced adversity in childhood turn out to be 'competent' as adults (Garmezy, 1988), 'resilient' (Cowen and Work, 1988), or 'abuse resistant' (Kruttschnitt, Ward and Sheble, 1987).

What is particularly persuasive, however, is evidence that discontinuity can itself be explained, that it is 'lawful' rather than simply random. Belsky and Pensky (1988) believe the evidence supports the position that discontinuity is indeed lawful, and is related to relationship experiences, either with spouses, school-mates, or some non-parental adult, which probably enhance feelings of worthiness whilst providing models of consideration and caring. As examples they cite Egeland *et al.*'s (1987) finding that the intergenerational cycle of child mistreatment was broken when women with abusive histories were involved in stable and emotionally supported marital relationships, and Crockenberg's (1987) findings that mothers with histories of parental rejection in childhood were protected from becoming angry and punitive towards their two year old children when they experienced high levels of social support from spouse or other significant individual.

Also relevant here are some of the findings of Rutter and Quinton and their colleagues on the adulthood outcomes for women and men who had been in care as children. They found a very significant effect, particularly for women, of a variable they term 'planning'—a composite variable combining planning for work (some definite choice of job or career) and for marriage (marriage after an acquaintanceship of six months or more, plus a positive choice of partner not just because of external pressure or a means of escape). In the male control group there was no effect of planning and in the female control group a just significant effect, but in the opposite direction. They concluded that planning is therefore a true protective mechanism i.e. one that is operative in the face of adversity but which has no effect in its absence. Planning was significantly related to marital support for ex-care women, and specific planning for marriage was related to marital support for ex-care men. There was no relationship for controls, probably because they mixed with a much more stable peer group and were therefore much less at risk of making a poor marriage, and also perhaps because controls had supportive families who were available to help guide them. Positive school experiences were also greater amongst ex-care men and women who planned (only significantly so for women) perhaps because they had so few other sources of self-esteem, satisfaction and accomplishment (Rutter *et al.*, 1990). As these authors say, there is growing evidence that, "...to some extent people select and shape their own environments... In so-doing individual characteristics are themselves modified" (Rutter *et al.*, 1990, pp. 152–3) and planning is an example of this.

There seem to us to be clear conceptual links here between Rutter *et al.*'s notion of planning, and Bennett *et al.*'s (1987) idea of deliberateness, described earlier. Both seem to relate to the notion of people making clear decisions about their lives, in a way that enables them to step outside of the particular circumstances that they have been brought up in.

This ability to step outside of a potential cycle of adversity is a particularly important idea, and relates to the suggestion that there could be circumstances under which adversity that may be harmful to some, can, under different sets of conditions, actually enhance adjustment in certain respects. This appears to have been the case, for example, for young people in the Oakland Growth Study who were already aged 8–9 years at the onset of economic depression. What seems to have happened is that many of these youngsters experienced a kind of 'accelerated development' as a result of taking on valued roles as paid employees outside the home (more common with boys) or in home care (more often the case for girls) at ages earlier than would otherwise have been the case (Elder and Caspi, 1988).

In this chapter we have attempted to sketch out the findings of previous research under five main headings. First, we examined research which described the range of experiences to which a child might be exposed with a problem drinking parent. We concluded that there is a wide range of negative experiences which children will acquire if their parents have a drinking problem. These experiences may include confusion, witnessing or experiencing violence, aggression or arguments, unpredictability, embarrassment, and relationship difficulties with the non-problem-drinking parent as well as the problem drinker.

We then reviewed the evidence suggesting that the offspring of problem drinkers were at risk of developing problems during childhood. We concluded that there was clear evidence from a wide range of studies and reviews, conducted in many countries, that having a parent with a drinking problem raises the risk of a child developing one or more of a large number of problems, difficulties and disorders during their childhood years. These difficulties are often summarised in terms of anti-social behaviour, emotional and psychological difficulties, and poorer school performance, although they are not confined to these areas alone.

We moved on to consider research on the adulthood outcomes for the children of problem drinkers, finding that most research had been conducted on alcohol-related outcomes. This research implies that the evidence of negative drinking outcomes for offspring once they reach adulthood is not clear, with the outcome depending to a great extent upon the sampling and the exact nature of the outcome criterion. Adults with alcohol problems report problematic childhoods and a greater likelihood of having a problem-drinking parent; and problem children with alcohol-misusing parents are more likely to develop problematic adulthoods involving alcohol misuse. Yet adults with alcohol-misusing parents recruited from community samples, although they report problematic childhoods, do not seem to report greater alcohol consumption than do comparison respondents. When the criterion is alcohol-related problems or dependence, some differences do emerge. Research on outcomes other than problem drinking is fragmentary and inconclusive, but there are some indications that there might be sex differences in outcomes, with daughters possibly being somewhat more at risk for depression, for eating disorders, for various psychiatric personality disorders, and for marrying a problem drinker. There are also some indications that for both sexes, there might be negative effects on self-esteem, particular types of depression, and interpersonal skills; and there has additionally been the suggestion that there might also be some positive effects on offspring such as increased achievement or autonomy motivation.

Following this we looked specifically at mechanisms that had been suggested for how parental drinking problems might lead to effects on the offspring, particularly during the latter's adulthood lives. We showed that there are a wide variety of possible mechanisms which have been put forward to explain the link between parental problem drinking and any long-term deleterious effects on the offspring. We concluded that, although the weight of evidence currently implies that a genetic contribution of some degree should not be ignored, there were strong possibilities that both an alcohol-specific, environmental, behavioural modelling mechanism, and a range of general environmental mechanisms (e.g. offspring are negatively affected by family discord), might be at work.

Finally, the wider literature on the effects on offspring of such childhood events and difficulties as parental discord, family separation, abuse of children by parents, and economic depression was examined. Those who have researched in these related areas have generally come to the conclusion in recent years that there are no straightforward paths from childhood to adulthood, no simple 'cycles' of adversity, and no inevitability in the transmission or problems from one generation to the next. Indeed it turns out often to have been the case that early accounts of the inevitability of intergenerational transmission were exaggerated, and that negative adulthood outcomes following childhood adversity are by no means certain. Often such outcomes are the exception rather than the rule. The picture of lifetime development that is emerging from this research is a complex one, involving multiple interactions between factors, many moderating and mediating variables, and complicated transactional pathways over time. Two themes, though, stand out. One is the importance, in conferring vulnerability, of inter-parent conflict and general family discord. The second is the importance of sex differences in responses to adversity. The review of this wider literature concluded by examining the concept of resilience, and describing some of the variables (such as positive relationship experiences, planning and deliberateness) which might be related to being able to overcome childhood adversity.

CHAPTER 3

DOING RESEARCH ON THE SUBJECT: THE DESIGN OF THE PRESENT STUDY

PURPOSE OF THE STUDY

It is clear from the material outlined in the previous chapters that what happens to the children of problem drinkers once they grow up to adulthood is of great interest, both practically and theoretically. When we started this study there was a great deal that was not known about this group of people. For example, we knew very little about a whole range of adulthood outcomes apart from drinking behaviour. There were also many things which were unclear concerning the childhood family lives of the offspring of problem drinkers, and the ways that these correlated with adulthood outcome. Hence, for example, we knew that many children of problem drinkers reported very unhappy, disharmonious family backgrounds, but it was not clear whether or not it was the parental drinking problem, or the family disruption, which might lead to any deleterious adult outcomes.

We were interested in a number of key issues. First, we wanted to know a great deal more about how these children adjusted once they reached adulthood. Did they find it difficult to make or to maintain close adult relationships? Did they have lower levels of self-esteem? Did they experience more psychological difficulties or problems in adulthood? Were their personalities affected in any obvious ways?

Second, we were of course interested in their behaviour and attitudes towards alcohol. Although we have criticised other researchers for over-emphasising this issue, it is still the case that this is an area where the evidence seems to suggest that these young people may be at particular risk. We decided, however, not to restrict our questions. There seemed no reason to suppose that, if someone was vulnerable towards developing a problem with a substance, he or she would necessarily turn to alcohol, and so the use of a wide range of other drugs was examined as well.

Finally, we were interested in examining in detail the relationship between different experiences in childhood, and the outcome in adulthood for children of problem drinkers. For example, the effects of maternal and paternal drinking problems on adulthood adjustment were compared, and the impact of family disharmony on adulthood outcome examined.

THE PARTICIPANTS—WHO THEY WERE, AND HOW THEY WERE RECRUITED

Problems of Recruitment

The task of recruiting a large number of people each of whom had a parent with a drinking problem is replete with problems: it was necessary to locate people who were now adult, but who in the past had had a parent with a drinking problem, and who might be willing to tell us about often distressing and disruptive incidents in considerable detail.

There were a number of possible ways in which we could have recruited such a group of people, although each had considerable problems attached to them. For example, if there existed good centralised public records where all people treated for alcohol-related problems were listed, with their names, addresses, and family structures, we could have created a list of people who, when they were children, had a parent with a drinking problem. Or we could have searched the records of individual alcohol problems helping agencies and found people who were clients over the past thirty years, who had children who would now be adult. Another strategy might have been to contact alcohol treatment agencies and enquire about current (or past) clients of theirs with drinking problems who reported that they themselves had a parent with a drinking problem. A fourth strategy might have been to seek out the clients of a wide variety of agencies which help people with problems, not solely those related to alcohol. Hence we might have approached mental health services, social services, probation, marriage guidance and so on, locating people with current problems who reported having had a parent with a drinking problem. A final strategy would have been simply to advertise generally for adults who were the offspring of problem drinkers. There are, however, numerous problems with all these strategies. No centralised records exist listing who has been treated for alcohol-related problems. Trying to track down ex-clients of individual agencies to locate their now-adult children would be immensely difficult, and mostly impossible—after all, most specialist alcohol agencies are relatively new (probably averaging 10 years old or less), and hence might not have an ex-client group with children who were now adults. And of course there are important confidentiality issues here—a client would have given his or her name and address confidentially, so no agency could simply pass them on to us to investigate. Finally, even if we managed to cross all the hurdles, we would still be getting a sample of children of treated problem drinkers, and because there is a large amount of evidence which shows that many problem drinkers never receive any formal help for their drinking problems, it would mean that our sample would not be at all representative of all children of problem drinkers, only of those of treated drinkers, and only the contactable ones at that.

We could of course have tried to recruit people with current alcohol or other problems, but the difficulty with this method is that it pre-selects people who have problems in adulthood—and if one of our questions is, 'Do the children of problem drinkers have problems in adulthood?', then we clearly must not deliberately select people for whom the answer is known to be 'yes'. Also, much of the research in the past has been conducted on adults with current alcohol problems, and we have criticised this method in detail in the previous chapter. Even advertising for volunteers is not problem-free—we would not know people's motivations for volunteering, we would know nothing about the people who did not volunteer, and we would not know how serious the drinking problems were that our respondents claimed that their parents had.

As if all these difficulties were not enough, even if we had managed to collect a sample of adults who were children of problem drinkers, and found out about their current life adjustment, we would still not know how different this adjustment was to other people in the population who did not have such an upbringing. For example, if we found our sample to be on average somewhat depressed, we would need to have a control group of people who did not have a parent with a drinking problem, to know if this was a significant finding.

The Solution

It was clear that there was going to be no single, problem free method of recruitment of adults who were the children of problem drinkers. Instead it was decided to attempt to recruit using as wide a variety of sources as possible. In this way the sample might be more representative of the whole population of young adults who had parents with drinking problems than might have been the case if participants had been drawn from a single source. Furthermore, results could be compared to see if the source of recruitment altered the results obtained. If the results were the same irrespective of source, it would imply that the findings were robust. The only method deliberately avoided was the recruitment of people receiving treatment from alcohol problem treatment agencies; in that case the childhood factor of interest (being the children of problem drinkers) would be contaminated with one of the adulthood outcomes we wished to explore (having alcohol problems as young adults). In practice recruitment sources fell into two broad types: 'community/advertising' (such as public advertising, workplaces, community surveys) and 'clinical/agency' (such as probation, health services, social services).

Equal numbers of men and women were sought, so that hypotheses about gender differences could be tested. It was decided, furthermore, that people aged between 16 and 35 years should be recruited with equal numbers in four age-bands (16–20, 21–25, 26–30, 31–35). Such a range would include interviewees young enough to recall and describe their family experiences, and yet old enough for adult adjustment or maladjustment, including drinking problems, to have become apparent. Hence the study was one of 'young adults' but at the same time the age range was broad enough to allow an exploration of age effects. Certain adulthood outcomes might occur at a comparatively early age (late teens or early 20's) others not until the early 30's.

It was decided to recruit a control group (referred to from here on as 'comparisons') from exactly the same sources as our 'offspring' group, attempting to match for sex and age. Because it was anticipated that much of the treatment of results would involve within-offspring-group analyses, it was decided to recruit a comparison group which was half the size of the offspring group. It was decided that available resources would permit the conducting of 240 interviews—160 with offspring interviewees and 80 with comparisons.

Finally, we decided in a proportion of cases to attempt to interview more than one person in a family—i.e. to interview two or even three siblings. This would enable a comparison to be made between the accounts of the siblings, as well as enabling an assessment to be made of the reliability of certain pieces of information.

In summary, then, the aim was to recruit two groups (offspring and comparisons), in the ratio 2 : 1, with both groups being stratified by sex (equal numbers of males and females), age (equal numbers in four age bands of 16–20, 21–25, 26–30, 31–35), and source (equal numbers from clinical/agency and community/advertising sources).

How a Parental Drinking Problem was Defined

To be included in the 'offspring' group a respondent had to report having at least one parent who (now or in the past) had a drinking problem, with onset before the respondent was aged 21 or before he or she left home, whichever was the earlier. To be included in the comparison group, interviewees had to report that neither parent had had such a problem to their knowledge.

Although interviewees were placed in the offspring or comparison group according to their report of the existence or not of a parental drinking problem, many further questions were also asked to ascertain whether or not this statement was well borne-out on closer examination. We were of course limited in the evidence we could access: this was a volunteer sample, and there was no way of accessing any records that might be held concerning our respondents' parents. Indeed, 43% of the sample stated that, to their knowledge, their parents had never been treated for their drinking problems, nor attended Alcoholics Anonymous (AA), and so in any case there would probably exist no treatment records on these individuals. We had to rely, therefore, on respondents' answers to our detailed questioning about their parents' drinking. Nevertheless, if there was any doubt as to whether or not a parent did have a drinking problem, we simply excluded the interview from the analysis.

In order to start to address the issue of whether or not their parents had a drinking problem, all respondents were asked a series of preliminary questions. They were asked: to describe their parents' drinking, using one of the six categories of 'teetotaller', 'light drinker', 'moderate drinker', 'fairly heavy drinker', 'very heavy drinker' or 'problem drinker'; how often each parent would have a drink; how much each parent drank in general; and whether each parent ever drank 'more than was good for them'. If all of these questions provided answers which implied light to moderate drinking, no further questions relating to parental drinking were asked; but if one or more provided answers implied a possibility of heavy or problematic drinking, further questions were asked as follows: changes in parental drinking patterns throughout the respondent's childhood; frequency; binges; locations of drinking; treatment for drinking problems.

If a respondent defined a parent as a problem drinker, or described the existence of drink-related problems, he or she was assigned to the offspring group. Finally, a crucial question was whether or not a respondent had lived with a parent who was actively drinking in a problematic fashion for a minimum of six months (in almost all cases the period of exposure was of course much longer), before reaching the age of 21 or before leaving home (whichever was the earlier). If this criterion was not met, even though the person concerned might have volunteered for the project as a son or daughter of a parent with a drinking problem, the interview was not included in the analysis.

It is important to note that this definition of childhood exposure to a parental 'drinking problem', although constructed with care, is not identical to a confirmed diagnosis of alcohol dependence according, for example, to the latest version of the Diagnostic and Statistical Manual of Mental Disorders (Sher, 1991). Our definition is a psychosocial one, based upon a close relative's opinion, which we confirmed via detailed interviewing, that a parent's drinking constituted a problem. Where the focus of research is on a social group such as the family, as is the case with the present project and much of our other research (e.g. Orford *et al.*, 1992), this is appropriate.

It is relevant at this point to say a word about our use of the term 'drinking problem'. The reader will already have noted, and readers from the USA may have been struck by, our repeated use of this term and our avoidance of the term 'alcoholism' which is the preferred term in the USA and in other parts of the Americas as well as in a number of other countries. This question of language and definition is a difficult and controversial one. The term 'alcoholism' is most closely associated with a model of drinking problems which views such as a problem as akin to a disease, with characteristic symptoms, disease progression, and aetiology which may or may not include important components of genetic transmission and biochemical abnormality. According to this disease view, it is important to get the diagnosis right, and to be precise about whether a particular instance fits the criteria for alcoholism according to DSM or other similar systems. This could be particularly important for research on intergenerational transmission, since it may be the case that important mechanisms of transmission only operate when alcoholism, or alcoholism of a particular type (see Chapter 2), is present in the parental generation. Furthermore, use of the term 'alcoholism' may have advantages for children and other family members, since its use may appear to clarify what is wrong and provide a clearer idea of what should be done. The philosophy of the widespread self-help organisation Alcoholics Anonymous and its co-organisations for family members, Al-Anon and Al-Ateen, rests heavily upon the disease model.

Our position on this, shared we believe by most workers in the field in Britain, is that, despite these potential advantages, the disease model has not been successful in illuminating the origins of alcohol problems, nor has it led to advances in treatment or prevention. Indeed many believe that it often impedes effective intervention by using the label 'alcoholic' and insisting on a rather rigid abstinence approach to treatment in all circumstances, when in fact a more varied and flexible approach is called for. Furthermore, in our view the disease model over-simplifies and obscures a complex subject and leads one in certain directions which may not be helpful in the quest for an understanding of the nature of such problems. For example, we think it likely that drinking problems have much in common with non-substance forms of addictive behaviour such as excessive gambling or hypersexuality, and that many of the 'symptoms' of addictions such as excessive drinking are caused by the reactions of individual consumers and significant others to behaviour that exceeds normality or expectations. This is not the place to embark upon an extended discussion on the nature of drinking problems: for this the reader is referred to the book, Excessive Appetites, written by one of us a few years ago (Orford, 1985). Suffice it to say that the field is still so fluid that these are matters of opinion. We ourselves espouse a psychosocial rather than disease view. This may have had some bearing upon the conduct of the research we shall describe, but on the whole we believe that an understanding of the lives of the young adults who participated in the present project is affected very little by the model of drinking problems adopted by us as researchers.

In practice it is likely that the large majority of 'problem drinking parents' whose offspring were interviewed for this project would have been diagnosed as 'alcohol dependent' according to DSM-IV, and all the remainder would have qualified for DSM 'alcohol abuse'.

The Final Sample

A very wide range of sources was approached (see Table 3.1 for a summary) in order to acquire volunteers, and in order to try to attain the required 50:50 division between advertising and clinical sources.

The source of respondents simply represents how they came to hear about the project. Respondents who came after they or their parents heard about or saw the project via some measure designed to attract the attention of the general public were deemed recruited from an advertising source; whereas respondents who came because either they or their parents were clients of a specialist 'agency' source—health, social services, self-help group, etc.—and hence heard about or saw the project via these agencies were deemed recruited from an agency/clinical source. Hence respondents in the 'clinical' group would *either* have heard about the project from

Table 3.1 Sources of Sample Recruitment

	Offspring (%) (N=164)	Comparison (%) (N=80)
Community/Advertising		
Media[a]	31	35
Firms[b]	4	12
Other participants[c]	7	10
Personal contact[d]	12	21
Total advertising	54	78
Clinical Agency		
Health services[e]	8	14
Social services and probation[f]	18	4
Voluntary agencies[g]	3	2
Self-help groups[h]	16	2
Total clinical	45	22
Unrecorded	2	—

[a] Media includes newspaper advertising, newspaper articles, radio and television appearances, advertising in libraries, placing an advertisement through the letter box of all houses within selected wards in one city, and advertising at the local University Open Day.

[b] 'Firms' included advertising within the 100 largest firms in the South-West of England, and amongst the staff and students of a number of local colleges and voluntary agencies.

[c] These were mostly the siblings, and sometimes the spouses or friends of earlier participants.

[d] A number of participants volunteered as a result of hearing about the project informally via the research staff; these were not close personal friends of the researchers.

[e] Health Service sources were Clinical Psychologists, Consultant Psychiatrists and General Practitioners.

[f] Social Workers, Probation Officers and Prison Welfare staff.

[g] Local Councils on Alcohol plus a voluntary organization providing residential care for adolescents.

[h] Al-Anon and Al-Alteen groups.

a parent who was now or had been in the past a client of one of these clinical agencies; *or* they would have heard about it because they were now or had been in the past clients themselves.

From over 350 16–35 year olds recruited as potential interviewees, the first 250 who enabled the criteria outlined above to be met were interviewed. After discarding cases over whom there was still doubt about the parental problem drinking status, the final sample size was 244, comprising

164 offspring of problem drinking parents, and 80 comparison respondents. Details of parents' drinking will be given in the following chapter: for now, we may simply note that of the 164 in the offspring group, 29 reported that the problem drinking parent was the mother (or step-mother), 112 the father (or step-father), and 23 both.

The final sample was made up as shown in Table 3.2. In practice, men proved more difficult to recruit than women, particularly amongst those over 20 years old; and advertising sources were more productive than agency ones, particularly for the comparison group.

Although no attempt was made to stratify the sample by marital or social status, the aim was to achieve a sample that was mixed in these respects. In practice, the sample consisted of 45% single, 42% married or cohabiting, and 7% divorced or separated (6% missing data); and 45% professional/managerial (I/II on the Registrar General's coding), 11% routine non-manual (IIIN),. 20% skilled manual (IIIM), and 21% semi- or unskilled manual (IV/V) (3% missing data). This represents a socially mixed sample, although in comparison with the general population, professional and managerial groups are somewhat over-represented, and blue collar occupations are under represented.

It needs to be noted that although the Registrar General's classification of occupations has the advantage of being well known and hence useful in providing a description of the sample that is easily understood, it has notable disadvantages. As an index of social status, it relies solely upon the

Table 3.2   The Sample in Terms of Age, Sex and Source

	Offspring (%) (N=164)	*Comparisons* (%) (N=80)
Sex		
Male	43.9	50.0
Female	56.1	50.0
Age		
16–20 years	21.9	26.2
21–25 years	25.0	23.7
26–30 years	30.5	25.0
31–35 years	22.5	25.0
Source		
Community/Advertising	54.3	77.5
Clinical/Agency	43.9	22.5
Unrecorded	1.8	0.0

nature of the occupation of a single member of the family who is assumèd to be the main bread-winner—usually the husband/father. The figures given in the previous paragraph are based upon the longest occupation of the research participant's father. For purpose of analysis of the data (Chapters 4–6), however, we used what we believe to be a more satisfactory measure of the socioeconomic status of a participant's childhood family, based upon both the occupation and education of both father and mother (see Chapter 4 and Orford and Velleman, 1990).

Finally, we note that the 244 participants came from a total of 213 families. In 19 families (13 offspring, 6 comparisons) we interviewed 2 adult children, and in 6 families (all offspring) 3 adult children.

METHODS

Because of the detail in which we were interested, we decided to use an intensive interviewing method, as opposed to, for example, using a postal questionnaire. We knew that locating such a sample of people would be difficult and so, once located, we wanted to glean as much as possible; we wished to discover a considerable amount about both the childhood and adulthood life of each participant, and this would be both time consuming, and highly individual—a postal questionnaire could not possibly do justice to this material; and much of the information we wanted might be upsetting, and it was likely that only careful and sensitive interviewing would reveal the material we wanted. In addition, a number of questionnaires and checklists were used to maximise the reliability and validity of information obtained on certain topics.

It was further decided to re-interview people after 12 months. Again this was for a number of reasons. One interview would only provide a single snap-shot of our respondents' adjustment, whereas a second interview would make it possible to: assess, by repeating some questions, the degree of confidence we should place in our respondents' recollections; gauge the stability of adulthood adjustment at least over a shortish period of 12 months; and test certain hypotheses about causal influences on adjustment (for example concerning the effects of stress and social support during the year between interviews).

The Interviews

The basic method employed, then, was two long interviews, conducted 12 months apart, covering both retrospective recollections of the family of origin and current life adjustment. Interviews were held in people's homes, or at the University, whichever was most convenient to the participants.

The first interview took an average of about six hours to conduct, although the range of time taken was quite large—from about three and a half hours up to more than 20 hours. Long interviews were often conducted over more than one interviewing session, with 22% of interviews taking more than one occasion to complete. It often comes as a surprise to people not familiar with this kind of research that such long interviews are possible. It is our experience, from this and other research, however, that those being interviewed about such personal matters have rarely if ever had a chance to talk about them in this way before. Due to this, participants have a remarkable tolerance for interviews lasting for several hours. Furthermore the interviewer's task of facilitating such an interview is interesting, and rewarding, and constitutes a job that is more than averagely satisfying.

At the end of the first interview, participants were asked whether they had any objections to being contacted and re-interviewed in twelve months' time, and at the same time they were asked to provide an alternative follow-up address besides their current contact address. Eleven months after their first interview, an attempt was made to contact each person to arrange a follow-up interview. Eighty-nine per cent of the sample were successfully re-interviewed. This interview was shorter—it took about four hours on average to complete, and the range of time taken was smaller—from about two hours, up to about six hours. Because of this, only 10% of re-interviews took more than one occasion to complete.

If the interviewee gave permission, each interview was tape recorded; but as well as this, detailed notes were written by the interviewers during the interviews, and the interviews were then coded using a detailed coding frame, utilising both the notes and the tapes.

The contents of the interviews were informed by the literature available at the time (see Chapter 2), exploratory interviews with 15 young adults who had had parents with drinking problems (eight women, seven men, drawn from the same range of sources as those in the main sample), and consultations with 20 practitioners (social workers, psychotherapists, residential workers) with experience of talking to young adults with adjustment problems. Topics were chosen in order to provide as good a picture as possible of those experiences in childhood and the aspects of current adulthood life adjustment believed to be of most importance, and also to enable tests to be made linking these two domains. A number of major areas were focussed upon. The first interview was divided into roughly two halves, the first concerning childhood, the second adulthood up to the present.

There were certain areas in the realm of childhood experiences which we particularly wanted to examine. First of course was the offspring's experiences relating to the parental drinking, including details about both the parental drinking itself (what, when, where, etc) and the effects that this drinking had on parental behaviour. A second area of concern which we have already drawn attention to in Chapter 2 covers such matters as violence, family discord and parental separations. A third area was that of childhood adjustment—how did our interviewees respond to these various pressures? Did they develop any psychological or physical problems? Finally, we wanted to understand the demographic context in which these issues arose—examining such issues as the education and jobs of their parents, the existence of siblings and other close family members, and in general the sort of environment in which the interviewees grew up.

The second half of the interview concentrated on participants' adulthood adjustment, looking at the history of their drinking and drug-taking, examining how stable versus disruptive their adult lives had been so far, looking at self-esteem and personality development, at the existence of psychological difficulties, and at general feelings of satisfaction and dissatisfaction with how their lives had developed so far.

The re-interview focussed almost entirely on the interviewees' lives over the past year, since their first interviews. The second interview covered very similar topics to the adulthood section of the first interview, but only examined these topics as they related to the past year.

The interviews were mainly conducted by four graduate interviewers (two graduates of psychology, one of English, one of computer studies), although one of us (RV) also carried out a small number. Another key feature of this study was the training of the research interviewers to employ a semi-standardised interview which coupled the best features of an 'in-depth' or 'clinical style' interview for eliciting emotions and difficult past experiences, with the features of a 'structured' or 'survey' interview for collecting facts and opinions. Areas of inquiry were specified and these were explored using 'open' questions; but interviewers knew that they would have to code highly specific information and so specific probes and clarifications were utilised as required in order to obtain this degree of specificity (eg, the timing of onset of the parental drinking problem, or the extent of joint family activities). In addition, the use of standard format questionnaires, check-lists, and card-sorts (twelve in the first interview, six in the re-interview) increased the quality of the structured information which was obtained. Rutter and his colleagues (e.g. Rutter, Cox, Egert, Holbrook and Everitt, 1981) have shown that it is possible to train interviewers to obtain both 'high quality facts' (to use their terminology) and to elicit feelings and attitudes.

Our confidence in the results of this study rests heavily upon the time and care which was given to the interviewing task. The four interviewers involved were carefully trained and their work was discussed in a team meeting on a weekly basis throughout the project, in order to ensure comparability. Great care was taken to establish good rapport and to create the best possible conditions for accurate recall of events (Baddeley, 1982; Robins *et al.*, 1985). For example, participants' biographies were carefully and slowly reconstructed during the interviews and factual information, such as whether a parent's drinking constituted a problem when the respondent was of a particular age, was asked about in relation to other, salient life events. In addition, questions about aspects of childhood experience which might otherwise be difficult to recall with any certainty, such as whether or not a parent often drank at home, were asked about in full, and only after considerable discussion of the wider circumstances of family life and parental drinking. Further details of the development of these interviews are given, and methodological issues discussed, in Velleman and Orford (1984;1985).

Reliability of the Interview Data

Many people would contend that interviewing people about the subjects that we covered is a useless thing to do for three reasons: (1) because people cannot recall details of the past at all accurately; (2) because even if they could, interviewers could not reliably ask people questions about the past in a way which would allow comparisons between people unless they used a highly structured interview (with all its concomitant problems, such as of lack of flexibility and reactivity, reduction in interaction between interviewer and respondent in constructing the interview, and interference in the creation of a relationship between interviewer and respondent); and (3) because interviewers could not reliably code the answers (even if they could obtain them reliably) without over-simplifying these complex and intricate variables.

Others would contend, more generally, that interviews themselves are not a valid method of obtaining good quality data, being far too subjective to yield useful or scientifically valid information. We disagree strongly with this stance. We believe that it is important to continue the gradual move in clinical and social psychological research away from exclusive reliance on laboratory based experimentation, or postal questionnaires, towards research in which people actually talk to other people, make relationships with them, and ask them meaningful and real questions about their lives. Nevertheless, the latter type of research does raise very important questions; and one of the most important is whether in such research it is possible to collect reliable information, particularly when asking for information about past happenings.

The best known evidence against retrospective reporting as a research method was the study by Yarrow *et al.* (1970) which compared mothers' reports of their children's development with clinic and nursery school records made as much as 30 years earlier. Correlations were generally low and systematic biases were found in the direction of mothers reporting fewer problems and over-estimating children's abilities. But institutional records are often unreliable, and other studies have shown that reliable recall is more likely for events that carry some importance for the individual, and *whether* events have happened is more accurately recalled than *when* they occurred. Results are inconsistent regarding the possibility of systematic bias in recall. Wolkind and Coleman (1983) found that currently anxious or depressed women reported more parental marital problems than women who had been depressed but were now well, and Robins (1966) found that adverse childhood events were more commonly reported by those with current psychosocial problems than by those without. However, in a later, more systematic evaluation of recall of childhood events after 30–50 years, by siblings with and without current psychiatric problems, Robins *et al.* (1985) have not replicated the finding of a biasing effect of current mental state and have found good agreement between siblings for factual data, and for parent behaviours such as marital disputes or involvement in community activities. Quinton (1988) concluded that until more is known about this issue, "... it is preferable to place most weight on discrete events located within broad time periods, to concentrate on obtaining clear descriptions of events and relationships rather than on generalised recollections, and to use the reconstructive nature of memory (Bartlett, 1932) to locate events within a coherent life history framework" (p. 279).

In the present study, the issue of reliability was examined in the following, six, separate ways. Clearly not all of the information gained could be subjected to each of these reliability checks, but samples of information were assessed using each of these methods.

1. Internal Consistency

The internal consistency of each of the questionnaires and check-lists used within the study was examined in the conventional way by calculating their 'alpha' coefficients. These ranged from 0.78 to 0.93 (with the exception of two of the personality sub-scales which had alphas of 0.72 and 0.65), and all levels of internal consistency were judged to be acceptable. Another way of examining internal consistency is to look at what interviewees said about themselves with reference to two different time periods. For example, people were asked about the degree of division between their home lives and their peer relationships for two periods: up to age 11 and post-11. Although one would expect an increase in the amount of home-peer 'division' reported as interviewees grew older, with the peer group becoming increasingly important and with adolescent needs for privacy and independence growing, nevertheless a substantial correlation would be expected. This indeed was what was found—70% of respondents reported the same level of home-peer 'division' in the two time periods, and 95% reported the same or *more* 'division' in the later period as in the earlier. The correlation between the 'division' ratings for the two periods was 0.67 which was highly significant statistically.

2. Reliability of Interview Administration

This was examined by analysing the results of the study by interviewer. We selected more than 20 variables to examine in this way. Approximately half of these were variables which we predicted might give significant differences between the interviewers (eg smoking: two of the interviewers were smokers, two were not, and it is conceivable that interviewers who did or did not smoke might have a different approach to asking about the existence of problems relating to smoking). The other half were variables which we predicted would not give significant differences (eg. sex, age left home). Examining this number of variables it would be expected that purely by chance some interviewers would see more respondents who, for example, left home early, or whose parents had a high level of education. That is what we found—a small number of moderately significant differences which we feel do not reflect any systematic interviewer biases.

3. Reliability of Coding

This was examined by looking at a random sample of six per cent of all the interviews, and basing the estimate of inter-coder reliability on a second interviewer coding from a tape-recording of another interviewer's interview.

The overall reliability (based on summing results from all the variables form which we have both an initial and a second rater's codes) shows 78% perfect agreement for the first interview (91% to within one scale point), and 86% perfect agreement for the re-interview (96% to within one scale point). More detailed analyses separating out the complexity of the coding reveal, not surprisingly, that inter-rater reliability is lower in the case of more 'subjective' variables.

For example, over relatively 'objective' issues such as what interviewees said about the number of siblings they had, or about when they left home, there was 100% agreement between the two coders. On the other hand, some variables are much more 'subjective', and there was less agreement on these variables. The level of absolute agreement fell to as low as 38% in the case of interviewees' descriptions of the negative sentiments expressed about their parents' relationships (a four-point scale based on a content analysis of words used throughout the interview). Agreement to within one scale point, however, was much higher (88%) and in the case of the positive sentiments expressed about the parents' relationship, the absolute level of agreement was equally high (88%). It should be noted that absolute agreement is a harsh test: correlations between ratings were always statistically highly significant.

These inter-coder reliability coefficients are at acceptably high levels, and are at least comparable with other researchers' data. But there are a number of major problems with measuring reliability in this way with such detailed and contextual data. Interviews are performed in an interpersonal context of which a tape-recording can necessarily only be a partial record. Hence the second rater will often receive only partial information from the recording, will receive almost no information about non-verbal communications, and will not be as personally involved in the interview process, being an observer rather than a participant. When we examined the direction of disagreement in simple cases where the code used was a binary one (presence *vs* absence) we obtained some support for this view. We predicted that the first interviewer, being party to more information, would be more likely to code 'presence'; and indeed this was the case in 80% of the instances. Hence our criticism of this method of assessing reliability is that one would not necessarily expect a very high inter-coder reliability given the full context of the interview versus the rating of a tape recording. The fact that an acceptably high reliability was mostly found suggests that the care taken with continued training, and discusion about the interviewing and the coding, paid high dividends.

4. Reliability of Recall

If people are asked the same question about the past, on two occasions separated by a year, do they give the same answer? There is evidence from experimental psychology that there is considerable stability of long term memories (e.g. Bahrick *et al.*, 1975; Waldfogel, 1948). With a variety of variables, we attempted to ask the same question in the re-interview that we had asked in the first interview. The results again showed that there was a large measure of agreement, but that this agreement was far from perfect. We shall look at just three variables here, as examples: a supposedly 'objective' variable (age left home) and two more 'subjective' ones (divided home-peer relationships, and violence between parents).

'Age left home' was measured on a 5-point scale (under 16, 16, 17, 18 or 19, 20 or older). Participants gave exactly the same 'age left home' over the two interviews in 65% of cases, rising to 92% agreement if a one-point discrepancy on the scale was allowed. Similarly, what they said about divisions between home and peer group after the age of 11 was coded on a 4-point scale (not divided, some division, moderately divided, highly divided): there was a 50% absolute agreement over the two interviews, or 84% to within one scale point. Finally, violence between parents was coded on a complex 19-point scale that combined information on the severity, frequency and duration of violence: there was a 57% absolute agreement over the two interviews, or 75% to within one scale point.

It needs to be stressed again, however, that less than perfect agreement is not surprising, considering the different contexts in which this information was gathered. In the first interview, the questioning took the form of a biographical, life-history approach where questions led on from one another, and where the actual age at which the person 'left home' would have been clarified to both the interviewer and (more importantly) the interviewee. In the re-interview, however, these questions appeared 'out of the blue', and hence there were no contextual cues enabling the respondent to reconstruct memories as there had been 12 months earlier (and this is a very important dimension in improving memory, as shown by research in the area of eye-witness testimony). Furthermore, in many cases the interviewers were also different for the two interviews.

5. Stability Over One Year

In other instances questions were asked on both occasions which related, not to childhood events, but to aspects of current life. This provided an opportunity to test the stability of accounts given by participants over a 12 month interval. For example, assessment of self-esteem using the Rosenberg (1965) scale was quite highly stable over that interval (Year 1– Year 2 correlation of 0.70); positive mental health (a complex variable described in Chapter 5) moderately stable (0.66); and satisfaction with current marriage less so (0.46), although still highly significant statistically.

6. Agreement Between Siblings About Recall of Childhood Events

Looking at data from the 25 families where two or more siblings were interviewed, we found an overall perfect agreement of 67% across all variables, and agreement to within one scale point (when there were at least 4 points on the scale) of 84%. These findings parallel those in the other areas of reliability: although agreement is far from exact, siblings do in general appear to be describing similar childhood events.

Again, however, perfect agreement is not to be expected in data from different members of the same family: children of different ages and temperaments are exposed to different circumstances and perceive, and later reconstruct, events from somewhat different perspectives. Even a variable as apparently ' objective' as 'number of siblings' produced less than perfect agreement. Taking three members of one family which we interviewed as an example: there were three children in this family, all of different ages. The parents separated and divorced, and eventually, after some two or three years, the mother re-married, to a man who also had two children by his first marriage. Because of their ages, and their stages of leaving home, the two older respondents did not define their new step-siblings as siblings, whereas the youngest respondent, who had a new family life with her step-siblings, did.

There are many who would argue that the search for reliability is doomed to failure since it is pointless to expect adult memories to reflect the truth of what happened in childhood. It is certainly clear that all experience, even at the time, is to some degree subjective and constructed rather than being a perfect mirror of an objective reality. All *recall*, therefore, is doubly subjective and re-constructed. We have some sympathy with this view, but on the other hand we must distinguish between the subjective and constructed nature of experience, and the reality of certain events and actions. If someone's mother is regularly beaten up by her drunken husband to the point of, on occasions, being hospitalised, there is a clear 'reality' here which existed irrespective of any subjective interpretation or retrospective reconstruction. Our aim in those parts of the present research that concerned themselves with retrospective reports of events in the participants' childhoods (as opposed to perceptions, attitudes and which were also asked about) was to obtain, by careful interviewing, information of good quality which reflected childhood events and circumstances as they actually occurred.

CHAPTER **4**

RECOLLECTIONS OF GROWING UP WITH PARENTS WITH DRINKING PROBLEMS—RESULTS I

What was it like growing up in a home where one or both parents drank excessively? How did the parents behave towards their children, and how did the children attempt to deal with this behaviour? Did they develop many problems as children? How did their childhoods compare with those recalled by young people whose parents did not drink excessively? The many hours of detailed interviewing which these 244 young adults contributed to the research produced a large amount of information. This chapter will examine what they told the interviewers about their childhoods.

Interviewees were asked about a variety of topics. We were interested, of course, in parental drinking, and in drink-related behaviour, so participants in the offspring group were asked many questions about when the problem drinking started, and how long it lasted; where and when drinking took place; whether or not any treatment or help for the drinking problem was received; and what impact the drinking had on life at home, and on the child's experience. We were also interested in learning about how these young people had coped with living with a problem drinking parent.

Our interests extended beyond the parents' drinking however. We asked many questions concerning the family environments in which offspring and comparison children had grown up, knowing that much previous research had suggested that family disharmony, violence and separation might be important mediators determining the extent to which there might be negative consequences for children either in childhood or adulthood.

We were also interested in general issues of childhood adjustment. Did these children have many childhood problems? What were their friendship networks like? Did they themselves start to use alcohol or drugs as children? Did offspring and comparison interviewees differ in these respects?

Throughout, some questions were phrased in ways that required factual answers whilst others were far more open, requiring participants to simply talk in their own words about issues or events. For example, when asking an interviewee to tell us about his or her parents' relationship, we asked some highly specific questions concerning, amongst other things, the frequency of rows, or the frequency of expressions of affection. But the interviewee was also asked to tell the interviewer in his or her own words about the parental relationship—what it was like, whether or not the parents were thought to have been happy together, or suited to one another, etc.—hence providing a much richer picture of what the interviewee actually thought about the parental relationship than could have been obtained from a series of 'closed' questions alone.

EXPERIENCES OF PARENTAL DRINKING

The Extent of Exposure to Drinking Problems as Children

During the first interview participants (offspring group only) were helped by detailed questioning to carefully reconstruct their experiences relating to parental problem drinking. This allowed the interviewer to clarify, and subsequently to code on a special chart, each person's recollection of the development of and, if applicable, improvement in, the parental drinking problem. Table 4.1 shows the codes used and three illustrative examples. In one of the three cases shown, the problem was thought to have been present more or less throughout childhood; in another it developed relatively late on; and in the third exposure was reduced by separation during the interviewee's teens. The mean age of offspring interviewees when they, *in retrospect*, thought that their parents had *probably* developed drinking problems was 3.5 years (sd = 5.0); and the mean age when they *definitely at the time* were aware that their parents had alcohol problems was 9.6 years (sd = 7.5). Mothers with drinking problems were recalled as developing their problems later in the interviewees' lives than were fathers, both 'probably, in retrospect' (average for mothers 6.7 years, for fathers 2.7, $p < 0.002$) and 'definitely, at the time' (average for mothers 12.0 years, for fathers 8.2, $p < 0.005$).

The most common pattern reported was a drinking problem which started either before the child's birth or during early childhood (although the child was usually not aware of the problem until sometime later) and which then continued uninterrupted until either the child left home as a young adult, or (less commonly) until the child was separated from the parent by parental separation or death. This continuing pattern of parental problem drinking spanning both early childhood and adolescence was the

Table 4.1 Three illustrations of method of charting active years of a parental drinking problem during the years of upbringing

Age	Year by year code		
	P 162 Daughter	*P 226 Son*	*P 234 Daughter*
Before born	4	3	4
0	4	3	5
1	4	3	5
2	4	3	5
3	4	6	5
4	4	3	5
5	4	3	5
6	5	3	5
7	5	3	6
8	5	3	6
9	5	3	6
10	5	3	6
11	6	3	9
12	7	9	9
13	7	9	8/10
14	7	9	6
15	7	9	mother and daughter
16	7	9	moved away
17	7	9	
18	7	6	
19	7	son to	
20	7	university	
21	daughter left home		

Key: 1 Don't know; 2 Definitely no problem; 3 Probably not a problem; 4 Probably a problem in retrospect; 5 Definitely a problem in retrospect; 6 Definitely a problem; 7 Definitely a problem—getting worse; 8 Definitely a problem—better than before; 9 Definitely a problem—crisis; 10 Abstains.

rule: relatively few people reported parental drinking problems that were confined to one period or another, or which did not continue uninterruptedly (9% of offspring reported exposure to parental problem drinking only before the age of 11; 13% reported exposure only from the age of 11 plus onwards; and 7% reported two distinct periods of exposure). The median number of years of exposure of the child to the parental problem between ages 6 and 15 (before 6 very few could be definite about the existence of the problem), was eight counting only 'probable' and 'definite' years (or five counting only 'definite' years).

Furthermore, only 39% of offspring respondents were aware that their parents with drinking problems received treatment or professional or specialist advice for these problems before the respondents were aged 21, and a further 7% thought that treatment or advice had occurred but could not put a date on it. The offspring group is therefore roughly equally divided between those who could recall their problem drinking parent received treatment or advice during the participant's childhood or adolescence and those who could not. Of those who could, only 60% (or 27% of all offspring) recalled that their parents received help from an alcohol-specialist treatment unit, voluntary agency or self-help group (and of this number, just over half recalled that their parents were members of Alcoholics Anonymous but believed that they had not received professional treatment).

Extracts from interviewers' reports from two of the interviews illustrate this common theme of parental problems continuing throughout much of a person's childhood.

P80

P [the research Participant] was definite that his father had had a drinking problem before P was born and he was aware of his father's problem as early as four years old. Until P's early teens, his father had been a daily drinker, drinking both at home and in pubs. He, "… would start as soon as the shops opened [where he would buy a couple of bottles of sherry or whisky], would drink through the afternoon into the evening [and then go to the pub and have] … a few glasses of beer". His father had never to P's knowledge had any treatment for his drinking, but since P was about 14 years of age his father's drinking had been better and from then on he drank whisky, about one and a half bottles daily, but he, "only drinks at night time", and would go for periods of three or four weeks without drinking at all.

P123

Although definitely of the opinion that his father had had a drinking problem throughout P's childhood, P was not aware that his father was drinking heavily until he was 16 or 17 years old. P had become so used to his father being drunk that it seemed normal. He was able to carry on a normal life, even though drinking approximately 20 singles a day. "If you didn't know what he was like [sober] you'd think he was maybe just a bit insecure". He very rarely drank at home and tended to be, "secretive about the amount he drinks". P only realised how much his father was drinking when working in a bar one Christmas, noticing that he would have five whisky doubles in a half pint mug at lunchtime and evening and drink them within half an hour. At that time his father had realised that his drinking was becoming a problem and had several periods of abstention. When P was in his very late teens and early twenties, his father had seen a family friend who had also had a drinking problem, and had recently seen his doctor about his drinking for the first time. Otherwise P believed that his father had received no help from outside the family throughout P's childhood.

Effects of a Drinking Problem on Parental Behaviour

Drinking affected parents' family conduct in many different ways, as the following illustrations show.

P73

P had early memories, from age four or five years, of her father's strange behaviour, for example him falling off a bike in the high street, probably drunk. She recalled finding him, several years later, by the 'fridge on the kitchen floor. She had felt really frightened. In her late teens, things were at crisis point. Her father started hitting her mother and her brothers had nearly come to fights over it. Her father was bound over by the police to keep the peace for five months and there were constant rows at home.

P76

Although his father drank every day, market day was "a dreadful day, everyone would get really drunk", otherwise it was, "just a fact of life, just how it was, didn't notice any difference". Later things got worse. "He'd go off and not come back at night, and he'd never done that before. One Christmas Eve really sticks in my mind when he smashed a new car. It was so incredibly lucky he didn't kill someone else. He managed to drive it home, God knows how".

P275

Until P was ten, she and her family lived abroad. Drinking was part of the social scene and her father would drink from dawn to dusk and more, drinking wherever he went, at home, others' homes and at work. P knew that her father would drink several bottles of vodka or gin at the weekend and that he hid bottles in the garage, garden or in his coat. She had an early recollection of him drinking out of a bottle. He always needed to drink before he went out and brought drink home with him from town. He slept a lot. He was ill with kidney problems when P was ten and for much of her teens he was in and out of clinics and hospitals and at one point was very ill and was given 24 hours to live.

As part of that section of the interview devoted to parents' drinking problems, all members of the offspring group were also asked to complete a questionnaire listing 61 ways that it was believed excessive drinking might adversely affect parental behaviour. From this long questionnaire a shorter scale (the Parental Behaviour Scale or PBS) was constructed consisting of the 16 items shown in Table 4.2. Items were chosen for this scale because they appeared to particularly reflect the impact of parental drinking upon the parent's behaviour at home, because they were items that offspring could answer with some confidence (the longer list included a number of items about which many interviewees said they could not be certain e.g. withdrawal symptoms such as sweating and feelings of sickness in the morning), and because they appeared from preliminary item analysis

Table 4.2   The parental behaviour scale

	Problem drinking parent		
	Father *(N=112)*	*Mother* *(N=29)*	*Both* *(N=23)*
When drinking would your problem-drinking parent (or would either of your problem-drinking parents):			
Come home very drunk?	56	32	48
Wake up the whole family when came back late at night?	22	21	15
Drink secretly or 'sneak drinks' at home?	32	69	58
Get very drunk at home?	30	61	48
Upset family occasions (Christmas, birthdays)?	37	58	52
Make a fool of selves at home, or were noisier than usual?	37	56	43
Come home with blood over face and clothes?[1]	19	19	6
Make a fool of self in public?	27	20	25
Talk rubbish, or talk on and on at people?	47	52	47
Let self get dirty, unkempt, or smelly?[1]	23	18	25
Get very possessive and jealous?[2]	32	44	26
Fail to join in with family activities?	33	33	37
Be late or inconsistent or unreliable or unpredictable, or break promises?	53	48	26
Have very changeable moods?	54	54	45
Ever get into debt?[2]	39	27	40
Ask you or your brothers or sisters for money?	13	19	10

[1] —% 'Regularly' or 'Sometimes'.
[2] —% 'definitely a problem'.
All other items—% Regularly.

to contribute satisfactorily to the total scale score (an alpha coefficient of 0.79 showed that the 16-item PBS had a satisfactory degree of internal reliability). Each item of the PBS was scored from 0 (never occurred or not a problem) to 3 (had regularly occurred or had definitely been a problem). Hence the maximum possible score was 48. In practice scores obtained ranged from a low of 2 to a high of 43, with a mean.of 26.2 (sd = 8.9) and a median of 27.

The contents of the PBS, as well as the numerical results obtained from it, show the extent of disruptive parental behaviour associated with parents' drinking problems. The lives of many young adults who had parents with drinking problems had been regularly disrupted by parents being drunk, upsetting family occasions, making fools of themselves, being unreliable, displaying changeable moods, and creating financial difficulties. It is equally important to note, however, that variability is high. Whilst there was a minority who reported that almost all the PBS items had occurred regularly, there was also a minority who reported six or fewer of these items occurring regularly or a larger number occurring occasionally.

Mention should also be made of a number of the questionnaire items that did not appear in the final PBS, since they round out the picture of the disruptiveness caused by a parental drinking problem. For example, comparatively common were: the parent going out early in the evening and reappearing much later (44% regularly); being very restless at night (39% definitely a problem); being irritable and short tempered (85% yes); argumentative or very critical (55% regularly); self-destructive and self-punishing (49% regularly); very self-pitying (41% regularly); ever felt depressed (45% regularly); felt very anxious (38% regularly); attempted suicide or made a suicidal gesture (36% at least once). Also common were reports that parents with drinking problems had: been charged with an offence of any sort (38% at least once); become less efficient at work (40% definitely a problem); ever lost a job due to drinking (34% at least once); had any medical problems thought to be related to drinking e.g. liver, stomach, heart (71% yes); and had any major physical changes due to drinking e.g. putting on weight, changes in appearance (63% yes). Finally, note should be taken of the proportions who reported that their parents with drinking problems had made sexual advances to them or to their siblings (7% at least once) and to their friends (9% at least once).

PBS scores were significantly correlated with number of years of 'definite' exposure to the parental drinking problem between ages six and 15 ($p < 0.001$), and negatively with estimated age when the parental problem had its onset (both 'probably in retrospect', $p < 0.02$, and 'definitely aware at the time', $p<0.01$). Scores of those offspring with fathers only with drinking problems, and those with mothers only, were not significantly different.

Where did Parents Drink?

The most common locations where drinking took place were pubs or other licensed premises (74% of the offspring group recalled that their parents with drinking problems often drank there, whereas 9% recalled that they never did or did so only once or twice). Fifty-nine percent of the offspring group recalled that their problem drinking parents often drank at home; whereas only 25% recalled that their parents never drank at home or did so only once or twice. Not surprisingly, mothers with drinking problems were significantly more likely to drink·at home ($p<0.001$), and fathers were significantly more likely to drink in pubs ($p<0.002$). Some researchers (Jacob, 1988) have focused on the variable of in-home *vs* out-of-home parental drinking as one of potential significance for the family, although in the present study PBS scores were not correlated with reports of parental drinking locations.

Coping with Parental Problem Drinking

The majority of the offspring group, then, reported many negative child-hood experiences relating to one or both parents' drinking problems. How did they deal with them? This is an important area for at least two reasons. First, understanding how children and adolescents deal with parental problem drinking may provide clues to the mechanisms that underlie why some children develop the types of problem that they do whereas others develop different problems, or why some indeed appear to be resilient enough not to develop any overt problems. Second, there may be continuities between the ways that some children cope with problems in childhood and the types of difficulty that they experience as adults. In Chapter 2 we reviewed a number of theories (for example, Clair and Genest, 1987, or Jarmas and Kazak, 1992) that suggest such a link. For example, children who learn to avoid conflict with problematic parents might develop a habitual coping mechanism of avoidance, which might mean that later in their lives they avoid other issues which need to be faced up to in a more assertive manner.

We spent quite some time on the issue of coping in the interviews, and the following are examples of the kinds of things that participants said:

P72

"He'd wear you down ... make sure you couldn't leave the room ... then, when he'd got you in tears he'd let you go. But then you'd get to an age where you won't cry ... argumentative, I wouldn't stand for it, I used to shout back. I was rebellious at 13. I'd stand up to him and anyone. I worked from 13 onwards for the money, and to be out, and started drinking at 14, really quite heavily".

Like many interviewees, this same young woman had a number of things to say, not all complimentary, about the ways in which other family members reacted.

P72

"Mum tried to keep a quiet life, tried to keep the peace. She sent the kids off to the pictures on Saturday afternoons, although she couldn't afford it. She couldn't stand up to him ... I don't know how she lives with him ... My brothers are quite big and strong. They were always stepping in to stop it. I was worried that one of them would kill him."

P77

"I used to pretend there was nothing the matter. I made sure friends kept out of the way and didn't annoy him. I felt it was my responsibility to make it easier ... deceitful ... *not* do things. I was very different from my sister. She was inclined to have confrontations. Especially later on she had more trouble and arguments with him. She did bring people in which led to rows. I was more independent. I'd ignore him ... avoid upsetting Mum. Rows upset her more than me. I just left him out, I adapted that way. My sister was struggling to have something more normal perhaps. I was on my own a lot. It was partly me and partly because of the situation at home."

P162, *who considered that both her parents had drinking problems*:

Earlier she had been very baffled, frightened and tearful about her mother's drinking. Later she was very angry and wished her mother dead. She remembers taking long walks, cutting herself off and becoming isolated from her family and also from friends. She only realised that her father had been 'an alcoholic' when she was grown up, but she had felt very angry with him if he was also drunk when her mother was. She had used her father as a 'leaning post' to cope with her mother.

Responses such as these were then coded as representing one or more of 13 different coping styles which were drawn up on the basis of previous research plus the 15 exploratory interviews that preceded the main study. These categories are shown in Table 4.3. The style of coping most frequently used was 'avoidance' (used by 56% of the offspring group), and this is perhaps not surprising if it is considered that most young people living at home have a very limited range of options open to them when trying to deal with the behaviour of a problem drinking parent. More surprising perhaps is the fact that the next most frequently used style was open 'discord', used by 43% of the group. Sons and daughters used the most commonly reported styles equally often; but daughters more often reported utilising some of the other individual coping methods than did sons. This seemed particularly the case with help-seeking: girls recalled themselves as significantly more willing or able to seek help from neighbours or relatives than did sons ($p < 0.05$, with none of the other differences being statistically significant).

Although these coping styles seem to make sense as independent entities, we also investigated, using the statistical procedure of factor analysis, whether or not there were a smaller number of higher-order themes or factors that might underlie these styles. In this case the factor analytic solution involving four factors seemed to make the best sense, both statistically and psychologically, and the results are summarised in Table 4.3. The naming of factors is a matter of interpretation and labels for factors should always be treated as provisional. We had no difficulty tentatively naming the first two coping factors as 'fearfulness and self-protection' and 'confrontation and self-destructive action' respectively, but the third and fourth gave us more difficulty. Factor three seemed to be associated with acting fearfully, and being highly interactive over drink, and it was provisionally termed 'involvement'. It may be that this factor relates to the difficulty which is commonly reported of sticking with one method of coping—many people had tried a variety of ways of coping, finding that none met with lasting success. The final factor, associated with avoidance, switching off, self-blame, help-seeking, and stoicism, we called 'detachment, internalisation and help-seeking' (or, for convenience, simply 'detachment').

EXPERIENCES OF THE CHILDHOOD FAMILY ENVIRONMENT

A very considerable amount of that part of the first interview that concerned childhood was taken up with asking questions about, and getting

Table 4.3 14 Different coping styles and 4 coping factors

Styles	Number (and percentage) reporting each coping style		Examples
	Sons (n=72)	Daughters (n=92)	
Avoidance	40 (57)	51 (55)	Refused to talk to him/her; left alone; stayed in bedroom; hid; went out
Discord	20 (43)	39 (42)	Rowed with him/her; threatened; hit
Switched off	14 (20)	23 (25)	Built shell around self; felt lonely; day-dreamed
Fear for the future	14 (20)	20 (22)	Afraid for the family; worried what would happen in future
Fearful inaction	17 (24)	16 (17)	Too afraid to do anything; terrified
Help-seeking	6 (9)	20 (22)	Sought help from neighbour or relative; escaped next door
Stoicism	6 (9)	13 (14)	Pretended all was well; put on a bold front
Anti-drink	5 (7)	14 (15)	Found the drink and hid it/poured it away
Action against self	6 (9)	12 (13)	Threatened to kill self; refused to eat; got drunk; made self sick
Self-blame	2 (3)	14 (15)	Was a martyr; blamed self; felt guilty
Indulgence	5 (7)	11 (12)	Gave him/her drink or money; made him/her comfortable
Emotional attack	1 (1)	4 (4)	Tried to show him/her up, make look rediculous, or make jealous
Protective action	2 (3)	1 (1)	Hid own money; took special care of own possessions

Risk and Resilience

Table 4.3 *(continued)*

Factors Name:	'Fearfulness and self-protection'		'Confrontation and self-destructive action'		'Involvement'		'Detachment, Internalisation and help-seeking'	
% of Variance:	14%		11%		11%		9%	
Coping Styles, and Factor Loadings	Fearful inaction	0.67	Emotional attack	0.66	Indulgence	0.67	Avoidance	0.71
	Protective action	0.64	Discord	0.62	Anti-drink	0.57	Switched off	0.61
	Fear for the future	0.63	Action against self	0.61	Fear for the future	0.52	Self-blame	0.42
	Stoicism	0.43			Self-blame	0.35	Help-seeking	0.36
					Stoicism	0.31	Stoicism	0.33

the interviewees to expand on, issues relating to their family environments. From these discussions a number of measures of family life were developed. These included measures relating to family relationships, to the stability of the family, and to a range of family experiences.

All the information presented so far in this chapter has been related to the offspring group alone. The information now to be presented about the family environment, on the other hand, was also collected from the comparison group.

Family Relationships

We were interested in a number of issues relating to family relationships. These included both negative factors such as the amount of aggression and violence in the family, and positive factors such as the amount of social and cooperative activities which parents engaged in with each other. Examples of things that were said are as follows:

P78 Offspring

This respondent could only remember one occasion when he was small when his parents seemed close. Otherwise there were always arguments, at least several times each week, whenever his father was drunk, unless he was too drunk to speak. There was regular violence between his parents which lasted over a period of several years. On occasion his mother would be bruised. Other times she fended him off with a rolling pin. He never hit the children, but the interviewee himself was violent towards his father on a number of occasions when he was much older. His father didn't want to have anything to do with the children. "I hated him but couldn't do anything about it...I was more afraid of him than anything. You had to be quieter if he was home. Sometimes he used to be silly and would make us laugh, but he was grumpy and obstinate when drunk". The atmosphere between the children and their mother was good as long as they were not with their father. Family activities and discussions took place without him. "Mum was very quiet, very organised, did everything". They felt sorry for her and tried to get her to leave their father but she wouldn't. He remembers thinking it was nice being at home with his mother, and that he wanted to stay with her forever.

P210 Offspring

Her parents, "always had a lot of rows—a blazing row every two weeks". They were, "basically incompatible, very little show of affection...I think there is very little feeling for each other". Over a period of two or three years there had been some seriously violent occasions. Her father had tried to throttle her mother on at least three occasions, and the police had been called. The interviewee herself had been hit by her father, she estimated approximately every six months or so, and once he had whipped her with a belt. Although she was scared of her father and didn't like being seen with him, she did describe him as 'sensitive' and someone who had a, "good sense of humour—the life and soul". Mother was the, "stronger of the two. She's not afraid of anything. We are on the same level. She understands everything". This participant sensed a big difference between her own family and other people's—"Every other family has things well worked out".

P317 Offspring, *both of whose parents had had drinking problems:*

"There was terrible tension all the time... [but] they always made it very clear that despite all the aggro they would never split up. They did love each other. It was a very close relationship... they were not inhibited with affection... they probably would kiss every day". There were rows several times each week, always about drinking. There was no real violence, but his mother was, "extraordinarily venomous when drunk", and would lash out at his father. Once or twice the latter had pushed the interviewee through impatience but nothing more. The family atmosphere was described as 'claustrophobic' and 'very liberal'—"I wanted us to be a more normal, conventional family". The atmosphere was divided fairly equally between 'terrible tension' and a lot of 'genuine care'. "The whole alcoholism thing was some kind of game they played". Although his parents never did anything much together, never went out, "The whole of their life was a joint activity. They were sharing things all the time... We talked endlessly in circles... a constant analysis of what was going on... Being liberal was a lie, it's a confusion of being open—not really of dealing with a problem... [Father would say] we are a family... propaganda from my father".

P189 Comparison

This interviewee described her parents' relationship as, "pretty good I think... very affectionate". They had arguments, about once every month or two, "which they never tried to hide". Her parents shared a number of interests and as a family they did a lot together. There were day trips together, taking part in sports together, and it was a family tradition to always have breakfast together with both parents every day. The family atmosphere was, "nice, hectic... we are a close family, all very interested, a caring family". Her mother was very comforting and motherly, and they had always had a very close relationship. Her father had always been very interested in her, particularly in homework, and they would play sports together, but their relationship had not been so close, particularly in her teens, when there were things she could not talk to her father about.

P190 Comparison

This informant thought that his parents loved each other very much, although they had had their ups and downs. There had not been much outward show of emotion, however—they were "not that type of family". His mother was a very good mother, very sensible, and it took a lot to get her to argue. Father, on the other hand, was very dominant. Things had to be right for him and he would shout if they weren't. There were lots of raised voices, perhaps once a week. The children wouldn't argue with their parents, what Dad said went. Father used corporal punishment as a last resort, but it was fair. They didn't do a lot together as a family. They were fairly separate, tending to do their own thing. His mother had devoted her life to her family and had worked very hard to be a mother, mediating between the children and their father. The latter could have been more friendly—he was verbally aggressive, although very loving—and it would have been nice if he had been around more. They were, "not a close family at all, not a cuddly type family".

In fact, some twenty different aspects of family life were eventually coded. To simplify the analysis these were clustered into the six groups shown in Table 4.4.

The most striking thing about these results is the very large differences between offspring and comparison groups on almost all variables. The offspring group reported very much more disharmony in parental and family relationships than did the comparison group—they described both the parental relationship that they observed, and the family relationships that they were part of, in very much less positive terms, and they reported more negative experiences with fathers. There was a highly significant difference ($p < 0.0005$) between the two groups on an overall measure of family harmony–disharmony which was created by factor analysing the relationships between the six variables shown in Table 4.4. One major factor emerged, which was clearly interpretable as relating to family harmony–disharmony, and all respondents were scored on this factor.

Nevertheless, although it is the case that the offspring group generally described more disharmonious family environments and the comparison group generally described more harmonious ones, it is also important to stress that both offspring and comparison groups had members who showed the full range of scores. Substantial numbers of the offspring group reported harmonious parental and family relationships, and substantial numbers of the comparison group reported disharmonious relationships. Having a parental drinking problem increases the *probability* of recollecting a disharmonious childhood family environment, but it does not guarantee it.

Given the evidence reviewed in Chapter 2 of the likely importance of violence as a mediating factor in determining the extent that children and adolescents are affected by parental problem drinking, this area was examined in some depth. As Table 4.5 shows, the offspring group again reported considerably more violence in all the major categories than did the comparison group; but it also appears to be the case that more violence was

Table 4.4 Recalled parental and family relationships, comparing offspring and comparisons

Variable and range for each scale	Offspring (N=164)		Comparison (N=80)		t-test value
	mean	sd	mean	sd	
Parental positives (0 to 9) (e.g. frequency of joint activities, and of overt expressions of affection, between parents)	2.90	2.3	5.00	2.7	−6.33***
Family positives (0 to 9) (e.g. frequency of joint activities, and of open discussions, within the family)	3.25	2.4	5.09	2.6	−5.55***
Parental and family negatives (0 to 9) (e.g. frequency of arguments, amount and severity of violence, between parents or within the family)	4.70	1.8	2.23	1.8	9.89***
Negative experiences (0 to 12) (See Table 4.6, NCE)	4.17	2.4	1.68	1.6	9.64***
Relationship with mother (−4 to +5) (e.g. frequency of joint activities, of emotional closeness, and parental withdrawal)	2.02	2.1	2.63	2.2	−2.14*
Relationship with father (−4 to +5) (e.g. frequency of joint activities, of emotional closeness, and parental withdrawal)	0.38	2.2	2.19	1.8	−6.90***
Index of Harmony/Disharmony (Factor Score, standardised)	−0.40	0.8	0.82	0.9	−10.04***

$* = p < 0.05$; $*** = p < 0.001$.

Table 4.5   Recalled violence and aggression within the family of origin, comparing offspring and comparisons

Variable	Offspring (N=164)		Comparison (N=80)		CHI²-test value
	No.	%	No.	%	
Parent-to-parent violence					
Any violence	108	(66)	17	(21)	42.8***
Any prolonged violence	78	(48)	6	(8)	38.2***
Any regular violence	45	(27)	4	(5)	16.9***
Any serious violence	48	(29)	7	(9)	13.0***
Any regular and prolonged	43	(26)	4	(5)	15.6***
Any serious and prolonged	34	(21)	2	(3)	14.2***
Any serious and regular	20	(12)	2	(3)	6.2*
Serious and regular violence over a prolonged period	19	(12)	2	(3)	5.6*
Parent-to-child violence					
Any violence[1]	95	(58)	62	(78)	9.0**
Any violence[2]	68	(42)	14	(18)	13.8***
Any prolonged violence[2]	50	(31)	12	(15)	6.8**
Any regular violence[2]	34	(21)	4	(5)	10.1**
Any serious violence[2]	32	(20)	7	(9)	4.6*
Any regular and prolonged[2]	29	(18)	4	(5)	7.4**
Any serious and prolonged[2]	23	(14)	5	(6)	ns
Any serious and regular[2]	17	(10)	3	(4)	ns
Serious and regular violence over a prolonged period[2]	14	(9)	3	(4)	ns

$* = p < 0.05$; $** = p < 0.01$; $*** p = 0.001$.
[1] (including controlled corporal punishment)
[2] (excluding controlled corporal punishment)

recalled *between* the parents than between the interviewee and either parent. Nevertheless it is the case that substantial proportions of the offspring group reported violence over a prolonged period both towards them and between their parents, and that for a substantial minority (roughly one in ten) this violence was also serious and was regularly meted out. It is also worth noting that, when there was violence reported between parents and children, there was more violence reported as directed towards male children.

It is difficult to over-emphasise the importance of these findings. Research into the area of violence generally has shown that individuals exposed to severe family violence and aggression as children are more likely than others to be violent in their own families as adults; and other research has shown that family violence in childhood can often lead to severely deleterious effects on childhood self-esteem and general behaviour (see Chapter 2).

A final and interesting finding relating to this area is that if controlled corporal punishment is included as violence, the comparison respondents move from reporting vastly less violence to reporting significantly higher levels than the offspring group. This relates to the interesting debate within family research concerning the relationship between control and support. There is an indication here that the offspring families might be less able to exert control using punishment than the comparison families (see Foxcroft and Lowe, 1991, for a similar finding), and also less able to offer support, in that they are much more likely to expose their children to higher levels of violence.

The Range of Childhood Family Experiences

All the interviewees were asked to complete the checklist of items shown in Table 4.6, which was designed to show the immediate impact of parental or family problems upon the child him- or her-self. As can be seen from the Table, the offspring group reported significantly more of all but one of these negative childhood experiences (NCE) than did the comparison group, and when a scale was constructed by adding together all the items, the offspring group scored significantly higher (an alpha coefficient of 0.78 showed that the 12-item scale had a satisfactory degree of internal reliability).

Although the worry and uncertainty, feeling of family instability, experience of being caught between the interests of two parents, and the adoption of certain adult roles—all of which are reflected in the NCE measure—were reported far more frequently by offspring of parents with drinking problems than by members of our comparison group, the age of onset of

Table 4.6 Negative childhood experiences (NCE) within the family of origin, comparing offspring and comparisons

Childhood experiences	Offspring (N=164)		Comparison (N=80)		CHI²-test value
	No.	%	No.	%	
Arrangements going wrong	80	(50)	19	(24)	14.7***
Lack of social life for the family	109	(68)	30	(38)	19.8***
Moving house a lot	42	(26)	15	(19)	1.5ns
Being on own a lot	77	(48)	19	(24)	12.7***
Forced to participate in parents' rows	73	(46)	7	(9)	32.1***
Being pulled between parents	81	(51)	15	(19)	22.0***
Worry re: parent losing job	37	(23)	3	(4)	14.2***
Fear of having to do without	36	(23)	5	(6)	9.7**
Keeping secrets from one parent to protect the other	53	(33)	8	(10)	14.7***
Putting parent to bed	46	(29)	1	(1)	25.3***
Having to take care of parent	43	(27)	6	(8)	12.1***
Having to act older	99	(62)	17	(22)	34.5***
Total NCE scale score					
	Mean	sd	Mean	sd	('t')
	4.17	2.4	1.68	1.6	9.64***

** $=p<0.01$; *** $=p<0.001$.

these problems during childhood and the total number of years of exposure to a parental drinking problem were not significantly correlated with NCE within the offspring group. NCE was significantly correlated, however, with scores on the PBS scale ($r=0.44$, $p<0.001$).

Family Stability

Given the findings we have described above, it would have been a reasonable hypothesis that offspring families would also have been characterised

by an increased rate of marital separation and divorce. Interestingly, however, although there was a high rate of this type of family instability in the
offspring group, there was also a level in the comparison group which was
virtually as high: 36% of the offspring group experienced a parental separation during their upbringing, compared with 28% of the comparison group,
a difference that is not statistically significant. If separations caused by the
death of a parent are excluded, the difference increases in size (32% offspring, 21% comparison) but is still not significant.

A second measure of family stability is the length of time over which a
child experienced a stable family (i.e. one where there were no parental
separations for whatever reason—we termed this 'continuous parenting').
The average length of continuous parenting for members of the offspring
group was 14.6 years, with the comparison group averaging 15.2 years—
again not a significant difference.

These findings underline the importance of utilising a comparison
group in this type of research—without one it would have been a simple,
but probably mistaken, step to conclude that the high level of family discord found within the offspring group was responsible for an unusually
high rate of separation and divorce.

Gender Issues

Whether or not the participant in the research was a male or female was
largely unrelated to the variables presented above—sons and daughters of
problem drinkers reported, on average, similarly negative childhood environments and tried to cope in broadly the same ways. One of the few differences, as noted above, was that more males than females reported that
violence was directed towards them. We shall see in Chapters 5 and 6,
however, that young men and women who have had parents with drinking
problems appear to face somewhat different risks as young adults, and
childhood variables such as family discord and relationships with fathers
and mothers may not carry identical significance for the two sexes.

Where there were differences, however, was in terms of the gender of
the problem drinking parent. This is an important issue to examine for a
number of reasons. First, many commentators have suggested that the children of problem drinking mothers would be more severely affected than if
the drinking problem parent was the father. The reasons for this suggestion
have ranged from a belief that the mother is more important than the father
in terms of maintaining family unity, to one which implies that, as the
mother is more likely to drink at home, this would have a greater impact

on the developing child. Another reason why this issue is important relates to the suggested relationships between the gender of the problem-drinking parent and that of the child—the suggestion, for example, that children will be more likely to imitate the behaviour of parents of their own sex; or alternatively, that they will be more likely to be influenced by the behaviour of opposite sex parents.

Dividing the interviewees into four groups (80 comparisons, 29 with only a mother and 112 with only a father with a drinking problem, and 23 having two problem drinking parents), and comparing them with each other on the measures of childhood family environment, it was found that all offspring groups differed significantly from the comparison group on most measures, and, as shown in Table 4.7, that the three offspring groups also differed significantly from each other on a number of them.

Table 4.7   Recalled parental and family relationships by sex and number of problem drinking parents

| | *Offspring*
Problem drinking parent | | | | | |
| | *Father only*
(n=112) | | *Mother only*
(n=29) | | *Both*
(n=23) | |
	mean	*sd*	*mean*	*sd*	*mean*	*sd*
Scale, and possible range						
Parental positives (0 to 9)	2.81	2.4	2.49	1.7	3.87	2.6[a]
Family positives (0 to 9)	2.94	2.3	4.20	2.4	3.58	2.7[b]
Parental and family negatives (0 to 9)	4.66	1.9	4.66	1.9	4.93	1.5[c]
Negative experiences (NCE, 0 to 12)	3.70	2.3	5.48	2.4	4.83	2.2[d]
Relationship with mother (-4 to $+5$)	2.39	2.0	0.86	2.0	1.66	2.0[e]
Relationship with father (-4 to $+5$)	-0.13	2.1	1.90	2.1	0.91	2.2[f]

[a] $F=2.60$ (ns); 'both' significantly different (*) from 'fathers' and 'mothers'
[b] $F=3.63$ (*); 'fathers' significantly different (*) from 'mothers'
[c] $F=0.22$ (ns); no group significantly different from another
[d] $F=7.96$ (***); 'fathers' significantly different (*) from 'mothers' and 'both'
[e] $F=7.20$ (***); 'fathers' significantly different (*) from 'mothers'
[f] $F=11.52$ (***); 'fathers' significantly different (*) from 'mothers' and 'both'
* $=p<0.05$; ** $=p<0.01$; *** $=p<0.001$.

Where the mother alone had the drinking problem, interviewees had significantly higher scores on the negative childhood experiences (NCE) scale than if the father alone had the problem, and they recalled the relationships with their mothers as significantly less positive than did interviewees with mothers without a drinking problem (see Table 4.7).

If the father alone had the drinking problem, on the other hand, interviewees recalled their relationships with their fathers as significantly less positive than did interviewees with fathers without a drinking problem. This 'fathers only' group also recalled significantly less positives within the family environment as they grew up, as compared to both those with 'mothers only' and comparisons (see Table 4.7).

The third group were those where both parents had drinking problems. On the negative childhood experiences (NCE) scale, the 'both' group scored between the other two offspring groups. Relationships with the father were significantly better if both parents as opposed to only the father had the drinking problem; and perceived positives in the parents' relationship were greater if both parents as opposed to only one parent had the drinking problem (see Table 4.7).

Also investigated was whether or not the gender of the offspring interacted with that of the problem drinking parent. There were very small differences in the main between sons and daughters for each category, and none of these differences were statistically significant.

Two other tendencies in these results are worthy of note however. One is for relationships with fathers with drinking problems to be recalled as having been particularly negative, more so than is the case for relationships with mothers with such problems. The other, not shown in the table, concerns relationships with the non-problem-drinking parents. Here sons with 'mothers only' with problems stand out from other offspring sub-groups as recalling comparatively negative relationships with their fathers (mean of 1.43), scarcely different on average from their relationships with their problem drinking mothers (1.36). All other sub-groups recall on average significantly better relationships with their non-problem parents than with their drinking problem parents (Orford and Velleman, 1991).

Childhood Family Environment and Coping

We described earlier how the children of problem drinkers coped with their parents' behaviour. Relationships between coping and other variables—family relationships, family experiences, and family stability—were examined. Of the four coping factors that emerged from the factor analysis, the third and fourth factors correlated with none of the family environment measures, but the first two did relate significantly to a number of them. 'Fearfulness and self-protection' correlated with: a more negative relationship with father (0.22, $p < 0.005$), a higher score on the scale of parental and family negatives (0.22, $p < 0.005$), and being located at the more disharmonious end of the overall measure of family harmony/disharmony (0.16, $p < 0.05$). There were also relationships with almost all of the parent-to-parent and parent-to-respondent violence measures (with correlations ranging from 0.30, $p < 0.0005$, for 'serious, regular and prolonged parent-to-parent violence', and 0.28, $p < 0.0005$, for 'serious and regular parent-to-parent violence', to 0.25, $p < 0.005$, for 'serious, regular and prolonged parent-to-respondent violence'), where the relationship is always between more violence and the more fearful and self-protective end of the coping factor scale. Most of these correlations rise in magnitude when only those interviewees who had fathers with drinking problems are examined; and there are no significant correlations at all when only interviewees with 'mothers only' are examined.

'Confrontation and self-destructive action' correlated with many of the same measures: a more negative relationship with father (0.18, $p < 0.05$), a higher score on the scale of parental and family negatives (0.28, $p < 0.0005$), and being located at the more disharmonious end of the overall measure of family harmony/disharmony (0.22, $p < 0.005$). There were again relationships with many of the parent-to-parent and parent-to-respondent violence measures, although here the higher correlations were with the parent-to-respondent measures, not the parent-to-parent ones (with correlations ranging from 0.29, $p < 0.0005$, for 'any parent-to-respondent violence excluding corporal punishment', and 0.27, $p < 0.0005$, for 'prolonged parent-to-respondent violence', to 0.22, $p < 0.005$, for 'serious and prolonged parent-to-parent violence'), where the relationship is always between more violence and the more confrontative and self-destructive end of the scale. Once more, most of these correlations rise in magnitude when only those interviewees who had fathers with drinking problems are examined; but this time there is one significant correlation when interviewees with 'mothers only' are examined (0.43, $p < 0.05$, with being located at the more disharmonious end of the overall measure of family harmony/disharmony).

CHILDHOOD ADJUSTMENT

It is clear that both groups, but most particularly the offspring group, contained individuals who had many negative experiences to deal with in their childhoods. Much previous research (see Chapter 2), both specifically with the offspring of problem drinkers and more generally with children who are subjected to distressing experiences such as child abuse, parental violence, or family separation, suggests that children exposed to such experiences are at increased risk for the development of childhood adjustment difficulties. This issue was examined in detail within the present study.

A number of areas were asked about. These included the presence of physical and psychological problems and symptoms during childhood, difficulties in the development of childhood friendships, social isolation, and issues concerning any unevenness in the transition from adolescence to adulthood. The following were amongst the things said by offspring informants:

P80 Offspring

This young man said he, "never liked taking friends home", although he had brought some friends home, and, "wouldn't like to take a girlfriend home". He would leave home, but his mother was, "dependent on my money". When he was younger, he was, "quite quiet really. I didn't mix with too many people. I had the odd friend but didn't hang around in crowds". Now he liked crowds. At secondary school he had, "got into a hell of a lot of fights". He found that, "kids respect you more, after a fight", and, "hang around you". He thought that, "people don't seem to be too friendly towards me because of Dad's drinking". He now had three or four good friends at work but felt very lonely. He said he himself had started to drink in his mid teens, and at the age of 17 or 18 was a very heavy drinker, drinking, "a hell of a lot", about 10 pints of beer or so when he went out.

P133 Offspring

In her teens this participant's mother had left home and her father was home only at weekends. During the week she and her siblings were in the care of two young women not much older than themselves. They were on their own a lot during the week and used to have lots of friends round all the time. Instead of their parents looking after them, they would sort things out for themselves. She felt very mature at school because she was, "making decisions at home that most kids have made for them".

P162 Offspring, *both parents with drinking problems:*

This informant was one of a relatively small number who described a very troubled adolescence. She said she had, "bottled it all up about her parents' drinking", had not told her friends about the family, and from about age 14 had gradually cut herself off from all her friends. She took several overdoses in her teens, the first at age 14, and was off school for two years suffering from anorexia. She saw a child psychiatrist and was in hospital for several weeks in her late teens. Amongst the events of the next year or two she mentioned stealing money from her parents, living with her boyfriend for some months, and drinking all the time together, and taking another overdose.

P217 Offspring

Although in the first two years of secondary school this interviewee had been bullied and only had a few close friends, by the time he was 13 or 14 he had developed a strong sense of, "belonging to a group, who were very important to me". He would bring male friends home readily (but not girls), but would never talk to friends about his home life or vice versa, because, "I didn't want to…I lived for evenings and weekends", when he could be with friends.

P219 Offspring

This participant described how from the age of eight he would go out with boys several years older than himself, spending a lot of time outside the home. He was still, "knocking around with older friends", in his early teens. He, "couldn't relate with kids my own age". He started smoking cannabis when he was 11 and drinking in pubs at 13. From this age on he was away from home a lot. He, "spent a hell of a lot of time out…[Home] was just a like a hotel, just ate and slept there…never spoke about home life".

Physical and Psychological Problems and Symptoms during Childhood

All interviewees were asked about 34 childhood symptoms. These were commonly described problems of childhood, including those most often previously reported as particularly common amongst children of problem drinking parents and/or children of disharmonious parents. These symptoms and the proportions of offspring and comparisons reporting each, are shown in Appendix 1.

The offspring group reported experiencing a significantly larger total number of symptoms during childhood or adolescence than did the comparison group (means of 5.73 *vs* 4.03, $p < 0.001$), and they were also more likely than comparisons to report having experienced 28 of the 34 individual problems (statistically significant in the case of eleven of them). The comparison group reported only three problems more frequently than offspring (in no case statistically significant). Of the eleven symptoms showing significant differences, 'emotional detachment' showed the most significant difference (32% *vs* 10%, $p < 0.001$). Looking at the sexes separately, there was no significant difference between offspring and comparison sons in terms of the total number of reported symptoms (5.85 vs 4.50, n.s.), but there was a significant difference between offspring and comparison daughters (5.63 vs 3.55, $p < 0.005$).

Factor analysis of these data revealed two factors which made sense statistically and were also in line with a great deal of previous research on childhood problems. The first factor, which we called 'anti-social behaviour', had 13 out of the 34 symptoms moderately or strongly associated with it. The second factor we termed 'withdrawn, demoralised and having problems at school', and this had 11 out of the 34 symptoms associated with it. The symptoms which characterise these two factors are indicated in Table 4.8. Figure 4.1 shows that members of the offspring group obtained higher mean scores than comparison interviewees on both these two factors; that offspring daughters obtained significantly higher mean scores than did comparison daughters on both factors, although the differences were not found significant for sons. Sons (irrespective of their parental problem drinking status) obtained significantly higher scores than daughters on the anti-social behaviour factor; and daughters (irrespective of their parental problem drinking status) obtained significantly higher scores than sons on the withdrawn, demoralised and school problems factor.

Development of Childhood and Adolescent Friendships

This area was asked about in three ways. First, a number of open-ended questions were asked about interviewees' social lives and friendships as children and adolescents, and the extent to which these activities were shared with their parents. Due to the views expressed in the preliminary interviews, we were interested in whether or not there was a division between our interviewees' home lives and their friendships, and whether this had been more prevalent in the lives of our offspring interviewees. Many young people report a high degree of interaction between these two important facets of their childhood lives, home and friendships (for example having friends coming home with them for meals, having parties at home). Yet it was striking in the preliminary interviews how many offspring interviewees reported a lack of this interaction, due to the uncertainties inherent in having a problem drinking parent. In the full study we found, as hypothesised, that members of the offspring group reported a significantly greater degree of division between home and peer group than did comparisons. This was the case both before age 11 ($p < 0.0005$) and after this age

Table 4.8 Childhood symptoms loading at +/−0.3 or higher on each of two factors

Factor 1—'Anti-social behaviour'		*Factor 2—'Withdrawn, demoralised and having problems at school'*	
Variable	*Loading*	*Variable*	*Loading*
Destructive behaviour	0.75	Concentration difficulties at school	0.68
Aggression	0.69	Distractability	0.61
Stealing	0.61	Anxious	0.61
Other self-injurious behaviour	0.60	Frequent waking	0.57
Delinquency	0.58	Inability to do homework at home	0.55
Temper tantrums	0.49	Depressed	0.53
Truancy	0.43	Prone to crying	0.44
Head Banging	0.39	Arithmetic difficulties	0.42
Hyperactivity	0.38	Emotional detachment	0.36
Sleepwalking	0.35	Nightmares	0.33
Bedwetting	0.32	Accident proneness	0.31
Rocking prior to sleep	0.32		
Nightmares	0.32		

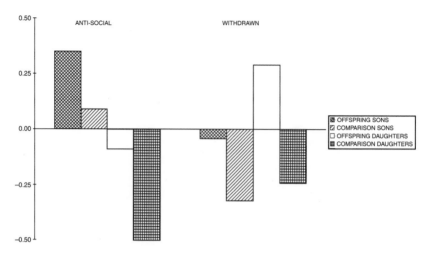

Figure 4.1 Mean scores on the two childhood symptoms factors—'anti-social behaviour' and 'withdrawn, demoralised, and having problems at school'.
Anti-social behaviour: significant difference between offspring and comparison daughters ($t=3.19$, $p<0.01$).
Withdrawn, demoralised, and having problems at school: significant difference between Offspring and Comparison daughters ($t=3.38$, $p<0.001$).

($p<0.0005$), which were asked about separately. For both offspring and comparisons, there was more home-peer division reported for the adolescent years than for earlier childhood, probably reflecting normative age-related changes in friendship behaviour towards increased separateness and privacy from parental influence as the child grows older.

Secondly, it had been suggested by previous research, and again by our preliminary work, that the offspring of problem drinkers were more likely to be socially isolated, a parent's embarrassing behaviour making the child shun the company of other children. In fact, however, when participants were asked about this, the proportions of the two groups recalling that they had felt isolated were not significantly different, either as younger children (offspring 45%, comparisons 41%) or as adolescents (offspring 42%, comparisons 41%). Thirdly, the interviewees were asked whether they had experienced any of the twelve friendship difficulties (shown in Table 4.9) that preliminary interviewing had suggested might be common amongst the children of problem drinkers. The offspring group reported on average almost twice as many of these friendship difficulties as did the comparison group—a statistically significant difference ($t=6.35$, $p<0.0005$). There were few sex differences. Comparison sons reported a significantly higher mean number of friendship problems than comparison

Table 4.9   Friendship difficulties reported by offspring and comparisons

Experiences	Offspring (N=164)		Comparison (N=80)		CHI²-test value
	No.	%	No.	%	
Feeling different from your friends	109	(69)	48	(60)	1.91ns
Feeling apart from the life that everyone else led	93	(59)	33	(41)	6.61**
Finding out that other children were discouraged from being friendly because of your parent	21	(13)	4	(5)	3.88*
Being embarrassed seeing your parent when with friends	83	(53)	24	(30)	10.90***
Your parent showing you up in front of friends	83	(53)	20	(25)	16.40***
Your parent showing you up in front of opposite sex friends	60	(38)	14	(18)	10.39**
Your parent showing their problem once in front of friends	56	(35)	4	(5)	26.11***
Your parent showing their problem on a number of occasions in front of friends	47	(30)	2	(3)	24.12***
Feeling embarrassed about your home	68	(43)	19	(24)	8.52**
Being worried about bringing friends around	102	(65)	29	(36)	17.20***
Trying to meet friends outside as much as possible	79	(50)	20	(25)	13.66***
Never bringing friends around	51	(32)	11	(14)	9.46**
	Mean	sd	Mean	sd	t-test value
Total friendship problems scale score	5.39	3.1	2.85	2.5	6.35***

$* = p < 0.05$; $** = p < 0.01$; $*** = p < 0.001$.

daughters (3.58 vs 2.13, $p < 0.01$), although both were significantly lower than the corresponding offspring group means (5.51 vs 5.30, n.s.). Comparison group sons were more likely than comparison daughters to report, for example, having felt apart from others' lives, and feeling embarrassed about their home. Hence the offspring–comparison contrast in terms of childhood friendship problems was greater for daughters than for sons.

An overall measure of 'difficulties in childhood adjustment' was created by summing standardised scores on the measures of: the development of symptoms and problems; the existence of friendship problems; and the division between home and peer relationships. As predicted, the offspring group also had significantly higher scores than comparisons on this measure ($t=6.21$, $p<0.0005$).

Early Drug and Alcohol Use

Interviewees were asked a number of questions about their own use of both alcohol and a range of different drugs. A detailed drinking history was built up for all interviewees—when (if at all) they started drinking alcohol in the first place, when they first started drinking regularly, through to when (if at all) they developed any type of alcohol problem. A similar, although not quite so detailed, record was built up of each interviewee's drug history, examining the use of prescribed drugs, cannabis, and other illicit drugs.

Table 4.10 shows the percentages in each of a number of 'early use' or 'early problem use' categories for both the offspring and the comparison interviewees, up to the age of 18. It can be seen that, although only a smallish minority of either group were involved in these activities (with the exception of starting to drink alcohol), and only two of the differences shown in the table reach a level of statistical significance (prescribed psychoactive drugs at age 17 or earlier, $p<0.05$, and moderate drinking at age 17 or younger, $p<0.005$), it is always the case that more offspring than comparison interviewees reported the early use of drugs or alcohol. It is also the case that if the number of interviewees are examined who reported use of any one out of the four (cannabis, other illicit drugs, prescribed drugs, and fairly heavy alcohol) by the age of 17 or younger, almost half of the offspring group fall within this category as opposed to only just over one quarter of the comparison group ($p<0.005$). As we shall see in the following chapter, however, even these modest differences tend to narrow and often disappear altogether at later ages.

Leaving Home Early

Finally we examined the possibility that living with a parent with a drinking problem could affect the transition to adulthood and that this might be reflected in the age of leaving home. It was found that interviewees from the offspring group tended to leave home at a younger age than comparison interviewees: 12% of the offspring group had left home at age 15 or younger, as opposed to 5% of the comparison group. By age 17 the equivalent figures were 37% and 23% (a significant difference, $p<0.005$)

Table 4.10 Early alcohol and drug use by offspring and comparisons. Numbers using prescribed, cannabis, and other illicit drugs, and having started using alcohol, moderately drinking, fairly heavy drinking, problematically drinking, and becoming abstinent from alcohol, by different ages; and numbers reporting at least 1 out of fairly heavy alcohol use, cannabis use, other illicit drug use, and prescribed drug use, by age 17 or younger

	Offspring			Comparison			Chr²
	Sons	Daughters	Total	Sons	Daughters	Total	Offspring vs Comparison
N	72	92	164 (%)	40	40	80 (%)	
Use of:							
Prescribed drugs							
age 15 or younger	6	11	17 (10)	2	3	5 (6)	
16	2	5	7 (4)	—	1	1 (1)	
17	1	5	6 (4)	1	—	1 (1)	
			30 (18)			7 (9)	4.11*
Cannabis							
age 15 or younger	4	12	16 (10)	—	2	2 (3)	
16	6	4	10 (6)	1	3	4 (5)	
17	6	2	8 (5)	4	—	4 (5)	
			34 (21)			10 (13)	3.25
Other illicit drugs							
age 15 or younger	—	5	5 (3)	1	1	2 (3)	
16	7	2	9 (5)	1	1	2 (3)	
17	10	4	14 (9)	1	3	4 (5)	
			28 (17)			8 (10)	2.02

Table 4.10 *(continued)*

	Offspring			Comparison			Chi^2
	Sons	Daughters	Total	Sons	Daughters	Total	Offspring vs Comparison
N	72	92	164 (%)	40	40	80 (%)	
Alcohol:							
—Started							
age 15 or younger	40	40	80 (49)	16	19	35 (44)	
16	17	14	31 (19)	11	11	22 (28)	
17	9	16	25 (15)	6	3	9 (11)	
			136 (83)			66 (83)	0.06
—Moderate							
age 15 or younger	9	7	16 (10)	1	1	2 (3)	
16	13	3	16 (10)	3	3	6 (8)	
17	8	10	18 (11)	1	2	3 (4)	
			50 (30)			11 (14)	7.99**
—Fairly heavy							
age 15 or younger	5	8	13 (8)	2	2	4 (5)	
16	8	1	9 (5)	3	—	3 (4)	
17	5	8	13 (8)	1	1	2 (3)	
			35 (21)			9 (11)	3.18

—Problem							
age 15 or younger	3	3	6 (4)	1	1	2	(3)
16	7	2	9 (5)	1	—	1	(1)
17	4	2	6 (4)	3	1	4	(5)
			21 (13)			7	(9)	0.52
—Becoming abstinent							
age 15 or younger	—	1	1 (1)	—	—	—	
16	—	—	—	—	—	—	
17	1	5	6 (4)	—	—	—	
			7 (4)			0	(0)
'precocity'[1]			80 (49)			22	(28)	10.52***

[1] 'precocity' = at least 1 from cannabis, other illicit drug, prescribed drug, fairly heavy alcohol use, by age 17 or younger

$* = p < 0.05$; $** = p < 0.01$; $*** = p < 0.001$.

and by age 19, 74% and 61% (in each case the percentages are of those participants who had reached that age by the time of the study). This effect was, if anything, more pronounced for young women than for young men. For example 9% of women interviewees from the offspring group had left home at age 15 or younger, as opposed to 3% of the comparison group. The equivalent figures by age 16 were 17% and 5%, and by age 17 were 36% and 18% (a significant difference, $p<0.05$).

Childhood Adjustment and Coping

Significant relationships were found between several of the above mentioned measures of childhood adjustment and two of the four coping factors described earlier. 'Confrontation and self-destructive action' correlated with the first factor which emerged from the factor analysis of the 34 childhood symptoms: 'anti-social behaviour' (0.23, $p<0.005$), and friendship problems (0.27, $p<0.001$), and also with the overall measure of 'difficulties in childhood adjustment' (0.19, $p<0.05$). 'Detachment', correlated with the second factor from the 34 childhood symptoms: 'withdrawn, demoralised and having problems at school' (0.23, $p<0.005$), and also with a greater level of division between home life and outside friendships after age 11 (0.23, $p<0.01$), with a younger age of leaving home (0.17, $p<0.05$), and with the overall measure of 'difficulties in childhood adjustment' (0.21, $p<0.01$). When results are analysed separately for sons and daughters, a pattern emerges, with the correlates of 'confrontation and self-destructive action' being stronger or only significant for sons, and the correlates of 'detachment' being significant only for daughters.

THE IMPORTANCE OF FAMILY DISHARMONY

We have outlined above how having a parent with a drinking problem increases considerably the chances of a young person reporting both parental and family disharmony, and the experiencing of problems and difficulties of his or her own in childhood or adolescence.

One suggestion, that emerged from the review of relevant previous research in Chapter 2, was that family disharmony is the factor that might account for the increased risk of problems in adjustment to be found amongst the offspring of parents with drinking problems. Accordingly the overall reported family disharmony variable, described earlier, was examined closely. The results tended to confirm its central importance.

For one thing disharmony was found to correlate significantly, in the sample as a whole (offspring and comparisons combined), with a number of other measures outlined above. For example, it correlated highly significantly with the overall 'difficulties in childhood adjustment' measure (0.64, $p<0.0005$) and with each of the specific dimensions of childhood adjustment difficulty: 'antisocial behaviour' (0.22, $p<0.001$); 'withdrawn, demoralised and school problems' (0.38, $p<0.0005$); divided home and peer relationships (0.57, $p<0.0005$) and 'friendship problems' (0.61, $p<0.0005$). Within the offspring group, it also correlated significantly with two of the four coping factor scores, namely the 'fearfulness and self-protection' factor (0.16, $p<0.05$), and the 'confrontative and self-destructive action' factor (0.22, $p<0.005$). Another coping factor—'detachment, internalisation and help-seeking' was correlated significantly with certain components of family disharmony (rows between the parents; negative views about the family as a whole) and with some aspects of adjustment such as a greater reported division between home and peer life and with higher scores on the 'withdrawn, demoralised and school problems' factor.

Secondly, the question was asked which of the two variables—family disharmony or parental problem drinking—was the more strongly associated with childhood and adolescent problems. The question was approached in two ways. One consisted of dividing the whole sample into those with relatively disharmonious and these with relatively harmonious families in the same ratio (164/80) as that of offspring to comparisons. This involved, in effect, reassigning 26 comparison respondents (33%) to the relatively disharmonious category, and 26 offspring (16%) to the relatively harmonious category. It was then possible to see whether the disharmony/harmony or offspring/comparison split was the more strongly associated with reports of adjustment difficulties. The results (see Table 4.11) show that it was the former that consistently emerged as the stronger. The differences in sizes of the correlations are not large, however, and in no instance is the difference statistically significant.

The foregoing analysis does not allow, however, for a complete disentangling of the complex inter-relationships between variables. Accordingly, a technique was used known as path analysis. This is a special application of multiple regression analysis, in which questions about relationships and possible causal influences are asked by examining the sizes of the regression coefficients with and without certain variables entered into the analysis at different stages. Whether or not, and at what stage, certain variables are entered into the analysis, depends on the model of causal influence

Table 4.11 Does offspring (*N*=164) versus comparison (*N*=80) or disharmony (*N*=164) versus harmony (*N*=80) correlate more highly with childhood adjustment?

	Difficulties in childhood adjustment	Childhood problems	Anti-social behaviour	Withdrawn, demoralised and school problems	Friendship problems	Divided home from peers
Disharmony/ Harmony	0.51***	0.23***	0.16*	0.23***	0.46***	0.49***
Offspring/ Comparison	0.37***	0.19**	0.15*	0.20**	0.38***	0.29***

* = *p*<0.05; ** = *p*<0.01; *** = *p*<0.001.

that is being tested. A particular model is deemed by statisticians to be useful if, when the results of analyses at several stages are added together, this provides the best fit with the simple correlational data. The path analysis model that was tested is shown in Figure 4.2 and the model providing the 'best fit' for the present data is shown in Figure 4.3.

The model tested shows a likely causal link from parental drinking status (offspring *vs* comparison) to family disharmony, and likely causal links from both these variables to childhood difficulties. Alternative models, proposing that disharmony led to parental problem drinking or that the two variables were unconnected, were examined but did not match the correlation coefficients as well as the model shown in the Figure. The path diagram

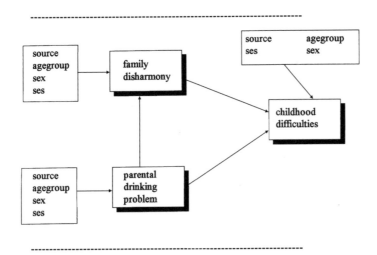

Figure 4.2   The path analysis model for childhood difficulties.

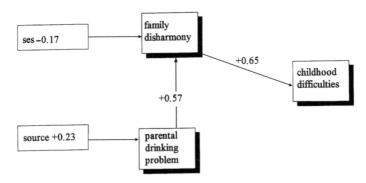

Figure 4.3:   The pathways to childhood difficulties.

Table 4.12 Childhood difficulties: a summary of direct and indirect paths and simple correlations

	Path analysis			Simple correlations	Direction of effect: Childhood diffs. associated with:
	Direct path	Indirect path	Total effect		
Family disharmony	+0.65	—	+0.65	+0.64	disharmony
Parental prob. drink.	+0.00	+0.37	+0.37	+0.37	offspring
Source	+0.02	+0.09	+0.11	+0.10	clinical
Agegroup	+0.01	+0.08	+0.09	+0.08	older
Sex	+0.07	−0.02	+0.05	+0.05	males
Ses	+0.04	−0.08	−0.04	−0.07	lower SES

shows that both direct and indirect pathways exist between the variables. The most important of these pathways and how the sum of direct and indirect paths match up with the simple correlation coefficients, are summarised in Table 4.12. (Some small effects not shown in Figure 4.3 are included).

The best fit model suggests that the existence of childhood difficulties is probably influenced directly by childhood family and parental disharmony, but that the negative effects upon adjustment of having a parent with a drinking problem, *per se*, are only seen indirectly, *via* their effects on family disharmony. This implies that if a parental drinking problem leads to disharmony, the chances of a child having adjustment difficulties is substantially heightened; but if the drinking problem does not lead to disharmony, then the child may be at no more risk than the average comparison child.

Coping as Mediator or Moderator

We looked for evidence that the ways offspring had coped with their parents' drinking problems at home, as recalled by them at interview, either mediated or moderated the relationship between family disharmony and childhood difficulties. No evidence could be found for either mechanism. If ways of coping mediated the disharmony–difficulties relationship, this should show up in the form of reduced disharmony–difficulties correlations when coping is statistically partialled out. The four coping factors identified earlier (Table 4.3) were examined separately, and so were data for male and female offspring, but in no case did partialling out the effect of coping in this way reduce the correlations at all.

Coping might, on the other hand, moderate the disharmony–difficulties relationship, and if so this should show up in the form of a significant effect of the disharmony–coping *interaction* effect in the prediction of childhood difficulties, over and above any main effects of disharmony and coping separately. This is tested by multiple regression. Again none of the analyses carried out showed such an effect. Indeed coping showed only one main effect: for women offspring only, coping factor 4 (detachment) added significantly to disharmony in the prediction of childhood difficulties.

LOOKING BACK AT GROWING UP IN FAMILIES OF PROBLEM DRINKERS: A SUMMARY

It is easy to over-generalise about growing up in a family where at least one parent has a drinking problem. Although in many cases the scene is bleak, there is a great deal of variability in children's experiences, and not all offspring who took part in the present study reported family disharmony or childhood adjustment difficulties. Indeed, the variability extends to all of the information presented above—the offspring group reported a wide range of degrees of severity of the parental problem, of ages at which the parental problem started, of locations in which the alcohol was consumed, and in all other respects also.

Nevertheless, when the parental and family relationships and childhood difficulties of the children of problem drinkers who participated in this research are compared to those reported by a comparison group it is found that the former generally reported significantly more discordant childhood environments, more negative childhood experiences, and substantially less happy and cohesive childhood family lives. They frequently described negative and often violent parental and family relationships. Items which showed the greatest differences between the two groups included: negative sentiments expressed about the relationship between parents; frequency of parental rows and arguments; amount and severity of parent to parent violence; and scores on the check-list of parent-to-parent aggressive acts.

The offspring group were also more likely to report having had a variety of adjustment problems and difficulties in childhood and adolescence than were the comparison group, with the most significant difference being in terms of the overall 'difficulties in childhood adjustment' measure. The items which showed the greatest differences between the two groups included: a parent showing the child up in front of friends; separateness between the home environment and outside social activities, especially in adolescence; and 'emotional detachment' as a childhood problem.

All the information reported in this chapter originates from retrospective accounts, one of the criticisms of which is that the current concerns of interviewees might in some way colour their memories or their reporting of events. There are at least two reasons, however, for thinking that the general picture that emerges is broadly accurate. First, it concurs with the results of much research carried out with offspring of problem drinkers whilst the respondents are still children. This research was reviewed in Chapter 2. Secondly, although it might be thought that those people recruited from clinical sources might be more likely to construe their pasts in a negative way in order to explain problems in their current lives, it was found in the present study that the clinical *vs* community recruitment source variable correlated only very modestly and not statistically significantly with overall difficulties reported in childhood adjustment.

This chapter has also attempted to examine more closely the complex interrelationships between parental problem drinking, disharmony in the family, and difficulties in childhood adjustment. Again in line with research, reviewed in Chapter 2, conducted with offspring whilst they are still children living at home, is our demonstration in this chapter that both a disharmonious childhood family environment, and the fact of having had a parent with a drinking problem, are associated with reported difficulties in childhood adjustment.

Where the present analysis goes beyond previous research is in producing results consistent with the suggestion that *all* the association between parental problem drinking and childhood problems might be mediated *via* parental and family disharmony. This would mean that if young people had parents with drinking problems then they would be more likely to experience a disharmonious set of parental and family relationships, but *only if such disharmony occurred* would they be more likely to report childhood difficulties.

There are a number of other results outlined above which deserve comment. We have shown that, as compared to the comparison group, a high degree of separation was reported to have occurred between the home lives and peer relationships of members of the offspring group. This could not be attributed to the offspring group being more socially isolated, since there were no differences between the two groups in terms of the number, frequency and perceived quality of social situations experienced.

Hence there were many offspring respondents who reported being socially relatively well integrated with their age peers but who more or less deliberately separated off their friendships outside the family from their immediate family relationships. It may be useful to think of this as a facet of coping, a topic discussed at some length earlier in the chapter. As we showed there, the style of coping most frequently utilised was 'avoidance' (e.g. avoided him/her, refused to talk to him/her, hid, stayed in bedroom, went out, left home) reported by 54% of offspring, and this style was moderately but significantly correlated with division between home life and peer relationships. Another popular coping style (23%) was 'switched off' (e.g. built a shell around self, day dreamed, felt lonely), which could be viewed as another form of avoidance. 'Avoidance' and 'switched off' both loaded strongly on the fourth factor from the factor analysis of these coping styles ('detachment') which correlated significantly with the overall 'difficulties in childhood adjustment' measure, and with the individual measures of home versus peer life division, and with childhood emotional problems ('withdrawn, demoralised, and having problems at school'). It seems likely that one major way in which young people respond to and attempt to cope with a parental drinking problem is by attempting to avoid it or separate it off from the rest of their lives. Another is by being 'confrontative and self-destructive', a factor which also correlated with overall childhood difficulties, and specifically with childhood 'anti-social' problems.

Another feature of the early lives of members of the offspring group—namely the tendency to leave home at an earlier age than members of the comparison group—could be seen as representing another facet of the phenomenon of coping by escaping from the direct impact of adversity. When offspring are young they are inclined to escape by avoidance and separating off their outside lives from their home lives, and when they get older some escape by leaving home earlier than they might otherwise have done. This idea is given more weight in that the fourth coping factor of 'detachment, internalisation and help-seeking' correlated negatively with the age of leaving home.

The comparative absence of influence of the gender variable in many of the findings of this chapter provided another interesting result. Reviews by one of us (Velleman, 1992a,b), and evidence reviewed in Chapter 2, strongly suggested that there were significant differences between the ways sons and daughters reacted to the stresses of both problem drinking and disharmonious parents, yet the information we have reported in this chapter has shown no significant correlations between sex and any of the problem measures. Furthermore, our data have also shown that sex of respondent did not on the whole influence reports of the amount or type of family disharmony, although the regression analyses have shown that there are stronger effects of disharmony on the overall measure of 'difficulties in childhood adjustment' for males than for females.

The results presented in this chapter reinforce those emanating from studies of the children of problem drinkers while they are still children—having a problem drinking parent can lead to highly disrupted family environments, and to a great deal of family disharmony. The stories told to us also testify to the fact that these memories do not disappear with time—up to 10, 20 or 30 years later, offspring can still clearly recall and describe the experiences and feelings which they had as children and adolescents.

This chapter has outlined what interviewees—offspring and comparisons—told the interviewers about their childhoods. The main reason we selected a group of young adults, however, was in order to address questions about their adjustment as adults, and it is to this area that the next chapter turns.

CHAPTER **5**

THE CHILDREN OF PROBLEM DRINKING PARENTS AS YOUNG ADULTS—RESULTS II

How are these children of problem drinking parents, many of whom, looking back, describe a childhood troubled by parental disharmony and their own distress, functioning as young adults? In this chapter we shall be drawing upon the answers and accounts that the research participants gave when asked about their current lives and psychological functioning.

As was the case when asking for recollections of childhood, a variety of information was asked for. For a start, we wanted some basic information about the overall context of our participants' lives: whether they were married or cohabiting, in work or education, for example. Secondly, since one of the main objects of the study was an examination of the intergenerational transmission of drinking problems, there was of course a particular interest in the details of drinking as young adults. Hence we asked a lot of questions about the frequency of drinking, quantities consumed, drunkenness, and worries about the development of drinking problems, as well as questions about the use of other kinds of drug, both prescribed and illicit.

Our interests, however, were not confined to drinking and drug-taking. Armed with the knowledge that research in this field had, in general, suffered from focussing too exclusively upon those outcomes, most of the adulthood sections of the interviews were devoted to other matters. The topics covered were chosen because in each case a reasonable hypothesis could be formulated to the effect that offspring of parents with drinking problems, compared to those without, would have a different outcome. We concentrated on those areas of young adult life or functioning where offspring of parents with drinking problems were thought to be at particular risk. Hypotheses were based upon existing research evidence and/or upon opinions expressed by the panel of professional experts who were consulted prior to beginning the study and our pilot sample of young adult offspring, regarding the adulthood risks that the latter are likely to face. For example, it was widely believed, and often stated in the research literature, that children of problem drinking parents were very likely to suffer from feelings of low self-esteem as adults. Hence, we focussed on self-esteem, assessing it in two different ways, although in the meantime other research had not been very supportive of this hypothesis, as we saw in Chapter 2.

Another commonly held view was that offspring of parents with drinking problems, as adults, would have difficulties in forming close, rewarding, trusting and confiding relationships. Our pilot group of offspring were themselves particularly persuaded of the correctness of this hypothesis. It had also been mentioned repeatedly in the professional literature, although it had never previously, to our knowledge, been tested in any detail. As a consequence we devoted considerable interview time to this topic, asking questions about current marriage and close relationships, friendships, and social activities. Self-esteem and adulthood relationships were two of the most important areas covered but there were a number of others which will be introduced as the present chapter unfolds.

As with our questions about childhood, those that asked about current life and functioning were sometimes phrased in a way that required a factual, even numerical, answer whilst others were 'open-ended' allowing the interviewee to expand on his or her answer unrestrained by a fixed-choice answer format. For example, when asking about adulthood alcohol use we asked, amongst other things, how often the person drank and what was the largest quantity of alcohol consumed on one occasion in the last 12 months. But participants were also asked to enlarge on any worries they might have about the possibility of developing drinking problems themselves, and what their attitudes were towards potential sexual partners who appeared to drink a lot. Similarly, when asking about adulthood friendships, we asked, amongst other things, how often people had contact with each of their three closest friends. But interviewees were also asked to expand on the nature of their current relationships with partners and close friends and their levels of satisfaction with these relationships.

In this chapter we draw upon data from both first year and second year interviews. Sometimes information is combined from the two interviews to give a fuller picture of the matter in hand. This is the case, for example, with drug-taking: for one thing combining data from two years enables us to be more confident that a certain kind of drug-taking was a reasonably well-established pattern and not just very temporary. In other instances data from the two interviews are treated as two separate opportunities to test an hypothesis. For example, one of the measures of self-esteem was repeated on the second occasion which gives a second chance to test (with a slightly reduced sample size) an hypothesis that the two groups of participants differed in terms of that variable.

Marriage, Children and Work: the Basic Context of People's Lives

Table 5.1 shows the proportions of young men and women, offspring of parents with drinking problems, and comparisons, who were of different marital or cohabiting status, their histories of marriage and major cohabitations, whether they had children, and whether they were in work, education or unemployed. Our hypotheses with regard to these data were governed by our expectation, perhaps naive in retrospect, that children of problem drinking parents (the offspring group) would carry into adulthood an unsettledness, of which difficulty in making relationships would be part, and that this would make it somewhat more difficult for them to settle into a stable life of marriage or cohabitation and a career involving settled work or continued education.

The results shown in Table 5.1 do not support that view. Indeed, for women, the results are if anything in the opposite direction. For women, but not for men, there was a significant correlation between having had a parent with a drinking problem and married (or cohabiting) status. As we saw in the previous chapter, offspring women also left home earlier. It looks as if having a parent with a drinking problem may prompt some young women to leave home a few months or a year or two earlier than they might otherwise have done, and to form marital relationships and have children more often as young women. Offspring, men and women combined, had more children than comparisons.

For men, there were no significant offspring versus comparison differences in terms of marriage and children, but there was one significant difference in another area of adult life, namely how a person's socioeconomic status (SES) as a young adult compared with that of his or her parents. The transmission of socioeconomic status from one generation to the next is itself a complicated subject with many factors operating. For example, many of our participants were growing up during a time when educational standards and opportunities for work of a higher status were increasing, although this may have been less the case for the younger members of our sample. Hence, the average member of our sample might be expected to have a somewhat higher status level, at least as judged by educational level and work status, than his or her parents. Against this background of rising status, we were interested to see whether those who had had parents with drinking problems were comparatively disadvantaged and had achieved less than comparisons. To obtain a measure of SES relative to parents we simply subtracted an index of parents' SES from an index of the respondent's

Table 5.1 Marriage, children and work, by offspring *vs* comparison, and by sex

	Current marital status: married or cohab. %	Marital/co-hab. history: no. of long-term relationships Mean	Has children? %	Number of children? Mean	Work/education status: In work %	In education %	House-wife %	Unem-ployed %
Offspring								
Sons (N=72)	43[1]	1.50[4]	32	0.58[6]	63	11	—	25
Daughters (N=92)	69[1][2]	1.90[4]	47	0.96[6]	52	14	23	10
Total (N=164)	57[3]	1.73	40[5]	0.79[7]	57	13	13	17
Comparison								
Sons (N=40)	42	1.40	20	0.28	70	13	—	18
Daughters (N=40)	42[2]	1.50	33	0.48	45	30	8	18
Total (N=80)	42[3]	1.45	26[5]	0.38[7]	58	21	4	18

Figures that share a superscript are significantly different: [3] [4] [5] and [6] at $p < 0.05$; [1] and [2] $p < 0.01$; [7] at $p < 0.001$.

own, current SES. Putting a number on a person's or a family's socioeconomic status is itself fraught with difficulties. We decided to base our index of parents' SES upon both the work status *and* educational level of both father *and* mother. In the case of the respondent's own, adulthood, SES we combined educational level with job status of self *or* spouse, reasoning that married women who were working as homemakers (which is not easily classifiable in terms of most job status scales) should at least be given the benefit of their husbands' job status. What we found, after working through these complexities, was that offspring males were significantly less likely than comparison males to have increased their socioeconomic status compared with their parents ($t=2.74$, $p<0.01$). There was no difference for women.

Drinking and Drug-Taking as Young Adults

Extracts from interviewers' reports illustrate this area.

P73 Offspring

P stopped smoking three months previously, had a few puffs of dope aged 15–17, LSD once aged 18 and had a bad trip, and described her drinking as fairly heavy at age 17 and 18. She would go out to get drunk four times a week, barley wines and brandy with babycham. Since then she described herself as a moderate drinker. Last week, which was typical, she had 19 units [one unit is the equivalent of a half pint of average strength beer, a medium sized glass of wine, or a single pub measure of spirits]; and got drunk on 7 units once in the last year. She thinks she is in no danger from drinking—"I have foreseen the consequences, I know when to stop". She is generally mildly positive about drinking—"having a laugh is okay", but is strongly against drunkenness—"it repulses me, I'm angry that he (Father) hasn't the willpower to try and give it up". She reckons she has seen what it can do, but does enjoy it, and thinks it is okay. At the second interview, one year later, she was smoking 5 cigarettes a day, had taken cocaine once or twice (which she found "very nice") and speed less than once a month ("I do like it, I don't ever want more. I don't ever worry about it"). She had drunk 12 units of alcohol in the last week and this was a bit more than usual because they had just moved house and there was still Christmas drink around. She had had 20 units on one occasion, 10 units perhaps once every other month, and 8 units about once a week. "I like drink, its bad for your health, bad for your system and all that—but it doesn't put me off. I'm not concerned that *I'm* going to get addicted".

P272 Offspring

He smokes between 16–25 cigarettes a day, and has unsuccessfully tried to stop. At 16 he sniffed glue regularly (more than weekly) for a year and this is rated as a strong statement of a problem. At 18 he once took amphetamines and once LSD, and has taken hash monthly from 17 until the present, and this is no problem. At 17 he drank two pints once a week, and from 18, 2–4 pints three times a week with more on occasions. He had 13 units last week, drinking on four days. Quite a few times in the last year he would have drunk roughly 15 pints, and he has ended up in hospital in intensive care (it doesn't say whether this happened just once, but against glue sniffing there is mention that he has something wrong with his heart). His tolerance has increased. He does not think he is in danger.

P284 Offspring

R smokes about 8 cigarettes a week—about 4 each evening at the weekends—and never buys her own. She takes no drugs. She drank on occasions at age 13 and 14 and since 15 has been going out to pubs and parties more than when younger, so she drinks a bit more. She drank five units last week, on two days. She says she drank a whole bottle of vodka at a skittles do once in the last year, and has felt sick after drinking about 20 times, and experienced other effects of intoxication less often. She doesn't feel in any danger. Drinking is "okay as long as you are careful". Drunkenness "depends on the circumstances—if it's acceptable it's okay. It's a bit stupid to get really drunk. They can make a fool of themselves. For example if everyone's a bit drunk that's okay but to see someone very drunk at a posh dinner-dance is horrible". She thinks she is more aware of alcoholism than other people. It has made her very careful, i.e. she is aware how much she drinks and if she ever realised she was drinking too much would stop. At the second interview, P told the interviewer that she had drunk 36 units, on four days, last week which is more than usual because she had a very busy week. The maximum was 24 units—she knows she drank half a bottle of vodka and then, "lots and lots of drinks which were spiked". She drinks roughly half that amount approximately once a week. She claims that drinking doesn't affect her—if she starts to feel ill she'll stop: "I enjoy it. I have no worries—I do drink a fair bit really, but I always know inside me when to stop".

Present and past use of alcohol, tobacco, and a range of other drugs— illicit, purchasable at chemists' shops, or medically prescribed—were asked about in considerable detail. A summary of the major findings is contained in Table 5.2. The most striking thing about these results, at first glance, is the apparent lack of the expected differences between offspring and comparison groups. Very similar proportions of the 2 groups had ever used each of the 6 categories of drug shown in the Table, or had ever used them more than very occasionally or briefly. The same was the case for the proportions still using the different types of drug at the time of interview. The same was also true of replies to specific questions about alcohol use, which was focussed upon in particularly close detail. For example, we adopted a procedure, which has become standard in survey work concerned

Table 5.2 Six types of adulthood drug-taking reported by offspring of parents with drinking problems, and by comparisons; Group: O, Offspring; C, Comparison

	% Ever used		% Ever used more than occasionally or briefly		% Use ever considered a problem		% Still using		% Present use excessive or risky	
	O	C	O	C	O	C	O	C	O	C
Alcohol	98	100	74[a]	71[a]	14	9	94	99	17	11
Tobacco	72	68	64	54	28[b]	25[b]	56	55	18	6
Prescribed psychoactive[c]	52	46	10	18	11	16	8	10	15	21
Home medicines psychoactive[d]	NA	NA	31	28	NA	NA	71	79	7	6
Cannabis	46	50	15	13	5	5	24	26	11	6
Other illicits[e]	35	28	9	5	8	5	10	8	9	4

Figures are percentages, rounded up to the nearest whole figure, based on the total sample (N=164 offspring, 80 comparison).
[a] Drinking ever defined as at least 'moderate'.
[b] Current smokers only, 'would like to give up'.
[c] Including sedative-hypnotics, minor tranquillizers, anti-depressants, major tranquillizers.
[d] Including paracetamol, asprin, benylin and codeine, kaolin and morphine.
[e] Including amphetamines, cocaine, heroin, solvents, hallucinogens.
NA, not available.
Reproduced with permission from Orford and Velleman, 1990.

with alcohol use, of asking about the amount of alcohol consumed in the seven days prior to interview. Although most authorities consider people to be at moderate health risk at somewhat lower consumption levels, we used the more conservative level of the consumption of, for men, 30 or more 'units' of alcohol in the last seven days and for women, 20 or more, as our definition of heavy drinking. By this criterion, identical proportions of offspring and comparison interviewees (13%) were drinking heavily at the time of the first interview, although the proportions had increased slightly and a small gap had appeared by the time of the second interview (18% offspring, 15% comparisons). A somewhat higher proportion of offspring than comparisons admitted at the first interview that they had consumed a very large quantity of alcohol (men—30 or more units, women—20 or more units) on at least one occasion in the previous 12 months (20% offspring, 12% comparisons), but this gap had narrowed by the second year (15% offspring, 13.5% comparisons). At the first year interview identical proportions reported drinking some alcohol virtually every day (11% offspring, 11% comparisons).

When reports of current excessive or risky drug use are examined in greater detail, however, differences begin to emerge which are generally in the direction of offspring reporting the heavier, more frequent, or more risky use of drugs. The details are shown in the final column of Table 5.2. For example, twice as many offspring (9% versus 4% of comparisons) were judged by us to be current excessive or risky illicit drug users. We excluded from this group those who were only using cannabis or who had in recent months used at most two other types of illicit drug, and at most only very occasionally (no more than once every few months). Amphetamines, the most commonly used drugs, were used by just over half of this group, with cocaine, heroin, 'glue', 'magic mushrooms' and LSD, each being used by a minority.

Almost twice as many offspring (11% *vs* 6% of comparisons) were currently regular users of cannabis, using once a week or more often. A further, unexpected finding, was that, although virtually identical proportions of offspring and comparisons were current tobacco users, three times as many offspring (18% *vs* 6% of comparisons, chi squared = 5.86, *p* less than 0.05) were heavy smokers, consuming more than 25 cigarettes a day. There was also a modest difference between the groups on our scale of 'risky' alcohol use, 17% of offspring and 11% of comparisons being classified in terms of this scale as current risky drinkers. The scale was constructed by combining information about quantity, frequency, heavy occasional drinking, and health or social alcohol-related problems.

There was also a difference, in the expected direction, at the other end of the drinking continuum, with more offspring (20.5% *vs* 14% comparisons) reporting that they were current abstainers or comparatively infrequent, light drinkers—drinking at most fortnightly and never more than four units on one occasion. The 16 informants who were in prison at the time of the first interview were excluded from this comparison for obvious reasons.

Amongst these abstainers and infrequent, light drinkers were a number who described having had personal problems with their own use of alcohol in the past, although they had now overcome these. In the sample as a whole there were ten people with such alcohol problems in the past, of whom all but one were offspring. If these numbers are added to those informants considered to be drinking in a risky fashion at the time of interview, the offspring–comparison difference begins to look more substantial (22% and 12.5%, respectively, now drinking riskily or with alcohol problems in the past), although, like all the other group differences discussed in this section so far other than the one relating to heavy smoking, this difference is not substantial enough to be statistically significant with the sample sizes involved in this study.

Although there are differences to be found between the two groups when reports of current alcohol, tobacco, cannabis and other illicit drug use are examined in detail, these differences are not as substantial as we had expected. It is interesting to note, furthermore, that the figures shown in Table 5.2 for medically prescribed and over-the-counter psychoactive drugs are no greater for offspring than for comparisons; indeed in the case of prescribed drugs the modest differences that do exist are in the opposite direction. This is particularly interesting since, as was noted in the previous chapter, a greater number of offspring had been prescribed psychoactive drugs as adolescents—18% of offspring, but only 9% of comparisons, reported using prescribed psychoactive drugs for the first time at age 17 or younger. It seems that offspring were well in the 'lead', in terms of prescribed drug use, during adolescence, but that they lost this lead and were overtaken by comparisons in early adulthood. This is all the more remarkable given that somewhat fewer of the comparison respondents were recruited from clinical sources. The same phenomenon was found, although to a less marked degree, with advancing age, of ever have used, or ever having used regularly, the other categories of drug that we were interested in. The graph for 'ever using' cannabis is shown in Figure 5.1.[1] This shows clearly the way in which offspring, from their mostly retrospective

---

[1]This analysis is complicated due to the reducing numbers of our sample available to examine for the later years; hence this Figure is based on a smaller, closely matched sample of 64 offspring and 64 comparisons. Further details are to be found in Orford and Velleman, 1990.

Risk and Resilience

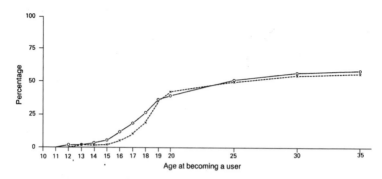

Figure 5.1 Cumulative probabilities of ever having used cannabis at different ages for offspring (solid line, *N*= 64) and comparisons (dashed line, *N*= 64). Reproduced with permission from Orford and Velleman, 1990.

accounts, were more likely than comparisons to be takers of cannabis up to around the age of 19 or 20—although it should be noted that only small-ish minorities of either group were involved—but that comparisons caught up in their late teens and early 20s.

In fact, of the five drug groups for which we could make the calcula-tion (insufficient information was available in the case of home medicines) it was the prescribed drugs that members of the sample were most likely to have stopped using after having ever used at an earlier point in their lives. As Table 5.2 shows, only 8% of the offspring group and 10% of the comparisons were still using prescribed psychoactive drugs at the time of interview, although around 50% of both groups had used them in the past. At the other extreme is alcohol, a drug which members of our sample very rarely gave up using once started, with between 94% and 99% still using. Another interesting statistic, also shown in Table 5.2, is the proportion of users of a category of drug who considered that their use constituted a problem or that they should give up. This statistic varies from a low of 5% for cannabis to 28% for tobacco, with other illicit drugs, prescribed drugs, and alcohol occupying intermediate positions. It is interesting to note that only about one fifth of those who had ever used an illicit psychoactive drug other than cannabis, considered this to have been a problem, and over 70% had apparently stopped using such drugs by the time of interview.

Whilst offspring–comparison group differences in terms of individual drug groups are not dramatic, and rarely statistically significant, we thought it possible that differences might show up more clearly in terms of the num-bers of people who were using regularly or heavily, or were having prob-lems, with more than one drug group. This did indeed turn out to be the case. The results were examined to see what overlap there was between those informants we had classified as current risky drinkers, as heavy smokers, regular users of prescribed drugs, regular users of home medicines, regular cannabis users, and users of other illicit drugs. In the whole sample 18% appeared in two or more of these categories. This we term multiple drug risk (MDR). MDR was more common amongst offspring than comparisons (22% versus 10%). There was, in addition, an effect of sex (males 27%, females 10%) largely due to differences in alcohol, cannabis and tobacco use, and a sample source effect (interviewees recruited from agency/clinical sources 25%, those from community/advertising sources 13.5%) largely due to differences in the use of tobacco, prescribed drugs, and illicit drugs other than cannabis. Combining these three factors—offspring versus comparison, sex, and recruitment source—provides us with sub-groups with very different rates of MDR. At the low end are female comparisons recruited from community/advertising sources, with an MDR rate of 3%. At the other extreme, with an MDR rate 12 times as great (37%) are male offspring recruited from agency/clinical sources. A form of statistical analysis known as log linear analysis was used to help disentangle the relative contributions to MDR of these three factors. This analysis revealed that the sex effect was the strongest ($p<0.001$), that the effect of offspring versus comparison was weaker but still independently significant statistically ($p<0.05$), and that the effect of sample source just failed to achieve significance. Interactions amongst the factors did not add significantly.

Testing Parental Modelling Theory

The previous section offers some, although weak, support for a degree of intergenerational continuity in drinking and drug problems. As the review of previous research in Chapter 2 showed, one of the leading explanations for such continuity has been in terms of behavioural modelling theory. To test the adequacy of this theory in explaining the intergenerational continuity found in the present results it is necessary to take into account the sex of the offspring, the sex of the problem drinking parent, and the nature of the relationship between the offspring and each parent. This enables the following three hypotheses, derived from modelling theory, to be tested:

—that modelling will be along *same-gender* lines (boys will model themselves on heavy drinking fathers; girls, heavy drinking mothers);

—that modelling will depend on the *degree of positive relationship* with either parent (the more positive the relationships with the problem drinker parents, the more likely it is that offspring will model themselves on their behaviour);

—that modelling will interact with the *availability of the role model* (specifically: that more exposure to parental problem drinking at home; exposure to problem drinking over a greater number of years; or exposure to more than one parental problem drinking role model, would lead to a greater liklihood of problem drinking in the offspring).

In fact, there was no evidence of same-gender modelling. Instead the main effect that can be seen is that sons, whether of fathers or mothers with drinking problems, are much more likely than daughters to have a raised risk: 25% of sons of problem-drinking fathers and 21% of sons of problem-drinking mothers were drinking in a 'risky' fashion, as opposed to 8% and 6% of daughters of these two types of parent; similarly the figures for risky use of illicit drugs other than cannabis were 13.5% and 14% for sons, compared to 5% and 6% for daughters; and for multiple drug risk were 35% and 36% for sons versus 9% and 6% for daughters.

Table 5.3 shows the evidence relating to the second hypothesis. Correlations are generally positive indicating that offspring with the more positive relationships with their problem drinking parents, and those perceiving a greater degree of similarity between themselves and their problem drinking parents, were generally more likely to score more highly on the four alcohol and drug indices. Men who were more positive towards their problem drinking fathers were significantly more likely to have higher alcohol problems scores. Some of the results for offspring of mothers with drinking problems are suggestive but the numbers are too small to achieve statistical significance. The strongest support for modelling in Table 5.3, however, concerns women who were more positive towards their problem drinking fathers and those who saw themselves as more like their problem drinking fathers. The following extracts from reports are illustrative.

P290 Offspring

"I thought F (Father) was great, but as I got older I suppose it diminished. I understood him. He tried to push us into things, not let us develop on our own. I loved him. I always thought a lot of him, was always very close to him. We seemed to be on the same wavelength". P could talk to F to "a certain extent—not about sex or anything like that, but I would talk to him about other things". She would do things with him two or three times a month and said she, "took after him in a lot of ways. F was someone to look up to—I always admired him. I suppose I always felt I had to keep up to his image of me—that was a bit difficult" i.e. as F was lacking in confidence he wanted P to make up for that weakness in him. "F affected the

Table 5.3 Relationship and similarity with problem drinking parent correlated with adulthood drinking and drug-taking variables

	Positive relationship with problem drinking parent				Perceived similarity with problem drinking parent			
	Fathers		Mothers		Fathers		Mothers	
	Sons	Daughters	Sons	Daughters	Sons	Daughters	Sons	Daughters
N	34–46	50–58	12–14	14–15	33–44	51–58	12–14	13
Problem or risky drinking	+0.06	+0.14	+0.44	−0.02	−0.01	+0.35**	+0.12	−0.47*
Problem or risky drug use	−0.16	+0.02	+0.31	+0.04	−0.03	+0.22*	+0.09	−0.46
Units of alcohol last week	−0.02	+0.33**	+0.21	+0.15	−0.01	+0.35**	−0.11	+0.31
Alcohol problems scale score	+0.45***	+0.20	+0.13	+0.19	−0.19	+0.11	−0.01	+0.06

$* = p<0.05$; $** = p<0.01$; $*** = p<0.001$.
Reproduced with permission from Orford and Velleman, 1991.

home life—if he was low, everyone else was" ... P thinks she now drinks too much, sometimes more than others. F always put P against drinking—he was "quite strongly against" her drinking. But because her father was a drinker, it made her look at it too lightly. She also said she started drinking when she was too young. She said if a man didn't drink at all, it would put her off him: it would perhaps make her feel as if she shouldn't be drinking and make her feel guilty.

P278 Offspring

Until 19 P used never to drink and hated people insisting on her drinking. She now drinks in moderation because she doesn't want to feel that M's (Mother's) drinking is causing her to be "abnormal" herself. She now describes herself as a light drinker, drinking every few days. She drank on five days last week totalling 12 units, never more than 4, with a maximum of about 8 last year. She feels in no danger, "I feel guarded against it—I never want to be degraded like that. It annoys me when people drink a lot but say they're okay. In moderation its good. It seems pathetic when people drink to get drunk. If someone gets drunk its okay, but it depends how—if they're silly, its nice, quite amusing, but if they get moody, self-critical, aggressive—its horrid". She thinks M's drinking is probably the cause of her having never got drunk and abstaining in the past. At home P never drinks at all which her parents think is childish.

P275 Offspring

F (Father) was very fair and very kind, well respected: "I looked up to him". He was a very nice man, everyone found him very charming—it was difficult to believe he had a problem. "We had a 'spirit is willing but the flesh is weak' relationship. I felt he let everyone down. You couldn't discuss things with F and get consistent answers". M (Mother) says that P is just like F, but P doesn't think so. At 16–17 she drank at parties during holidays and probably got very merry. At 18 she started going out to pubs but mainly drank tomato juice and gradually built up to age 24–25 when she was working on newspapers and went to the pub perhaps four times a week... She says she feels great danger from drinking because it's been in the family (it is M's opinion that both P's grandfathers had drinking problems). If P drinks a lot she gets very bad tempered, and she doesn't drink because of the worry that she might become dependent. She thinks moderate drinking is perfectly acceptable but that drinking does a great deal of harm in excess. She doesn't despise drinkers but feels very sorry for them. She thinks her background has had a great effect—P has a cautious approach to alcohol and a great respect for it as a result.

The final behavioural modelling hypothesis relates to the availability of the role model or models. There does appear to be a greater risk for those offspring who reported that two parents had drinking problems. For example no fewer than 43.5% of those with two parents with drinking problems reported past problematic or current risky alcohol use, with comparable figures for those with fathers only and mothers only with drinking problems being 20% and 17% respectively. Again, however, there are significant sex based effects here. Whereas for males there were negligible differences between those who had one parent with a drinking problem and those who had two, for females there were substantial differences. Women with two parents with drinking problems were more likely to have current risky or past problematic drinking (two parents 43%, one parent, 13%, chi squared = 7.45, $p<0.01$), and were more likely to have multiple drug risk (MDR: two parents 50%, one parent 15%, chi squared = 8.68, $p<0.005$). Similarly, women (but not men) whose problem drinking parent drank at home were significantly more likely than other women to have both current risky or past problematic drinking (parent drank at home: 26%, parent did not drink at home: 5%, chi squared = 6.63, $p<0.01$), and MDR (parent drank at home: 28%, parent did not drink at home: 11%, chi squared = 4.05, $p<0.05$). Using years of exposure to a problem drinking parent (between ages 5 and 15) as an index of length of exposure to modelling of heavy drinking yielded no significant findings in the expected direction. For males alone, however, there was a result in the opposite direction to that predicted: males with a higher than average number of years of exposure were *less* likely to be currently risky or past problematic drinkers than those with less than average exposure (16% *vs* 38%).

Are Children of Problem Drinking Parents more Likely to Marry People with Drinking Problems?

What evidence is there in the present data for a second kind of intergenerational transmission? Are the offspring of problem drinking parents especially likely to marry or partner people with drinking problems? In Chapter 2 this hypothesis, and the very limited evidence that exists to support it, were reviewed. It has often been said that daughters of problem drinking parents are particularly likely to form adulthood relationships with men with drinking problems.

In the present study only four participants, of those with a current partner, considered their partners to be problem or very heavy drinkers. A further nine were of the opinion that their partners were 'fairly heavy' drinkers. When the latter were included, it was indeed the case that more daughters of problem drinking parents (7 or 10% of those with a partner) than comparison women (1 or 4%) had current partners thought to be heavy or problem drinkers, but the numbers are clearly too small for us to be able to draw confident conclusions. What can be concluded, however, is that the large majority of daughters of problem drinking parents—and the same is true for sons—did not consider there to be anything particularly remarkable about their partners' drinking.

The findings were more interesting with regard to the participants' *previous* adult partnerships, although here of course there is an even greater chance that opinions about a partner's drinking include a large measure of subjectivity, coloured by the experiences of childhood. Keeping this proviso in mind, it was the case that a surprisingly large number of people, particularly offspring women, believed they had had a previous adulthood relationship with someone whose drinking constituted a problem. This was the case for 45% of offspring women, but it was also true for as many as 30%, 24% and 20% of comparison women, offspring men and comparison men respectively. It is interesting to note that there were seven women in all (6 offspring, 1 comparison) who described both a current heavy or problem drinking partner and a previous problem drinking partner. It is these women who most closely correspond to the popular stereotype of the daughter of a problem drinking parent who in adulthood seems repeatedly attracted to heavy drinking men. But it must be noted that this group constituted only about one in twenty of all daughters of problem drinking parents in our study (or 1 in 14 with current partners).

Is it the case, as many have supposed, that the offspring of parents with drinking problems have a high probability of *either* experiencing drinking problems themselves as adults *or* partnering other people who do? Table 5.4 shows the results of combining the data on the participants' own

Table 5.4   Own and/or partner's heavy, risky or problematic drinking by offspring *vs* comparisons and by sex

	Self: current risky/previous problem N (%)	Previous relationship with heavy/ problem drinker N (%)	Current relationship with heavy/ problem drinker N (%)	Any one of these N (%)
Offspring (N)				
Sons (71)	20 (28)	17 (24)	3 (4)	30 (44)
Daughters (91)	16 (18)	41 (45)	7 (8)	46 (52)[ii]
Comparison (N)				
Sons (40)	8 (20)[i]	8 (20)	2 (5)	13 (33)
Daughters (40)	2 (5)[i]	12 (30)	1 (3)	13 (33)[ii]

Figures sharing a common superscript are significantly different: $p<0.05$.

adulthood 'risky drinking' and their current or previous partners' heavy or problem drinking. Here it can be seen that just over half of female offspring (52%), and just under half of male offspring (44%), in the present study were positive in one or other of these respects; offspring informants, irrespective of gender, were significantly more likely to report one or other of these occurrences, and within these figures, offspring females were significantly more likely than were comparison females to do so. Figures for the comparison group, however, although they are somewhat smaller (33% for both men and women), do show that these experiences are quite common amongst young adults who have not had the experience of being brought up in families where the parent had a drinking problem.

Other Aspects of Adulthood Life Adjustment

As we were at pains to point out in Chapter 2 when reviewing the literature relevant to the present study and its interpretation, there may be effects in adulthood of having had a parent with a drinking problem other than harmful or risky drinking or drug-taking. In Table 5.5 are listed the relevant variables on which we had information from either the first or the second interview and which lent themselves to quantification.

The variables shown in Table 5.5 fall into eight topic areas. In each case there was good reason to expect that significant differences between offspring and comparison groups might be found. We predicted that offspring would, as a group, manifest greater instability as young adults and that this would be reflected in shorter periods of employment and of residence at one address, and shorter close relationships and friendships. We thought they might have more difficulties in their own marriages and partnerships, and might express greater difficulty in forming close relationships and obtaining emotional support from close friends. By comparison, the possibility that children of problem drinking parents might have greater difficulty adjusting to the world of work has scarcely been mentioned in the research literature. Since this is one of the principal domains to which young adults must adjust personally and socially, we spent time exploring this topic with participants, believing that offspring might manifest greater difficulties than comparisons in this area. A similar rationale existed for devoting time, particularly at the second interview, to the degree of participants' involvement in social activities and their level of satisfaction with these.

Moving to topics that are more personal than interpersonal or social, we attempted the difficult task of measuring self-esteem, using both a very

Table 5.5   General adulthood adjustment variables: offspring *vs* comparisons

Variable	Scale	Offspring (N=141–164)		Comparison (N=75–80)		Significance of difference (t or chi sq, as appropriate)
		Mean	SD	Mean	SD	
Stability						
Longest employment	0 to 5	2.79	1.6	2.80	1.7	ns
Longest address	1 to 5	3.30	1.5	3.50	1.5	ns
Longest relationship	1 to 5	3.49	1.7	3.03	1.8	ns
Longest friendship	1 to 5	4.07	1.4	4.01	1.4	ns
Age left home[a]		37%		23%		*
Relationships and Friendships						
Number of children	0 to 3 +	0.74	1.0	0.37	0.7	*
Marital status— single (1)/ not single (2)		1.60	0.5	1.45	0.5	*
Positives in current relationship	0 to 3	2.30	0.9	2.22	0.9	ns
Negatives in current relationship	0 to 3	1.40	1.0	1.60	1.0	ns
Ability to get close to others	0 to 4	2.19	1.0	2.24	0.9	ns
Emotional support from close friends	0 to 5	3.04	1.5	3.12	1.3	ns
Employment						
SES improvement	−4 to+4	0.15	1.6	0.44	1.6	ns
Job satisfaction	0 to 3	1.83	0.8	1.87	0.9	ns
Job dissatisfaction	0 to 3	1.11	0.8	1.18	0.8	ns
Satisfaction with work scale score	0 to 40	12.59	5.1	12.79	5.7	ns

Table 5.5   *(continued)*

Variable	Scale	Offspring (N=141–164)		Comparison (N=75–80)		Significance of difference (t or chi sq, as appropriate)
		Mean	SD	Mean	SD	
Social activities						
Social activity	0 to 4	3.14	1.2	3.38	1.0	ns
Number of social activities	1 to 47	15.44	8.9	18.38	8.5	**
Satisfaction with social life	−4 to +2	−0.54	1.6	−0.52	1.6	ns
Self-esteem and personality						
Self-esteem1[b]	10 to 40	22.23	4.6	22.12	5.0	ns
Self-esteem2[c]	0 to +48	7.76	5.2	7.08	4.6	ns
Anxiety	0 to 12	6.67	3.4	6.27	3.5	ns
Extraversion	0 to 12	7.43	3.4	8.72	2.8	**
Psychoticism	0 to 10	1.86	1.9	1.66	1.5	ns
Lie scale	0 to 12	3.94	2.6	3.84	2.5	ns
Adulthood problems						
Anxiety and depression	(standardised scores: mean=0; s.d.=1)	0.03	1.0	−0.06	1.0	ns
Deviance and delinquency	(standardised scores: mean=0; s.d.=1)	0.06	1.0	−0.11	0.9	ns
Life events						
Total life events	0 to 88	4.77	3.2	4.75	3.1	ns
Life satisfaction						
Life satisfaction	0 to 5	2.81	1.3	2.78	1.2	ns
Life dis-satisfaction	0 to 5	1.95	1.2	1.78	1.2	ns
Satisfaction/ dissatisfaction balance	−5 to +5	1.03	2.2	0.95	2.4	ns

*=$p<0.05$; **=$p<0.01$.
[a] % 'leaving home' at age 17 or younger.
[b] Rosenberg Self-Esteem scale. Higher scores indicate lower self-esteem.
[c] Ideal – Real self-discrepancy score. Higher scores indicate greater discrepancy.

well-known standard scale and an alternative procedure that was developed specially for this study. We also used a shortened version of the Eysenck Personality Questionnaire (EPQ) which provides four scale scores. We used the EPQ because it was at the time, and probably remains, one of the best known and most often used standard personality inventories. Two of its scales (neuroticism-stability and extraversion–introversion) have been long-established as two of the major dimensions underlying individual differences in adulthood personality. It was predicted that the kinds of experiences offspring had had in childhood would make them somewhat more anxious than comparisons as adults and that this difference would show up in terms of a difference in average scores on the first of these two dimensions. Incidentally, we prefer to think of this dimension of the EPQ as the anxious–calm dimension, since the word 'neuroticism' seems to us to carry extra, unnecessary connotations and to invite a prejudiced response.

Interviewees were also asked whether they were currently experiencing any one of 27 common psychological problems and, if so, which were causing them definite distress. An analysis of the pattern of inter-correlations amongst these 27 items (using factor analysis) suggested two main factors which we term 'anxiety and depression' (e.g. 'feeling anxious', 'feeling depressed', 'feeling panicky', 'worrying', 'waking up early in the mornings') and 'delinquency and deviance' (e.g. 'thefts', 'problems with police', 'shoplifting', 'fights'). The prediction was that offspring would report more psychological problems than comparisons.

At the second interview participants were asked about potentially stressful life events in the following areas: illnesses, injuries and accidents; bereavements; pregnancies; changes in relationships; separations; changes in living conditions; study or school events; financial circumstances; legal difficulties. Questions were asked about the circumstances surrounding each event that occurred in the preceding 12 months, and the likely stressfulness of such an event was subsequently rated (which is not necessarily the same thing as how stressful the person found the event subjectively). This measure was included principally to see whether recent stress in adulthood could be as strong a predictor as, or perhaps even stronger than, recalled experiences of childhood. But it was also thought possible that offspring might be living lives as young adults that involved more stress than comparisons.

Finally, we asked participants to summarise their feelings about areas of satisfaction and areas of dissatisfaction with their current lives. On the basis of what they said, both satisfaction and dissatisfaction were subsequently rated on four-point scales. Because these turned out to be very significantly negatively correlated with one another, the rating of dissatis-faction was subtracted from the satisfaction rating to produce an overall satisfaction balance score. Our final prediction was that comparison partic-ipants would describe their current lives, overall, as more satisfying than would offspring.

Before looking at the statistical findings, the following are relevant extracts from interview reports.

P233 Offspring

P had secure close friendships as a young child, but felt much less secure later because he was moving from place to place. In the past he has found it hard to get close to people—"whenever anyone shows me a bit of affection I immediately reject it, as I feel they are just getting at my confidence before rejecting me, but I can get close to people *now*. I've had difficulties in past years, but as I get older I'm getting more 'spiritually enlightened'. In the past I had great difficulty in trying to relate to people. I was very possessive. I got close enough to get hurt, but not close enough to hurt them". He has an active social life—on the committee of an 18+ group, part-time work for the Samaritans, an Amateur Dramatic Group, and Magical Society—all these within the last 18 months. He had a relationship which lasted two to three years—they lived together as man and wife and he became a father to her son. He has been out with girls from the 18+ club and has had two relationships with older married or divorced women with children—"I go for older women". He's currently flirting around a lot and sort of going out with one girl.

P73 Offspring

P married her present husband when she was 19. She described a good relation-ship. "I never tire of him, it's always good to think he's home". She said she had no difficulty in relationships with people and quite often went out. She would like a more social life, and felt she could be doing more—she is not working currently. But she didn't want anything, was happy and had a pretty good life really, "I've got it cushy". "We're very happy, he's my lifeline—I don't know what I'd do without him—I've got so much now that I didn't have before I knew him".

P272 Offspring

There is a mixture of satisfaction and dissatisfactions. The former include his girl-friend, and the fact he is attempting to sort things out, that he has still got friends despite the hassles he's caused, that his social life is good, and buying records—music influences him. Dissatisfactions include ups and downs with his girlfriend, wanting a better relationship with his parents, his sister's divorce two months ago which he feels he has something to do with, the fact he still has money problems, and being unemployed. He had 21 days in prison in the last year which he feels was three weeks wasted, and has lived in three different houses in the past few months. He ticked quite a number of problems, some coded as serious—eating too little, eating too much, both of which have occurred regularly throughout the year, and problems with the police and thefts which occurred for a period of up to three months during the year. The interviewer's impression was that P seems to live a very unsettled life. His sister and brother-in-law own the house where he lives, he doesn't eat regular meals and eats out a lot and this has made him develop "very bad eating habits" ... He has lots of friends and this didn't surprise the interviewer because he came across as a very charming, intelligent, confident person. His relationship with his girlfriend is very important. They have just got back together but there are some problems in that neither of their parents likes the other partner and so they have to live with their parents' disapproval. Gambling is a major problem for P—in the past he has lost several hundred pounds on one day ... He has done a lot of taking and driving away ... He hasn't done this for a little while and says it is a thing of the past.

P275 Offspring

P found it difficult to trust men. She didn't want casual relationships and needs to feel very secure in relationships. Apart from her husband she has never found somebody she wants or needs to confide in, although she can easily get to know people on a superficial, friendly basis.

As Table 5.5 shows, scarcely any of the predictions outlined above were fulfilled. None of our predictions regarding EPQ anxiety, psychological problems causing distress, social stability, emotional support from friends, and felt satisfaction with marriage or partnership, with work or other daily activity, with social activities, or satisfaction with life overall, were borne out by the results. Indeed, at the first year offspring men were somewhat more likely than comparison men to describe their marriages or partnerships as, on balance, more satisfactory than unsatisfactory, and at the second year, offspring (sons and daughters combined) were a little more likely to describe their current lives as, on balance, more satisfactory than unsatisfactory. However, the first of these two findings is based on a reduced sample of only those men with current marriages or cohabitations and both findings are of borderline statistical significance. In view of the fact that we were looking at nearly 30 individual hypotheses, it is quite likely that these can be attributed to chance. What does seem certain, however, is that there is no evidence here that offspring would describe their marriages and their lives overall in more negative terms than comparisons. Nor was there any support for the prediction that offspring would have lower self-esteem than comparisons. Although the differences on both self-esteem measures were in the predicted direction these differences were tiny in relation to variances and fell far short of statistical significance.

The two places where more significant findings did emerge were in one area where predictions had been less confident (amount of social activity) and in another where no prediction had been made (EPQ extraversion). Data on social activities were collected at the second interview in the form of a retrospective social diary of the week prior to interview. A count was made of all social activities taken part in during the week, defining 'social' to include, for example, meetings with relatives in the interviewee's own home or elsewhere, but to exclude, for example, such activities as shopping alone. Our measure of volume of social activity was simply the number of activities in the week, giving double weighting to longer-lasting activities i.e. those judged to have lasted for one hour or longer. There was a significant relationship between this measure and offspring versus comparison, with offspring recording the smaller volume of social activity. This was true for men and women combined (as shown in Table 5.5), and for men alone, although the difference was not statistically significant for women alone. In addition comparisons scored significantly more highly than offspring on the extraversion–introversion scale of the EPQ (offspring being significantly more introverted) when men and women were combined (Table 5.5), and the same was true for women alone but not for men alone.

A discussion of the possible meaning of these findings, as well as the general absence of positive findings, will be left until the end of this chapter and Chapter 7, where the findings from all aspects of the study will be discussed and placed in the context of the overall research literature and the development of ideas in the field. At this point, however, it may at least be noted that the findings of greater introversion and a lower average volume of social activity amongst offspring may be said to support each other in an interesting way. These 2 findings emerged from two very different procedures carried out 12 months apart. The EPQ is a standard, 'pencil-and-paper', self-administered questionnaire and was given to participants on the first occasion. The measure of social activity was obtained 12 months later and involved a detailed reconstruction, in conversation with the interviewer, of each of the last 7 days in turn. The first technique includes general statements about personality which the participant may or may not attribute to him/herself (e.g. 'Are you a talkative person?', 'Can you usually let yourself go and enjoy yourself at a lively party') whilst the second focusses upon discrete, very recent events. Although it could be argued that both have the limitation of relying upon the participants' self-reports—if this is a limitation it is of course one that applies to the whole study—the 2 techniques are very different in kind, and there can have been relatively little contamination between them. Hence, it is of particular interest that each produced differences between offspring and comparisons. The 2 measures were themselves significantly, but very modestly correlated in the sample as a whole ($r=0.19$, p less than 0.005), and it is possible that each was tapping some facet of a latent variable which we did not assess directly. Part of the concept of extraversion is that of 'sociability' or the feeling of being at ease in social situations. It is possible that a relatively low score on this scale and engaging in relatively few social activities are both indications of a preference for one's own company, or that of a partner, and comparative discomfort in other forms of social company. In the absence of a more direct measure of this concept, however, this must remain speculative.

Adulthood Adjustment Factors

We have been looking at quite a large number of individual variables to do with the participants' lives as young adults—the basic context of relationships and work, their drinking and drug-taking habits, and other aspects of their personal and social lives. Some differences between offspring and comparison participants have emerged but these have not always been in the places expected and overall there are nothing like as many differences as predicted. It is possible, however, that by looking at so many variables one by one in a piecemeal fashion, we are failing to see the wood for the trees. Are there underlying themes or factors that might better differentiate the two groups?

   With this question in mind, all the inter-correlations amongst a large set of adulthood variables were calculated and a factor analysis of the resulting matrix of correlations was carried out. Twenty-seven variables were included in the analysis, covering basic context, drinking and drug-taking, and other personal and social indicators. The age at which the young person had left the parental home was included, but work satisfaction, emotional support from close friends, and stressful life events experienced between the two interviews, were not. Some of the variables were treated slightly differently than was the case for earlier analyses: for example the two self-esteem measures were combined into a single index.

   How many factors should be extracted and examined following a factor analysis is always a matter of judgement since the analysis makes available a number of solutions based on smaller or larger numbers of factors. The 'best' solution depends both upon statistical criteria and the degree to which it appears to be interpretable in terms of factors that 'make sense' to the investigators. In other words, factors need to have both statistical and 'face' validity. Even then, there is no guarantee that other investigators would find the same factors in a different set of data, nor that the factors will necessarily prove useful in the long run in throwing light upon the processes of transmission from childhood to adulthood. Those questions can only be answered by further research, and by further analysis of the present data. In fact, as we shall see, the results of the factor analysis did turn out to be at least suggestive of processes that might be occurring in the course of transition from childhood to adulthood, and some of the extra risks that children of problem drinking parents might be facing.

Two solutions to the factor analysis were examined, one involving two factors, the other four. The two-factor solution was neat, made sense to us, and was in line with a great deal of previous research on personality and psychological problems. The first factor, which we called 'positive mental health versus demoralisation', is most clearly characterised by: high versus low self-esteem; a balance of positive versus negative feelings about overall life satisfaction and few versus many current psychological problems of the 'anxiety and depression' type. The second factor, which we termed 'conformity versus deviance', can be most clearly characterised in terms of variables such as: absence versus presence of current risky drinking, current illicit drug use, current regular cannabis use; and few versus many current psychological problems of the 'delinquency/deviance' type.

This solution, satisfactory though it appeared to be in some ways, turned out to be of little interest in terms of overall differences between offspring and comparisons. The scores of the two groups of participants were almost identical on each of these two major factors. The four-factor solution, on the other hand, turned out to be rather more interesting.

Table 5.6 shows the variables that characterise each of the four factors produced by the latter solution. In each case the variables with the strongest 'loadings' on the factor are shown first and other variables are shown in descending order of importance. Minus signs indicate negative loadings. For example, EPQ anxiety and life dissatisfaction characterise the negative end of factor 1 (demoralisation) whereas life satisfaction is characteristic of the positive end (positive mental health). Figures 5.2 and 5.3 show the average scores of male and female offspring and comparisons on each of these four factors.

There are a number of points to be noted about these results. The most interesting from our point of view is the emergence of the fourth factor since this is the one of the four showing the clearest relationship with having had

Table 5.6   Variables characterising each of the four adulthood adjustment factors

Factor 1 (14% of variance) Demoralisation versus positive mental health	Factor 2 (12% of variance) Age related social stability versus instability	Factor 3 (8% of variance) Excess, delinquency and sociability	Factor 4 (6% of variance) Problems in transition to adulthood
Personality (anxious–calm) Life dissatisfaction Life satisfaction(-) Self esteem Anxiety and depression Prescribed drugs: past problem/ current risky use Frequency of social activities(-) Current relationship problems Ability to form close relationships(-) Personality (extraversion– introversion)(-) Current relationship positives(-)	Longest relationship Longest employment Longest friendship Longest lived at one address Co-habiting/married Number of children Raised socio- economic status	Risky cannabis use Personality (lie)(-) Illicit drugs: past problem/ current risky use Alcohol: past problem/ current risky use Frequency of social activities Delinquency and deviance Ability to form close relationships Personality (extraversion– introversion Personality (psychoticism)	Tobacco: current risky use Age left home(-) Number of children Delinquency and deviance Raised socio- economic status(-) Alcohol: past problem/ current risky use

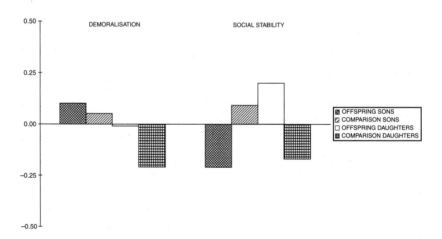

Figure 5.2   Adulthood demoralisation and social stability by offspring *vs* comparison and sex. Social Stability: significant difference between offspring and comparison daughters ($t = 2.00$, $p < 0.05$).

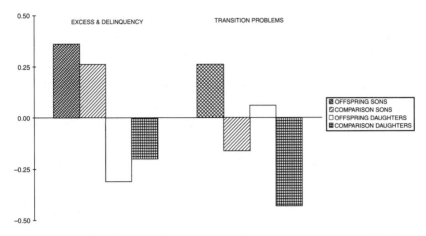

Figure 5.3   Adulthood excess/delinquency and transition problems by offspring *vs* comparison and sex. Transition problems: significant differences between offspring and comparison sons ($t=2.09$, $p<0.05$) and between offspring and comparison daughters ($t=3.78$, $p<0.001$).

a parent with a drinking problem. The relationship is significant for the whole sample, and for both men and women separately, being somewhat more significant for women. Offspring of parents with drinking problems achieved higher scores. Contributing to higher scores on this factor were: leaving the parental home at a relatively early age, being a heavy smoker, being a risky drinker now or having had some problem with drinking in the past, having relatively many psychological problems of the delinquency/ deviance kind, having relatively more children, and having made relatively little improvement in socioeconomic status in comparison with parents. This is an interesting combination of variables which could not easily have been foreseen, but it is certainly one that can be seen to make sense. There is, of course, danger in this kind of post-hoc interpretation of a factor that had not been predicted, but the exercise is legitimate provided conclusions are drawn very tentatively. Our cautious interpretation of this factor is that it may represent, at one end, a relatively unproblematic, perhaps careful and planned, transition from childhood and the parental home to adulthood and independence. At the opposite pole, towards which offspring are somewhat more likely to find themselves, is a relatively problematic, perhaps impulsive and unplanned transition.

Of particular interest, because of our initial concern with the intergenerational transmission of alcohol problems, is the finding that problematic or risky drinking loads, albeit modestly, on this fourth factor, but also figures, somewhat more strongly, in the third factor. If it is right to assume that these factors do represent underlying themes of some importance, the fact that problem or risky drinking contributes to both these factors suggests that this kind of drinking may be indicative of more than one kind of developmental process in young adulthood. Excessive drinking is very likely to be part of a youthful style of risk-taking and, probably mainly minor, delinquency. This style tends to be associated with more frequent socialising, relatively higher scores on the extraversion scale, and a belief that one is relatively well able to get close to other people. This is the pattern that corresponds to the positive end of Factor 3. Although there may be some risks involved in that lifestyle, it also appears to have positive elements to it, and having had a parent with a drinking problem is not correlated with it (although sex is, with men having significantly higher scores on Factor 3). On the other hand, heavy drinking may be part of the relatively problematic, impulsive and unplanned transition from the parental home to independence which we have tentatively identified as being the theme represented by Factor 4. The latter is more likely for the offspring of parents with drinking problems.

Although future research may not succeed in replicating these exact factors, the fact that risky or problem drinking splits between two factors in this way is important since it suggests why research, including our own, has found it difficult to establish a clear and strong correlation between having had a parent with a drinking problem and excessive drinking in adulthood. It is probably not drinking *per se* that is directly affected by having had a parent with a drinking problem, and the experiences associated with that, but rather a particular way of making the transition from childhood to adulthood. Drinking excessively can be a part of that pattern, but it is part of other patterns of young adulthood life as well.

Factor 1, which corresponds almost exactly to the 'demoralisation-positive mental health' factor from the simpler, two-factor solution of the factor analysis, is the most important in the sense that it is the single factor accounting for the largest proportion of all the variation exhibited by all the participants on all the variables combined. This may simply reflect our choice of variables, but it is likely that this factor represents a dimension of young adult life of great significance to the participants. The fact that having had a parent with a drinking problem is unrelated to it, is important. In view of the findings regarding extraversion and the frequency of social events, reported earlier in this chapter, it is perhaps surprising that offspring were not more 'demoralised' than comparisons. But these 'social' variables contribute modestly to scores on this factor in comparison with variables such as EPQ anxiety, life dissatisfaction and low self-esteem. Note, also, that extraversion, frequent socialising and believing that one has the ability to get close to people, contribute not only to 'positive mental health' but also to 'risk-taking, delinquency and sociability'.

Factor 2, which combines a number of the variables which were included to assess social stability, provides an interesting finding when the two sexes are analysed separately, as shown in Figure 5.2. For women, there was a difference on this factor, but in a direction opposite to that predicted. To our surprise, women offspring showed greater stability than comparisons. The result for men, although not strong enough to be significant, was in the other direction, with offspring sons showing a tendency towards lower stability than comparisons. We noted earlier in this chapter that women offspring were more likely than comparisons to be married or cohabiting and to have relatively more children, and the findings for Factor 2 derived from the factor analysis were in keeping with this.

Summary

Two general conclusions can be drawn from the results presented in this chapter. First, many of the differences that we had expected between offspring and comparison participants were completely lacking in our sample. It was *not* the case that offspring had generally poorer mental health as young adults, or specifically reported greater anxiety, or a greater dissatisfaction with life. Nor, overall, were they leading lives that were less stable than comparisons in terms of home, close relationships, friendships, work or education. Nor did scores on the relevant measures suggest lower self-esteem.

The second conclusion is that there are some differences to be found—although they are still not as dramatic as might have been expected—but these differences need to be understood within a broader framework for understanding adolescent–adulthood transitions and young adulthood styles of life. Offspring were more often than comparisons, heavy, risky or problematic users of each of a number of drug groups (including alcohol and tobacco), either separately, or combined in the form of 'multiple drug risk', but these differences were not as great as expected and were not always statistically significant. This seems to be at least partly because the risky use of substances is quite common amongst young adults, as part of a pattern that combines this risk-taking with a relatively sociable, outgoing leisure lifestyle. Young adults who did not have parents with drinking problems, especially young men, are just as likely as those who did to adopt this lifestyle. There is a further suggestion in the data that offspring may be somewhat less extraverted and gregarious than other young adults. If anything, this would serve to protect against risky substance use that was part of a general risk-taking, sociable style.

More dangerous for children of problem drinking parents, however, may be the way in which the transition from adolescence in the parental home to independence as a young adult takes place, and the dangers may be very different for young women and young men. Although this chapter has only presented evidence that bears indirectly on this point, we believe the results presented do suggest a hypothesis that this transition may be more hurried and unplanned, perhaps less calm and well thought out, than is the case for other young people. For women, this holds the danger of forming close relationships with men comparatively early, having boyfriends who drink heavily although these may not result in lasting relationships, getting married earlier than others, and having more children. Since there is no evidence in our data that the marriages of daughters of problem drinking parents are any less satisfactory than those of other young women, it may be wrong to think of this pattern as constituting a 'danger'. In fact, offspring women had, if anything, a more settled and stable way of life, although there may of course be other, hidden, costs involved. The risks of a relatively hurried and unplanned transition to adulthood are perhaps different for men. For them, differences showed up not in terms of marriage and children but in terms of a relative failure to improve their 'life chances', in terms of education and job status at least, relative to their parents.

A greater risk of heavy smoking and risky or problematic drinking also appeared to form part of this pattern of unplanned transition to adulthood. Of the two, it was heavy smoking that was most closely associated with this pattern. Although our data on childhood and adolescent smoking are not detailed enough for us to be sure, it may be that this reflects the peculiar characteristics of tobacco and the timing of its uptake during the life course. The regular use of tobacco starts very early, and a high proportion of users see its use as a problem for them, but a large proportion of early users continue with use into adulthood. We think it likely that children experiencing some of the family stresses associated with having a parent with a drinking problem, which were described in the previous chapter, are likely to be particularly at risk of becoming childhood or early adolescent smokers, of becoming heavy smokers early on, and of maintaining this pattern into adulthood. The large majority 'settle down' to a socially stable and mostly satisfying life, but heavy smoking is not incompatible with this and is likely to persist.

A number of these ideas are highly tentative, and in Chapter 7 we shall need to see what sense they make when put alongside other research findings and theoretical ideas. Before so doing, however, we shall continue to explore the results from the present study. The present chapter has focussed on differences between offspring and comparisons. In the following chapter we combine these two groups in the search for explanations of differences in young adulthood adjustment, beyond having had a parent with a drinking problem.

CHAPTER 6

EXPLANATIONS FOR DIFFERENCES IN ADULTHOOD ADJUSTMENT— RESULTS III

The last chapter has shown that, although there were some differences between the two groups in terms of their psychological adjustment as young adults, the offspring/comparison variable was not as useful as had been anticipated in explaining the variation in adulthood adjustments which were found. In this chapter we look more widely for an explanation of adulthood outcomes, taking the search well beyond the one factor of whether or not a person was brought up in a home where a parent had a drinking problem. Particular attention will be paid to the existence of disharmony in the family of upbringing. The review of previous research in Chapter 2 suggested that this was a likely leading contender for explaining difficulties in later adjustment, and Chapter 4 showed that to explain the results concerning *childhood* problems and difficulties, the existence of family disharmony was a more useful variable than knowing whether or not someone's parent had a drinking problem. Also examined are the influence upon adjustment of having had psychological problems as a child or adolescent as well as a range of more contemporaneous variables to do with life circumstances and satisfactions as an adult.

The ways in which human lives unfold are varied and complex, and the results presented in this chapter reflect that complexity. As a guide to the chapter, the following are the steps that it will take. Throughout most of this chapter, offspring and comparisons are combined in the analysis.

1. Disharmony in the family of upbringing and childhood psychological difficulties—two variables of particular interest—will be considered alone, and evidence presented of the link between these variables and a number of key adulthood adjustment variables taken one by one.
2. The link will be explored between these same two childhood variables— disharmony and childhood difficulties—and the overall adulthood adjustment factors identified in the previous chapter.
3. The picture will be made more complex by considering how these two supposedly key childhood variables interact with whether or not a parent

had a drinking problem, and with sociodemographic and sampling variables, in the prediction of adulthood adjustment factors. The multivariate statistical procedure known as 'path analysis' will be used here.

4. We then examine whether the ways offspring reported coping with their parents' excessive drinking mediated or moderated the relationships between childhood variables and adulthood adjustment.

5. Further complexity will be added by introducing into the model of life development being tested by the path analyses, variables that relate to adult life itself, such as whether a person is married or in a job, or how satisfied he or she is with various aspects of life circumstances.

6. Finally, admitting that no statistical model based upon discrete variables, however complex that model may be, can hope to do justice to the idiosyncrasies of individual lives, we present a number of individual 'cases' in a further attempt to throw light upon the ways people's lives develop after an upbringing that has involved living with a parent with a drinking problem.

FAMILY DISHARMONY AND INDIVIDUAL ADULTHOOD ADJUSTMENT VARIABLES

The same range of outcome variables that were discussed in the previous chapter were examined here. These related to marriage, children and work; to drinking and drug-taking as young adults; and to other aspects of adult life adjustment such as stability, relationships, work satisfaction, social activities, self-esteem, personality, psychological problems, stressful life events, and satisfaction and dissatisfaction with current life circumstances.

As Table 6.1 shows, fifteen of these relationships showed significant relationships with disharmony: respondents reporting disharmonious family relationships were more likely to have lower self-esteem at the time of interview, to see themselves as having less ability to form close relationships, on the relevant EPQ scales to be more anxious, more introverted, and more 'psychotic', to have more psychological problems in adulthood, both of the anxiety and depression type, and the deviance and delinquency type, to have a lower level of social activity, to be more dissatisfied with their social lives, to have left home earlier, to be less satisfied with their lives currently, to have a less positive balance between life satisfaction and life dissatisfaction, to be more risky in their use of tobacco and more likely to be at multiple drug risk. Since a large number of statistical tests have been carried out here, it is safer to rely only upon those that achieved a

Table 6.1 Adulthood adjustment variables: disharmonious *vs* harmonious backgrounds

Variable	Scale	Disharmonious ($N=141$–164)		Harmonious ($N=75$–80)		Significance of difference (*t or chi sq, as appropriate*)
		Mean	SD	Mean	SD	
Stability						
Longest employment	0 to 5	2.88	1.6	2.63	1.7	ns
Longest address	1 to 5	3.25	1.5	3.60	1.5	ns
Longest relationship	0 to 5	3.40	1.7	3.20	1.8	ns
Longest friendship	1 to 5	4.02	1.4	4.11	1.4	ns
Age left home[a]		37%		23%		*
Relationships and Friendships						
Number of children	0 to 3 +	0.70	1.0	0.46	0.7	ns
Marital status single (1)/ not single (2)		1.55	0.5	1.46	0.5	ns
Positives in current relationship	0 to 3	2.20	0.9	2.41	0.9	ns
Negatives in current relationship	0 to 3	1.51	1.0	1.36	1.0	ns
Ability to get close to others	0 to 4	2.08	1.0	2.46	0.9	**
Emotional support from close friends	0 to 5	3.18	1.3	3.24	1.5	ns
Employment						
SES improvement	−4 to +4	0.22	1.6	0.28	1.6	ns
Job satisfaction	0 to 3	1.86	0.9	1.81	0.8	ns
Job dissatisfaction	0 to 3	1.09	0.8	1.22	0.8	ns
Satisfaction with work scale score	0 to 40	12.36	5.1	13.26	5.6	ns

Table 6.1 *(continued)*

Variable	Scale	Disharmonious (N=141–164)		Harmonious (N=75–80)		Significance of difference (t or chi sq, as appropriate)
		Mean	SD	Mean	SD	
Social activities						
Social Activity	0 to 4	3.11	1.2	3.44	1.0	*
Number of social activities	1 to 47	15.76	9.1	17.77	8.2	ns
Satisfaction with social life	−4 to +2	−0.71	1.7	−0.20	1.4	*
Self-esteem and personality						
Self-esteem 1[b]	10 to 40	22.78	4.7	20.97	4.4	**
Self-esteem 2[c]	0 to 48	8.01	5.5	6.61	3.8	*
Anxiety	0 to 12	7.04	3.4	5.51	3.2	***
Extraversion	0 to 12	7.54	3.4	8.51	3.1	*
Psychoticism	0 to 10	1.95	1.9	1.46	1.5	*
Lie Scale	0 to 12	3.96	2.6	3.78	2.6	ns
Adulthood problems						
Anxiety and depression	(standardised scores: mean=0; s.d.=1)	0.10	1.0	−0.20	0.9	*
Deviance and delinquency	(standardised scores: mean=0; s.d.=1)	0.11	1.1	−0.22	0.8	**
Life events						
Total life events	0 to 88	4.90	3.4	4.49	2.9	ns
Life satisfaction						
Life satisfaction	0 to 5	2.65	1.3	3.09	1.2	*
Life dis-satisfaction	0 to 5	2.01	1.2	1.65	1.2	ns
Satisfaction/ dissatisfaction balance	−5 to +5	0.74	2.2	1.48	2.1	*
Substance use						
Risky or problem drinking	0/1	0.20	0.4	0.16	0.4	ns

Table 6.1 *(continued)*

Variable	Scale	Disharmonious (N=141–164)		Harmonious (N=75–80)		Significance of difference (t or chi sq, as appropriate)
		Mean	SD	Mean	SD	
Risky or problem drug traking	0/1	0.12	0.3	0.06	0.2	ns
Risky or problem us of prescribed drugs	0/1	0.23	0.4	0.26	0.4	ns
Risky use of cannabis	0/1	0.10	0.3	0.08	0.3	ns
Risky use of tobacco	0/1	0.20	0.4	0.03	0.2	***
Risky use of home medicines	0/1	0.07	0.3	0.06	0.2	ns
Multiple risky or problem drug use	0 to 5	0.91	1.0	0.65	0.9	ns
	0/1 vs 2+ᵈ	0.27	0.4	0.13	0.3	**

* = $p<0.05$; ** = $p<0.01$; *** = $p<0.001$.
ᵃ % 'leaving home' at age 17 or younger.
ᵇ Rosenberg Self-Esteem scale. Higher scores indicate lower self-esteem.
ᶜ Ideal – Real self-discrepancy score. Higher scores indicate greater discrepancy.
ᵈ The 6-point multiple drug risk/problem scale reduced to a 0/1 binary: where 0 = none or 1 risk; and 1 = 2 or more risks.

level of significance beyond the $p=0.01$ level, of which there are six shown in Table 6.1.

It will be recalled (Chapter 5) that only eight of these variables showed significant differences between offspring and comparisons, and of these only three were significant beyond the 0.01 level: social activities, introversion, and multiple drug risk. The pattern of statistically significant results is also very different. Whereas a number of variables which differentiated between offspring and comparison respondents were in the area which we have called 'the basic context of people's lives'—leaving home, being in a partnership with someone, having children—most of the significant results which differentiated those with harmonious from those with disharmonious backgrounds were in the areas which we had predicted would be affected by the existence of parental problem drinking. Respondents from disharmonious backgrounds reported more psychological difficulties, more difficulties in developing close relationships with others, greater anxiety, lower self esteem, heavier smoking, and more risky drug use.

CHILDHOOD DIFFICULTIES AND INDIVIDUAL ADULTHOOD ADJUSTMENT VARIABLES

A degree of continuity between childhood and adulthood adjustment was revealed by finding a number of significant relationships between reported childhood difficulties (the index combining friendship problems, divided home/peer relationships, and a number of common psychological problems of childhood) and a number of the same adulthood adjustment areas discussed in the previous section. Those who reported having had more childhood difficulties were more likely in adulthood to express less satisfaction and more dissatisfaction with their lives, and to report lower self-esteem, lower ability to form close relationships, fewer social activities and more dissatisfaction with their social lives, more anxiety and 'psychoticism', more psychological problems in adulthood, both of the anxiety and depression type and the delinquency and deviance type, and current risk or past problems with alcohol, illicit drugs and tobacco. Respondents with childhood difficulties had also left home earlier and had more children. All these differences outlined above were statistically significant, correlations ranging from 0.16 ($p<0.05$) in the case of alcohol risk or problems, and fewer social activities, to 0.36 ($p<0.0005$) for anxiety and depression problems.

FAMILY DISHARMONY, CHILDHOOD DIFFICULTIES, AND ADULTHOOD ADJUSTMENT FACTORS

Table 6.2 shows the correlations between the four overall adult adjustment factors and both family disharmony and childhood difficulties.

Table 6.2 Correlations between adulthood adjustment factors and family disharmony and childhood difficulties

	Factor 1 Demoralisation vs positive mental health	Factor 2 Age related social stability vs instability	Factor 3 Excess, delinquency and sociability	Factor 4 Problems in transition to adulthood
Disharmony/ Harmony	0.32 ***	0.04 ns	−0.03 ns	0.35 ***
Childhood Difficulties	0.39 ***	−0.01 ns	0.12 ns	0.27 ***

***=$p<0.001$.

One can see from this table that there are significant associations between two of the adult adjustment factors (factors 1 and 4) and both respondents' reports of disharmony or harmony in the family home, and the kinds of childhood difficulties which they reported having experienced. Hence the first factor—'positive mental health versus demoralisation' which seems to be the most important factor in that it accounts for the greatest proportion of the variation over all of the adulthood variables—is significantly related to family disharmony in a way that it was not with having a parent with a drinking problem (Chapter 5). Those respondents who reported family and parental relationships which we designated as harmonious were significantly more likely to describe themselves as being positively mentally healthy in young adulthood. This first factor is also significantly related to reporting the existence of difficulties and problems during childhood—the more likely a respondent was to tell us about difficulties during childhood, the more likely he or she was to be demoralised as a young adult.

The fourth factor, which we have interpreted as relating to a problematic, impulsive, unplanned versus an unproblematic, careful and planned transition to adulthood and independence, was correlated with disharmony/harmony at a significant level. (Note that the magnitude of the correlation, 0.35, is only marginally greater than the size of the correlation between adulthood factor 4 and parental problem drinking, which was 0.30). Our interpretation here is that young adults who recalled growing up in homes where relatively large amounts of parental and family upheaval was present, were more likely to then go on to show a relatively impulsive and unplanned transition from childhood and from the parental home, into adulthood and independence; and conversely, in more harmonious households, this transition was more careful and rather better planned. Similarly, there is a correlation between reporting the existence of difficulties and problems during childhood and this fourth factor—the more likely a respondent was to tell us about difficulties during childhood, the more likely he or she was to experience a more impulsive and unplanned transition from childhood to young adulthood.

Introducing Path Analysis

A problem with the foregoing analysis is that the relationships between the various childhood indices—parental problem drinking, disharmony, childhood difficulties—are not taken into account in this type of piecemeal correlational analysis. As was outlined in Chapter 4, path analysis, although it can never provide the last word on the subject, is one method for taking interrelationships between predictor variables into account and for beginning to test more complex cause and effect models of development.

The hypothesised path model with which we started and which was tested against the data is shown in Figure 6.1. This hypothesises a causal link from parental problem drinking to parental and family disharmony/ harmony, a causal link from both these variables to childhood difficulties, and a causal link from all three of these variables to adulthood adjustment. This model also suggests causal links between the demographic and sampling variables of socio-economic status, age-group, sex, and sample source, and each of the other variables in the model.

How did this model fare when tested against the data relating to the adulthood factors? As explained in Chapter 4, the adequacy of an hypothesised model, such as the one shown in Figure 6.1, can be tested by examining how closely the sum of the main direct and indirect pathway effects from one variable to another match the correlation coefficients actually obtained. A first step here was to consider the relationship between parental problem drinking and family disharmony. Our preliminary model suggested that the former was more likely to be cause and the latter, effect. Alternative models proposing that disharmony led to parental problem drinking, or that these two variables were unrelated, were examined, but they did not match the actual correlation coefficients as well as the model outlined above.

Attention then turns to the question of whether the model shown in Figure 6.1 fits the results obtained for each of the four adulthood adjustment factors considered separately. The four factors will now be taken in turn, and revised path diagrams presented for the three factors of greatest interest, namely factors 1, 3 and 4.

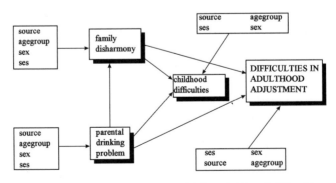

Figure 6.1   The path analysis model for adulthood difficulties.

Demoralisation *vs* Positive Mental Health

Figure 6.2 shows the path diagram for factor 1 (for greater ease of comprehension, only path coefficients of greater than ±0.1 have been shown in the diagrams). The diagram shows that both direct and indirect pathways exist between many of the variables; the most important of these pathways and how the sums of direct and indirect paths match up with the simple correlation coefficients are summarised in Table 6.3 that accompanies the path diagram (where all relevant coefficients are shown).

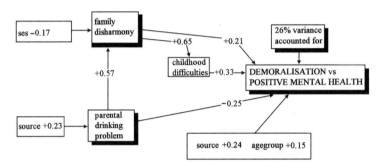

Figure 6.2 The pathways to demoralisation *vs* positive mental health.

Table 6.3 Demoralisation *vs* positive mental health: a summary of direct and indirect paths and simple correlations

| | *Path analysis* | | | *Simple correlations* | *Direction of effect demoralisation associated with:* |
	Direct path	*Indirect paths*	*Total effect*		
Childhood difficulties	+0.33	—	+0.33	+0.39	more problems
Family disharmony	+0.21	+0.21	+0.42	+0.32	disharmony
Parental problem drink	−0.25	+0.24	−0.01	+0.05	no total effect
Source	+0.24	+0.00	+0.24	+0.22	clinical
Agegroup	+0.15	+0.04	+0.19	+0.15	older
Sex	+0.04	+0.03	+0.07	+0.08	males
Ses	−0.00	−0.06	−0.06	−0.13	lower SES

A number of interesting findings emerge:

(a) as predicted, family disharmony is related both directly and indirectly (via childhood difficulties) to being at the demoralisation pole of this factor.

(b) The effects of parental problem drinking on this aspect of adulthood adjustment are only partly as predicted. The direct and indirect effects of parental drinking status appear to work in opposition to each other. If parental drinking problems led to family disharmony, and especially if this led to childhood difficulties in turn, then having a parent with a drinking problem increased the likelihood of being demoralised as an adult—an *indirect* effect. But if the drinking did not lead to disharmony, then there was almost no effect on childhood difficulties, and the *direct* effect of parental drinking status was opposite to that predicted (i.e. if there was no disharmony, having a parent with a drinking problem increased the likelihood of reporting positive mental health as an adult). Having a parent with a drinking problem increased the chances of being demoralised as an adult, *only if* there was family disharmony; otherwise having a parent with a drinking problem appeared, if anything, to strengthen adulthood mental health.

(c) There are some very weak indirect effects and two direct effects of the demographic and sampling variables: being in the clinical group, and to a lesser extent being older, meant that a respondent was more likely to be at the demoralised pole of this factor.

Age Related Social Stability

The second factor, which we have interpreted as measuring age-related social stability, is of less interest for our purposes, since age is the overriding influence. There are, in addition, small, direct effects of socioeconomic status and sex, with women and those of lower SES reporting longer relationships, periods of employment, friendships, continuous periods at one address, being married, and having more children.

Excess, Sociability and Deviance

The results relevant to adulthood factor 3 are shown in Figure 6.3 and Table 6.4. Again they show the hypothesised model to be confirmed in part only. Particularly noticable is the absence of any significant effects, direct or indirect, of having had a parent with a drinking problem.

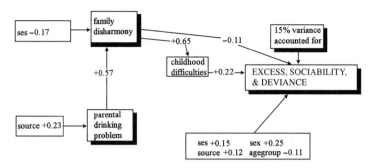

Figure 6.3   The pathways to excess, sociability and deviance.

Table 6.4   Excess, sociability and deviance: a summary of direct and indirect paths and simple correlations

| | Path analysis | | | Simple correlations | Direction of effect excess, etc. associated with: |
	Direct path	Indirect paths	Total effect		
Childhood difficulties	+0.22	—	+0.22	+0.12	more problems
Family disharmony	−0.11	+0.14	+0.03	+0.03	no effect
Parental problem drinking	−0.06	+0.02	−0.04	−0.03	no effect
Sex	+0.25	+0.02	+0.27	+0.28	males
Source	+0.12	—	+0.12	+0.12	clinical
Agegroup	−0.11	—	−0.11	−0.17	younger
Ses	+0.15	—	+0.15	+0.13	higher SES

The important pathways are those concerned with childhood difficulties, sex, and to a lesser extent socioeconomic status, age-group and from where the respondent was recruited for the study.

The main points of note are:

(a) the existence of childhood difficulties and being male both increase the likelihood of being at the more excessive end of this factor;

(b) being younger, of a higher socioeconomic status, and from a clinical source also all increase the likelihood of being at the more excessive pole;

(c) the direct and indirect effects of disharmony work in opposition to each other i.e., a disharmonious background would be more likely to lead directly to childhood difficulties, and thence to being at the excessive end of this factor, but a harmonious background would be more likely to lead directly to more excess, sociability and deviance. This finding highlights just how useful this type of analysis can be. The simple correlation alone implies that disharmony is unrelated to this factor; but the path analysis suggests that disharmony may actually be highly influential. The analysis suggests that if disharmony lead to childhood difficulties, then respondents were more likely to be at the excessive end of this factor, whereas if they managed to deal with the family disharmony in ways which did not lead to childhood difficulties, then they were slightly more likely to be at the opposite end of this factor—with less likelihood of risky or problematic use of alcohol or drugs, or delinquency or deviance;

(d) There are no significant direct or indirect effects of having had a parent with a drinking problem on this aspect of adjustment in young adulthood.

Problematic, Unplanned *vs* Unproblematic, Planned Transition to Adulthood and Independence

The results for the fourth adulthood factor are shown in Figure 6.4 and Table 6.5. Once again they show the hypothesised model to be confirmed in part only. The important pathways are those concerned with whether the respondent was offspring or comparison, with the existence of family disharmony, and with where the respondent was recruited, with smaller effects being shown for sex and socioeconomic status.

The most salient points are the following:

(a) having parents without drinking problems, having a harmonious background, being female, having a higher SES, and coming from an advertising source, all independently increased the likelihood of being at the more unproblematic, careful and planned transition to adulthood end of this factor;

(b) The one finding that is markedly different from the model and from the findings of the simple correlation analyses is the disappearance of childhood difficulties as an influential variable. The childhood difficulties variable is highly correlated with disharmony, and in this case appears to add nothing to disharmony in the prediction of an unplanned versus planned transition to adulthood.

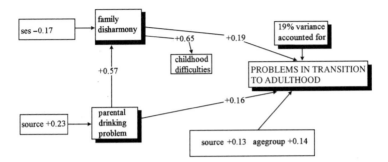

Figure 6.4 The pathways to problems in the transition to adulthood.

Table 6.5 Problems in the transition to adulthood: a summary of direct and indirect paths and simple correlations

	Path analysis			Simple correlations	Direction of effect transition problems associated with:
	Direct path	Indirect paths	Total effect		
Parental problem drink	+0.16	+0.13	+0.29	+0.30	offspring
Family disharmony	+0.19	+0.04	+0.23	+0.35	more disharmony
Childhood difficulties	+0.06	—	+0.06	+0.27	more difficulties
Source	+0.13	+0.07	+0.20	+0.22	clinical
Sex	+0.14	−0.01	+0.13	+0.12	males
Ses	−0.09	−0.02	−0.11	−0.13	lower SES
Age-group	+0.03	+0.04	+0.07	+0.03	older

THE INFLUENCE OF CHILDHOOD COPING (OFFSPRING ONLY)

As in Chapter 4, where we examined the influence of childhood coping on difficulties offspring experienced in childhood, partial correlation and multiple regression were again used to see if the ways participants reported coping with the experience of having a parent with a drinking problem added to the prediction of adulthood adjustment or served to mediate or moderate the relationship between childhood family disharmony and adulthood adjustment. Unlike other analyses reported in this chapter, this analysis of the influence of coping involves the offspring group only.

Demoralisation *vs* Positive Mental Health

The main finding here was the additional, independent influence of the fourth childhood coping factor—detachment—on demoralisation, an effect that was significant for both men and women (both $p<0.05$). It may be recalled that it was this same coping factor that provided significant correlations, for daughters, with childhood emotional symptoms, home-peer division in adolescence, and general childhood difficulties (see Chapter 4).

There was no evidence that coping mediated the disharmony–demoralisation relationship since correlations between family disharmony

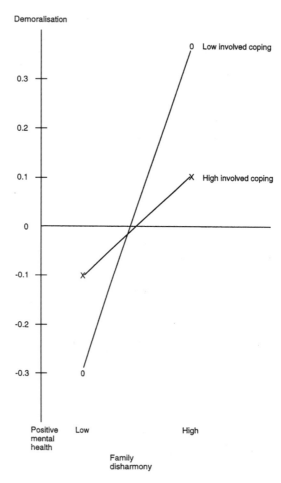

Figure 6.5 The relationship between 'involved coping', family disharmony, and demoralisation *vs* positive mental health, for women.

and demoralisation were scarcely at all reduced in size by partialling out, in turn, the effects of each of the four childhood coping factors. There was, however, evidence of one possible type of moderating effect, shown in Figure 6.5. This concerned coping factor 3—involvement—which, for women only, produced both a significant main effect ($p<0.05$) and a sig- -nificant coping x disharmony interaction effect. As Figure 6.5 shows, it was those women who reported higher family-of-origin disharmony and lower 'involvement' coping who were most demoralised as young adults. For those who recalled experiencing relatively harmonious homes as children, however, lower recalled 'involvement' in coping with the parent's drinking was associated with *better* mental health as a young adult.

Problematic, Unplanned *vs* Unproblematic, Planned Transition to Adulthood

Again, in the case of that aspect of adulthood adjustment that we believe centers on the nature of the transition to adulthood, the fourth childhood coping factor—detachment—provides an additional, independent source of prediction for men and women (both $p<0.05$). Once again there is no evidence of coping playing a mediating role, but there is one piece of evidence, for women only, that it might moderate the effect of childhood family disharmony. In this case the coping factor producing this result is factor 1—fearfulness and self-protection—and as Figure 6.6 shows it is those women reporting greater family disharmony as children and higher fearfulness and self-protection who experienced the more difficult transitions to adulthood. For those recalling relative family harmony, however, higher fearfulness and self-protection was associated with an *easier* transition to adulthood.

ADDING IN CONTEMPORANEOUS ADULTHOOD INFLUENCES

As outlined in Chapter 2, in recent years models of human development being considered in the research literature have become increasingly complex, viewing the adult not as a simple product of childhood influences, but rather as the present state of an individual life at a point on a complex pathway that includes relatively distant influences, such as those of the family of origin, and more proximate influences from recent adulthood.

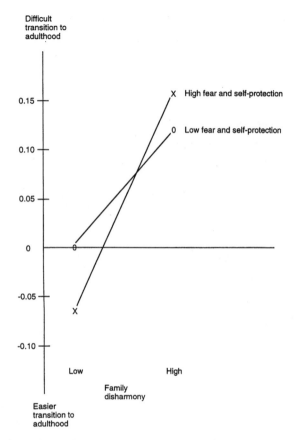

Figure 6.6 The relationship between 'fearfulness and self-protection coping', family disharmony, and difficult *vs* easier transition to adulthood, for women.

Hence we now present the results of path analyses that include, in addition to the childhood and sociodemographic and source variables that we have been considering in this chapter so far, the four adulthood circumstances variables and four adulthood satisfaction variables shown in Table 6.6 (a further slight variation on the analyses described above is that childhood difficulties is replaced by childhood problems, and these have been assigned to a level in the model consequent to family harmony and parenting drinking, and antecedent to adulthood variables).

Results here are confined to consideration of adulthood adjustment factors 1 and 4, the two factors influenced in some way by parental problem drinking. Results are now presented separately for women and men.

Table 6.6   Levels of an expanded path model, adding in contemporaneous adulthood variables

LEVEL 1—Sociodemographic and Source
Clinical *vs* Advertising
Age
SES
LEVEL 2—Childhood Influences
Family Disharmony
Parental Problem Drinking
LEVEL 3—Childhood Problems
Emotional
Conduct
LEVEL 4—Adulthood Circumstances
Married
In Work
Number of Social Activities
Total Life Events
LEVEL 5—Adulthood Satisfaction
Marital Quality
Friends' Support
Satisfaction with Social Life
Satisfaction with Work or other activity

Demoralisation *vs* Positive Mental Health

Results, for women and men respectively, for adulthood factor 1—demoralisation versus positive mental health—are shown in Figures 6.7 and 6.8.

For women (Figure 6.7) the results suggest an actual causal model in which current satisfaction with social life and satisfaction with marriage (being in a marriage with which a woman was dissatisfied being worse for mental health than having no marriage at all—Orford and Velleman, 1995), but particularly the former, play important roles in adult mental health, but with childhood problems (especially emotional problems) and childhood family disharmony continuing to exert important influence. The influence of childhood emotional problems is partly direct and partly indirect via its effect upon adulthood social and marital satisfaction. Parental problem drinking appears to have an overall positive rather than negative influence upon women's adulthood mental health.

For men, social and marital satisfaction are also important (as for women, an unsatisfactory marriage was worse than being unmarried) but

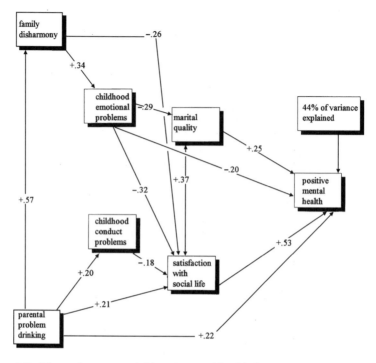

Figure 6.7 The pathways to adulthood mental health for women. Reproduced with permission from Orford and Velleman, 1995.

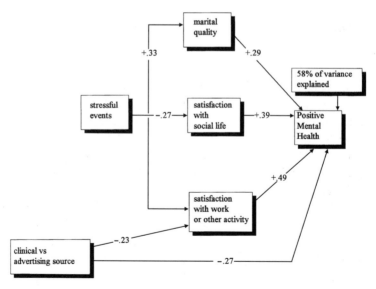

Figure 6.8 The pathways to adulthood mental health for men. Reproduced with permission from Orford and Velleman, 1995.

satisfaction with work or other activity is even more so (closer analysis showed that having no paid job was worse for mental health than having a job with which a person was dissatisfied—Orford and Velleman, 1995). Recent stress exerts a modest negative influence via reduced social satisfaction. Recruitment from agencies rather than by advertising is linked relatively strongly with demoralisation, part of this effect being indirect via lower satisfaction with work or other activity. What is of most interest to us for present purposes is the finding that, for men unlike women, no overall influence of childhood family disharmony nor of childhood problems remains.

Problematic, Unplanned *vs* Unproblematic, Planned Transition to Adulthood

When results were analysed separately for men and women, it turned out that the variables included in the present analysis produced a significant multiple correlation with a relatively problematic versus easy transition to adulthood for women, but not for men. Hence it was not possible to say that there were any significant direct effects of measured variables for men, and a path diagram could not be constructed with any confidence. For women, on the other hand, some of the same variables that figured in the causal path diagram for adulthood demoralisation versus positive mental health turned out to be important again for difficult versus easy transition. Notable amongst these were satisfaction with social life as a young adult (direct effect of −0.19) and childhood emotional problems, which had both a direct effect and an indirect effect via satisfaction with social life (total effect +0.24). Parental problem drinking had no significant direct effect. It appeared that its influence on the process of transition to adulthood was likely to be indirect, via such variables as childhood problems and an relatively unsatisfactory social life.

SOME INDIVIDUAL PEOPLE'S LIVES IN MORE DETAIL

The research interviews produced a great deal of qualitative data in the form of interviewer notes and tape-recordings. These data from a sample of 24 interviews with offspring of parents with drinking problems have been examined in detail for clues to understanding different forms of transition to young adulthood for people who have experienced this kind of adversity in childhood. Such qualitative analysis may complement the statistical approach and provide valuable additional insights into the processes of interest (Stiles, 1993; McKeganey, 1995).

The focus of this kind of analysis is upon the individual 'case'. We have found it convenient to depict the results from a single participant in the form of a 'path diagram' similar in form to those resulting from the statistical analysis of the whole offspring and comparison sample. In this case, however, each diagram represents just one person's account of his or her life, and the entries are personal to that one individual. Three illustrative personal path diagrams are shown in Figures 6.9, 6.10 and 6.11.

Each entry in the path diagram represents a theme or topic which was described at some length by the respondent and which seemed of importance

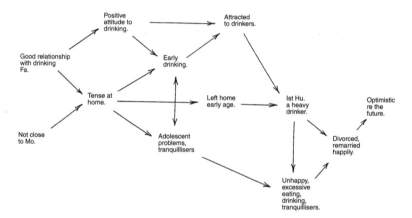

Figure 6.9   Illustrative personal path diagram: 1.

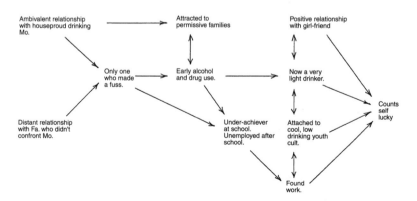

Figure 6.10   Illustrative personal path diagram: 2.

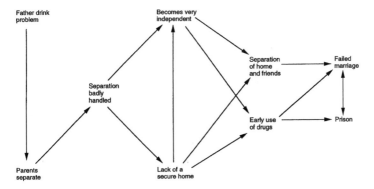

Figure 6.11 Illustrative personal path diagram: 3.

to him or her. The arrows represent hypothesised causal links between the elements. Occasionally these were explicitly stated by the person being interviewed. For example, the interviewee depicted in Figure 6.9 drew a link herself between her father's drinking, the way this had made her look at drinking too lightly, the fact that she herself had started drinking too young, and her feeling that she would be put off by a man if he didn't drink at all, perhaps because it would make her feel guilty about her own drinking. However, most of the links shown in these diagrams represent hypotheses made by ourselves in the course of analysis.

A number of themes and links recurred in the individual path diagrams, and these may be summarised as follows:

1. Even after considerable simplification, most of the diagrams are quite *complex* and no two are identical. Perhaps it would be surprising if it were otherwise, but this way of analysing data certainly brings home the point that individual lives are *unique* and that there is unlikely to be any simple solution to the problem of the environmental mechanisms of intergenerational transmission.

2. Many offspring interviewees described, not necessarily explicitly, ways of *escaping* their home situations. There were many references to staying with aunts and uncles, grandparents, friends or neighbours, or simply to staying out of the house as much as possible. There were examples of the non-problem drinking parent sending the child to boarding school or to a live-away job in order to remove him or her from stressful home circumstances. And there were numerous examples of offspring leaving home at a comparatively early age and, in the case of young women in particular, marrying very young.

3. Although these 'escape attempts' were often beneficial, they often appear to have been costly. There are many examples of offspring leading *unsettled* or unstable early adult lives, often associated with drug or heavy alcohol use, or with an early and unhappy marriage.
4. Although many offspring had experienced problems, sometimes quite severe ones, as young adults, most had achieved some measure of stability by the time they were interviewed. There was usually some *stabilising factor(s)* to which this might be attributed. Very frequently this was a marriage or partnership. Indeed individuals often attributed their stability explicitly to the influence of a partner who was stable, calm or supportive. Other such stabilising factors included educational success, job, and philosophy or religion.

SUMMARY OF THE FINDINGS REPORTED IN THIS CHAPTER

'Demoralisation versus positive mental health' emerged as the most important factor underlying the various indices of adulthood adjustment that were employed in the present study. This itself is both reassuring and confirmatory, in that such a factor has been found in much other current research despite differences in the precise measures used (e.g. Link and Dohrenwend, 1980).

The most important finding from the present chapter is that those respondents who recollected a disharmonious family background, and who recollected problems and difficulties experienced as a child, were considerably more likely to be demoralised as adults; and having a parental drinking problem was actually moderately related to *lower* demoralisation in the absence of family disharmony. These results show that disharmony within the family of origin is a far more useful explanatory variable for this principal mental health factor than is the fact of having had a parent with a drinking problem itself. These results emphasise and further extend the findings reported in Chapter 4 which demonstrated the importance of disharmony within the family of origin as an influential explanatory variable, showing how disharmony was more strongly associated with *childhood* difficulties than was parental drinking problems.

It is important to note that offspring respondents who did not report family of origin disharmony, were *less* likely to be at the negative pole of the demoralisation factor than were comparison respondents as a whole. One possible interpretation of this is that respondents may actually have been strengthened, or protected from becoming demoralised, by having a problem drinking parent.

Such an interpretation runs directly counter to the Adult Children of Alcoholics (ACOA) literature: "Children who are raised in this (alcoholic family) system learn, at a very early age, that they are worthless and that as individuals they are no good. To say that most ACOAs have a poor self image is an understatement; at every front the alcoholic family batters its children with negative thinking. The negative thinking becomes so ingrained in ACOAs that it becomes unconscious. This unconscious programming stays with these children all of their lives." (Kritsberg, 1988, p. 141). Our findings provide further evidence to substantiate the idea that the risks to adult offspring have been 'over-predicted'. Clearly some offspring will be damaged by their experiences, and our research reinforces the idea that, if family disharmony existed, and if in turn this led to childhood difficulties, then parental problem drinking would be associated with a poor adulthood adjustment. But it is possible that the over-prediction of risk to all offspring has been suggested on the basis of examining only clinical cases who would be, by definition, those with a negative outcome.

The main negative effect of offspring status which was not solely influenced or mediated by family-of-origin disharmony was the relatively high scoring position of offspring on the factor which we interpreted as indicating impulsive or unplanned transition to adulthood and independence (Factor 4). Both offspring status and family-of-origin disharmony were independently important in explaining factor 4.

Neither of the main childhood variables (disharmony or parental problem drinking) helped to explain sociability and excess (Factor 3) very well, even though risky adult alcohol and drug use both loaded on this factor. This was linked to being male, and to reporting having had childhood difficulties, and, less strongly, to coming from a clinical source (which included prisons), being younger, and being of a higher socio-economic status. These findings indicate that the routes to being at the positive pole of this factor (high on excess, sociability and deviance) are likely to be multiple, via childhood difficulties, via difficulties in later life, or via an 'affluent, youth rebellion'. The group of high scorers on this factor may including some young people who will 'mature out' without experiencing long-term difficulties. What is clear from the present findings, however, is that having had a parent with a drinking problem does not have much of a bearing on this aspect of young adulthood life.

The detailed case studies, as well as those statistical analyses that included contemporaneous variables to do with current life circumstances and satisfactions, provide a fuller picture of how the lives of the research participants unfolded and how it was that many made satisfactory life adjustments despite early adversity. In particular these analyses draw attention to the opportunities that people have for benefiting from positive stabilising factors in their young adult lives, especially satisfactory marriages, satisfying jobs, and good social lives. They also alert us to the risks that children of problem drinking parents run when they are motivated strongly by the wish to escape from the influence of a home dominated by a serious parental problem of this kind.

These results also suggest how the effects of childhood can, for some offspring, live on as a result of the indirect influence of the parental problem, and how the chains of events involved may differ for the two sexes. For example it appears from the present results that some daughters of problem drinking parents, who as a result experience emotional problems as children, may have relatively poor mental health as young adults both because these problems sometimes endure, but also because they are at greater risk of having poorer social lives and less satisfactory marriages than some other women of their age group. Some sons of problem drinking parents, on the other hand, who have experienced conduct problems as children, may as a result be at more than average risk of deviancy as young men. There is also some support in the present findings for the belief that how children cope with having a problem drinking parent in childhood may affect not only their own adjustment as children but also their health and well-being in the longer term. Detachment and internalisation as a form of coping in childhood was correlated with poorer adulthood mental health for both men and women, and for women from relatively disharmonious homes there was a suggestion that low involvement coping and high fearfulness and self-protection might put them at particularly high risk.

CHAPTER 7

HOW HAS OUR UNDERSTANDING ADVANCED? SUMMARY AND INTEGRATION

In the early chapters of this book, and especially in Chapter 2, we described the previous state of research about children of problem drinkers. In this chapter the results of our own research will be placed alongside the results of that conducted by others. The extent to which the present findings complement, or alternatively contradict, these other data will be examined and we shall draw some conclusions about the present state of knowledge in this field.

THE SAMPLES OF OFFSPRING AND COMPARISON YOUNG ADULTS RECRUITED FOR THE PRESENT RESEARCH

On the whole, the methods of recruitment used in the present research can be judged successful. Once helpful sources of participants were identified, it required only time (about two and a half years) and patience to recruit a good sized sample of both young men and women, spread across the age group 16–35 years as intended, and recruited from a variety of different sources. It was reassuring to find that neither age, nor sex, nor recruitment source—whether health, social, penal, or self-help agency on the one hand, or public advertising on the other—was significantly associated with any of the quantified variables concerning parental drinking history which were examined in Chapter 4.

Nevertheless, it should be noted that public advertising was somewhat more productive than agency sources; that there was a tendency for older members of the sample to have been recruited from advertising, and the younger members from other sources; and that advertising sources produced an excess of participants from higher social status families who were then probably somewhat over-represented compared with the general population.

Of particular interest is the fact that the majority of those respondents who reported that their mothers, but not their fathers, had had a drinking problem came via public advertising. Indeed, had we confined the sample to those recruited from agencies, only 10% would have fallen in this category (with a further 16% reporting both parents having drinking problems). There was an even more marked absence of 'mothers only' with drinking problems in the lower of our three family-of-origin social status groups. It is difficult to know to what factors to attribute these findings. Individuals in organisations and agencies who identified potential recruits for us may have more readily identified clients or contacts of theirs whom they knew to have fathers with drinking problems, and may have less readily identified those with mothers with drinking problems. The social status finding, on the other hand, may represent a real tendency for maternal drinking problems (unaccompanied by paternal drinking problems) to have been less common amongst families of lower social status in the previous generation.

Unlike participant's age and sex, lower family social status was related to a number of variables of interest, and most obviously to an earlier reported age of onset of parental problem drinking. It is unlikely that this effect can simply be attributed to early onset parental problems being associated with a decline in parental occupational status, since our index of family social status incorporated a number of different factors; and when age of onset was examined in relation to father's educational level alone, the effect remained. A more likely explanation is that participants from lower social status groups were less well shielded from the drinking problems, and from other related problems, due to reduced levels of privacy.

As well as more often being thought to have started later, parental problems were more often resolved before the offspring reached age 21 in the highest status group. Despite these differences in exposure, there was no relationship between family social status and our scale of the effects of parental drinking in the home, and the relationship with the index of the immediate impact upon the child (the NCE, or negative childhood experiences scale) was in fact positive, with participants from the higher social status families obtaining the slightly higher scores. This may be partly attributable to the higher proportion of maternal drinking problems in the higher status group, and additionally to the fact that higher status problem drinking parents (fathers as well as mothers) were reported to drink more regularly at home and less regularly in licenced premises.

A crucial question is whether the sample of offspring recruited was representative of young adult children of problem drinking parents. If the results obtained from this sample are to be used to draw general conclusions about the offspring of parents with drinking problems, then it is important to be clear about any ways in which the sample might not be representative of the total population of these offspring. The problem, of course, lies in the fact that we have very little way of knowing what this hypothetical 'population' might look like. By recruiting widely from a range of sources, avoiding recruiting participants who were identified on account of their own alcohol problems, but attempting to achieve a mix of those in touch with agencies because of mental health problems or offending as well as those identified by means that were quite independent of agencies, we believe the objective of building up a broadly based 'representative enough' sample was achieved. Certainly we know of no other way of achieving this aim. Any one recruitment source, used alone, would undoubtedly have led to a very biased sample. This is the case, for example, when samples are drawn exclusively from a clincial source, as has so often been the case in previous research. As discussed in Chapter 3, tracing all the offspring of a sample of treated problem drinkers would pose a number of insuperable problems and in any event would not result in a representative sample since treated problem drinkers are themselves unrepresentative of problem drinkers generally. A strategy relying totally upon a survey of the general population has attractions but in practice would be very time-consuming and costly, nor would it be free of bias since not all children of problem drinking parents would be willing to reveal the fact or take part in research.

We must also ask about the suitability of the comparison group. If this group was recruited in such a way that its members were unduly well—or badly—adjusted in some way then spurious conclusions might be drawn by comparing offspring with them. The attempt to recruit the comparison group from sources similar to those from which children of problem drinking parents were recruited was on the whole successful although the match was not perfect. In fact a lower proportion of comparison participants came via agency sources (22% *vs* 45%) which might have biased the results towards finding greater maladjustment in the offspring group. This strengthens our conclusion that overall, and with certain exceptions, the children of problem drinking parents studied here were, as young adults, as well adjusted as their peers. Had more comparisons than offspring been recruited via agency sources, rather than the other way round, we would be less confident in that conclusion since it could have been argued that offspring had been compared with an unusually and unfairly maladjusted group.

Nevertheless it has to be acknowledged that all participants in the present research were volunteers, selected and self-selected in complex and uncertain ways, as is usually the case in social science and health research. A number of more subtle but equally important selection biases might have occurred and these will be discussed later in the chapter when attempting to make sense of the findings in the context of the literature as a whole.

THE RANGE OF EXPERIENCES TO WHICH CHILDREN OF PROBLEM DRINKING PARENTS ARE EXPOSED

The present study has replicated the findings of a wealth of research on the childhood experiences of the offspring of problem drinking parents, much of which was reviewed in Chapter 2 (e.g. Bennett *et al.*, 1988; Cork, 1969; Moos *et al.*, 1990; Roosa *et al.*, 1988; Wilson and Orford, 1978). Many of the children of problem drinking parents who were interviewed by our research team were exposed to distressing and potentially harmful experiences, including parental arguing, quarrelling and fighting; violence; a negative family atmosphere; a reduction in the cohesion of family life; financial hardship; a low level of enjoyable joint family activity; and poor relationships with one or both parents.

A number of matters deserve closer mention. First it should be emphasised that it was factors to do with the quality of family life that so consistently distinguished the recollections of the two groups, and not the stability or breakdown of families. The proportions of children experiencing parental divorce or separation in the two groups were not significantly different although the proportion was somewhat higher in the offspring group. What characterised most of the offspring group in the present study was a parental problem that had persisted throughout most of the participant's childhood years, as often as not untreated as far as the child was aware, and often unacknowledged openly ('couldn't be sure'; 'never admitted'; 'got used to it'; 'thought it was normal') despite the family disruption or spoiling of family life with which it was often associated.

The presence of violence in the childhood family was something that was focussed upon in detail in the present research. The results confirmed the very significantly raised incidence of violence in the families with a problem drinking parent that has been found by others (e.g. Black *et al.*, 1986; Jones and Houts, 1992). The present results went further in demonstrating that it is violence *between* parents, but known about by the children, which is most frequently reported and which most markedly distinguishes the families of children of problem drinking parents from others. Furthermore the present results provide estimates of the proportions of such children who are likely to have been exposed to violence that was severe in kind, regular, or occurring over a prolonged period during childhood. (See Table 4.5 for details.)

One of the questions that has long given rise to speculation but which previous research has failed to clarify is whether it is worse to have a mother or a father with a drinking problem. Our results suggest that the answer is complex. Mothers' excessive drinking was found to be accompanied by a similar level of disruptive and disturbed parental behaviour as was that of fathers, but children of mothers with drinking problems were more likely to experience negative feelings of instability, worry, being caught in the middle of arguments between parents, and having to act as if older than their actual ages. On the other hand, as might be predicted from studies of the natural history of women's and men's drinking problems (e.g. Orford and Keddie, 1985), mothers' drinking problems were recalled as starting later on·in the participants' childhoods. What is more, children's individual relationships with their problem drinking parents tended to be better preserved when those parents were mothers than when they were fathers.

Much less frequently reported, and certainly much less frequently commented upon, in other research, however, is the high degree of variability in their childhood experiences reported by our research participants. It is certainly the case that some of the young adults interviewed for the present research were able to tell us in detail of a wide range of negative experiences which were related to parental problem drinking, amounting in some cases to the kind of 'regime of terror' described by John (see Chapter 1). Yet others, while very well aware that a parent had a serious drinking problem, reported that disruption and negative consequences were kept to a minimum. Effects upon adolescent frienships varied greatly: some avoided having friends round to their homes whilst others, like Mary (see Chapter 1), continued to invite friends home in a normal way. Another source of variation, amongst many that could be cited, is the extent to which either parent appeared to the child to be suffering from depression or some other mental health problem. It was not at all uncommon to hear that the problem drinking parent had been depressed and sometimes suicidal, and the same was true for the non-problem-drinking parents, especially mothers. These additional mental health problems, whether attributable to the excessive drinking or pre-existing, are considered by many to be of the utmost importance in conferring vulnerability upon the offspring (e.g. Merikanges *et al.*, 1994; Moos *et al.*, 1990; Sher, 1991).

This point about the great variation to be found in the experiences of children of problem drinking parents is a particularly important one. Many writers in this area (such as Black, 1979) suggest that all 'children of alcoholics' will be affected in similarly negative ways. This implies that all these children will experience the problem drinking of their parents in similar ways, or that the problem will make the parents act and react in essentially similar ways. The results presented in the research reported in this book, however, show that there is a huge variety of ways in which a parental drinking problem may be revealed in the family.

PARENTAL DRINKING PROBLEMS: EARLY EFFECTS ON CHILDREN AND ADOLESCENTS

Once again the results stemming from the present research fit well with the relatively clear cut conclusions reached by those who have reviewed the research into the association between parental alcohol problems and disturbance in their offspring whilst the latter are still children or adolescents (e.g. West and Prinz, 1987; Orford, 1990) and with other research reports on this topic that are continuing to appear (e.g. Barrerra *et al.*, 1993; Chandy *et al.*, 1993, 1995; Chassin *et al.*, 1993, 1996; Lynskey *et al.*, 1994; Reich *et al.*, 1993; Vitaro *et al.*, 1996). Our participants in the offspring group were much more likely than those in the comparison group to report that they had problems or difficulties during their childhoods, being more likely to: develop one or other of a range of psychological or social problems in childhood, have psychoactive medication prescribed for them, report difficulties with friendships, maintain a division between their home lives and their peer relationships, become involved in heavier drinking, and leave home early.

As Chapter 2 demonstrated, previous research has consistently shown that the children of problem drinkers have problems in three areas: anti-social behaviour or 'conduct disorder', school and learning difficulties, and emotional problems. Similar findings were produced in the present study. Offspring participants were significantly more likely to report having had childhood symptoms related to 'anti-social behaviour', and the same was true for symptoms falling in the 'withdrawn, demoralised, and having problems at school' cluster which included emotional problems as well as educational difficulties such as concentration difficulties at school, and inability to do homework at home. Emotional detachment was the symptom that most significantly distinguished the children of problem drinking parents from their comparison peers. A telling indicator of the vulnerability of offspring to psychological problems as children was the high numbers who were prescribed psychoactive medication at age 17 or younger.

In addition the present study has produced some results, that both confirm and go beyond previous findings, regarding the links that adolescent offspring make with the outside world in preparation for making the transition to adulthood. Findings relating to greater friendship difficulties,

a greater division between home lives and peer relationships, a higher frequency of involvement in drinking alcohol or taking prescribed or illicit
drugs at a young age (although this involved a minority of offspring and the
proportions in the two groups were not always statistically different), and a
higher probability of leaving home early, all reveal a higher level of adolescent difficulties amongst the children of problem drinking parents. It is
important to point out that the latter did not report being especially socially
isolated. The picture that emerged was rather one in which adolescents had
experienced difficulties in simultaneously relating well to family and
friends—for example, being shown up by a parent in front of friends was
one of the clearest indications of 'friendship difficulties' that distinguished
the two groups—and had chosen to insulate the world of friendships from
their difficult home circumstances.

One of the areas which has been less highlighted in previous research
is that of coping. The participants in the current study reported coping in a
wide variety of ways with the often disruptive upbringing that they experienced. It will be recalled from Chapter 1 that Mary had, in retrospect,
'coped' well by taking a lot of responsibility in the home, whilst John had
coped by distancing himself deliberately from what was going on in the
family, and Annie felt she had not coped very well at all. The most frequently used individual ways of coping were 'avoidance' and 'discord',
and we identified four clusters of ways of coping. This is a notoriously difficult area of research (Sher, 1991) but there is some intriguing overlap
between the concept of coping adopted here and the idea of 'defensive
roles' persued by Black (1979), and others, and reviewed in Chapter 2.
The 'acting out' role is the one most clearly confirmed by research so far
(e.g. Rhodes and Blackham, 1987), and it would appear to correspond with
the 'confrontation and self-destructive action' coping factor which we
found in the present data. This factor was one that appeared to have validity as a construct since it correlated, not only with the degree of family disharmony, but also with anti-social symptoms (sons only) and friendship
problems (sons and daughters). Others were relatively detached, self-blam-
ing, and inclined to seek outside help, and this coping factor correlated
with the withdrawn, demoralised and school problems cluster of symptoms
(daughters only) and with home-peer division after the age of 11 (daughters
only). Other roles suggested by Black and others—such as adjuster, placator, responsible child, hero, clown—have not yet been clearly supported by
research. The present findings suggest that ways of coping, as recalled later
from the vantage point of young adulthood, may be less clear cut than this.
Some of the children of problem drinking parents interviewed in the

present study described acting in a more 'fearful and self-protective' way. Others were more involved in trying to control the parent's drinking.

A conclusion that we came to in Chapter 2 was that previous research had neglected possible moderating and mediating variables and had, as a consequence, given the impression that parental drinking problems were linked to childhood maladjustment in a simple causative fashion. In particular the question had been raised whether much of the ill-effects of parental excessive drinking on children might not be due to the extent of family disruption or disorganisation, rather than to the parental drinking itself, even if the latter might be responsible for much of the family disruption (El-Guebaly and Offord, 1977; Wilson, 1982). This mediating hypothesis is one to which attention was given in the present research. Although others have found a significantly higher rate of family separation in the childhood experiences of children of parents with 'alcohol abuse' (e.g. Bergman and Wingby, 1993; El-Guebaly *et al.*, 1990; Kendler *et al.*, 1996), separation could not account for the parental drinking-child maladjustment link in the present data since separation had not occurred significantly more often for the offspring group. Family discord, or the quality of family life, as recalled by the young adult, was a different matter however. The 'path analysis' we used to help interpret the pattern of results obtained suggested that it was family and parental disharmony, and not parental problem drinking *per se*, that had the direct causal link with childhood difficulties. The effects of the parental problem drinking were indirect via its very substantial effects upon family disharmony. It is important to emphasise, however, that the effects of parental drinking upon family life were powerful and that the path analysis showed that the results were consistent with the view that drinking problems caused family disharmony rather than the other way around.

PARENTAL DRINKING PROBLEMS: EFFECTS ON OFFSPRING AS ADULTS

Whilst also stressing the variability to be found, the above discussion has underlined the contrast between the average picture of a discordant childhood home recalled by young adults who had a parent with a drinking problem and the homes of those without excessively drinking parents with whom they were compared. Although we have highlighted some areas not previously focussed upon—such as the division between home and friendships—this picture largely confirms the consensus of reports from previous research on the offspring of problem drinkers while they are still children. Our principal interest, however, was in the lives of the offspring of problem drinking parents as young adults. Hence the most important of the results of this current study are probably those reporting adulthood outcomes.

Substance Use: As the review in Chapter 2 showed, whether or not offspring report higher levels of excessive or problematic drinking as adults seems, from previous research, to be highly related to the source of the sample. We concluded from that review that: adults already identified as having alcohol problems were very likely to report retrospectively having had problem-drinking parents; and similarly that problem children with alcohol-misusing parents were more likely to develop alcohol misuse as adults. Yet adults with alcohol-misusing parents recruited from community samples, although they were likely to report problematic childhoods, did not seem to report very different drinking outcomes than did comparison respondents.

Although, in the main, drinking outcomes for these community samples were similar to comparison drinking rates, a pattern was beginning to emerge made up of two main components: first, an absence of substantial differences on measures of alcohol *consumption* between those with and without parents with alcohol problems; and second, a greater likelihood of reporting alcohol-related *problems* in offspring groups, both on self-report measures, and when these problems are assessed by others.

Although we utilised a wide variety of sources for our participants, it is clear that the study reported here falls into the 'community sample' section. Findings from the present study are substantially similar to those emerging from the recent literature, suggesting that the risk of inter-generational transmission of drinking problems may have been over-estimated previously as a consequence of relying too heavily upon clinical samples studied retrospectively (Sher, 1991). There was very little difference between the two groups—offspring and comparison—on measures of consumption. There were similar proportions in both groups who had ever drunk alcohol, and who were still drinking; identical proportions of the two groups were drinking heavily at the time of the first interview, and although slightly more offspring were drinking heavily a year later, these differences were not statistically significant. Almost identical proportions of the two groups reported drinking virtually every day.

It was when problematic drinking was examined that some differences emerged. As was reported in Chapter 5, a scale of 'risky' alcohol use was constructed by combining information about quantity, frequency, heavy occasional drinking, and health or social alcohol-related problems. There was a difference between the two groups on this scale in the expected direction (17.1% *vs* 11.3% of offspring and comparisons, respectively, being categorised as current risky drinkers—a ratio of approximately 1.5 to 1). There were also more offspring participants who reported having had problems with their alcohol use in the past, and when these two groups are combined—current risky or past problematic drinking—then almost twice as many offspring as opposed to comparison participants fell into this group (22.4% *vs* 12.5%).

These differences are modest and undramatic, and also statistically non-significant. Arguably, however, differences of this magnitude, if reliable as an estimate of the increased risk of adulthood problematic drinking faced by the offspring of problem drinking parents, are of considerable significance in the lives of those concerned and in terms of the prevention of psychological difficulties in the population. In fact the risk ratios found in the present study are much in line with those found by others. The early Cambridge-Somerville study, for example, although confined to a selected group of at-risk children, found the percentages of alcohol-misusing sons of alcohol-misusing and non-misusing fathers to be 22% and 12% respectively—also a statistically non-significant finding when taken alone. For sons with fathers with drinking problems, Russell (1990), in her review of previous research, found risk ratios for alcohol dependence symptoms in the previous year lying between 1.4 to 1 and 1.7 to 1. The corresponding ratio for males in the present research, for current risky drinking, was 1.4 (25% *vs* 17.5%). For daughters Russell found ratios varying more widely between 0.9 to 1 and 3.0 to 1. The corresponding ratio in the present study was in fact just outside this range at 3.5 to 1 (10.5% *vs* 3%). Parker and Harford (1987) found a ratio of 4.5 to 1 (9% *vs* 2%) for daughters of heavier drinking versus lighter drinking parents. Hence there are now a number of findings from the USA and UK that women, who are overall less at risk than men for aduldhood drinking problems, may be relatively more at risk than are men as a result of having been brought up by a parent with a drinking problem. In general it can probably be safely concluded that community studies, with comparatively unbiased samples, are confirming that the offspring of parents with drinking problems are at increased risk for drinking problems themselves as adults, but that the increased risk is fairly modest and that only a minority of offspring are affected.

Besides examining alcohol consumption and problems, drug use was also investigated in great detail. It was clear that we were only dealing with a minority of the sample here; but nevertheless there were some differences which revealed that the offspring group were the heavier users. Twice as many offspring were current users of illicit drugs other than cannabis; twice as many were current regular cannabis users; and three times as many offspring were heavy smokers.

This sizable difference in heavy smoking is of particular interest for a number of reasons. Of all the categories of substances asked about tobacco was the one thought by the highest proportion (38% of all participants who had ever smoked) to have been a 'problem' at any time (by comparison only 10% of lifetime cannabis users thought it had ever been a problem, and the same was true of 21% of lifetime users of other illicit drugs). Furthermore a comparatively high proportion of those who had ever used tobacco were still using it (79%, a figure exceeded only by the corresponding figure for alcohol at 97%) compared to the percentages still using cannabis (52%) or other illicit drugs (28%). Isohanni *et al.* (1991) have reported, from Finland, that teenage smoking correlates with family and parental problems, and Fidler *et al.* (1992) have reported, from Scotland, that amongst children with special educational needs, those with emotional and behavioural disorders were the most frequent and the heaviest smokers. Moos *et al.* (1990) have found a higher rate of smoking amongst the children of treated problem drinking parents than amongst community controls, and report that this difference remained after successful treatment of the parental problem by which time other group differences in the adjustment of offspring had disappeared. It seems very likely that, with all the attention that has been paid to the inter-generational transmission of the drinking problems themselves, an important form of transmission of health risk may have been overlooked. If tobacco is a mood-altering substance, readily available to children whilst they are still of an age to be living at home, and if its addictive properties are such that it is comparatively difficult to leave off once use has commenced, then we might expect the offspring of problem drinking parents, exposed to some of the family circumstances summarised earlier, to be at heightened risk of many years of heavy smoking. This it turn carries the risks of morbidity and premature death with which we are now familiar.

Due to the conceptual links between alcohol use and use of other drugs, as similar forms of 'substance use' or potential 'excessive appetites' (Orford, 1985), we examined 'risky drug use' as a phenomenon in its own right. Anyone who was a risky user of at least two out of alcohol, tobacco, prescribed drugs, home medicines, cannabis, or other illicit drugs, was categorised as showing 'multiple drug risk', and this was found to be more common in the offspring than comparison group (22% *vs* 10%). This was considerably more likely to be the case foŕ men than for women, although offspring status was still independently statistically significant.

At the other end of the spectrum, it was also the case that more off-spring participants were current abstainers or very infrequent or light drinkers (20.5% *vs* 14%). Although this difference was not statistically significant, it does tend to support previous suggestions and some earlier findings (Harburg *et al.*, 1990) that offspring may sometimes react against the example of their drinking parent in this way. It was the case, more gen-erally, that several adulthood outcomes involving alcohol or drug use in the present study (risky alcohol use, heavy smoking, regular cannabis use, more than occasional use of other illicit drugs, and adulthood adjustment factors 3 & 4) showed significantly greater variance for offspring than for comparison young adults.

Other Adulthood Outcomes: A point emphasised in Chapter 2 was the paucity of data on adulthood outcomes other than drinking, and accord-ingly this was an area on which we concentrated in the current study. Nevertheless, there are some data (presented in Chapter 2) from other stud-ies relating to non-drinking outcomes (e.g. Rydelius, 1981; Windle, 1990). Adults of both sexes who were the children of problem drinkers seem from previous research more likely to have poor sickness records—both days off, and general hospital visits—and be somewhat more prone to depression, and have some difficulties in their abilities to express emotions and to express themselves verbally in social settings if parents were reported to have been critical. There are some sex differences as well: adults who were sons of problem drinkers seem more likely to have a socially unstable out-come (to move home frequently, be registered with social services, and have a criminal record); adult daughters, on the other hand, seem more likely to have more children, and to be even more at risk for depression, and bulimic type eating disorders. Just as the risk of male-linked problems such as substance misuse may be increased more for women as a result of having a parent with a drinking problem, so the risk of female-linked prob-lems such as bulimia may increase relatively greatly for men (Claydon, 1987). There are also some very limited data suggesting that daughters might be more likely to marry problem drinkers. Finally, there has been a suggestion that there might be positive, personality strengthening, effects on offspring. Evidence for many of the supposed adulthood deficits of offspring of problem drinking parents, such as increased anxiety, reduced self-esteem, or interpersonal difficulties, has largely been negative, although the research involved may have been insufficiently sensitive (Windle, 1990).

As was stated in Chapter 2, however, all these findings need to be taken with a great deal of caution. Most are based on studies of University samples, of very young adults (often under 20 years of age), who have only very recently left home. Recent, more representative, community studies, however, have found some positive, but weak, effects in some of the areas where previous results have been negative. Tweed and Ryff (1991), using a questionnaire approach with a broadly based US community sample rather like the one involved in the present study, found small but statistically significant differences in anxiety and depression, although there were no differences between offspring and comparisons on the majority of measures of personality and psychological well-being that they examined, and there were few sex differences. In a community sample of women, also from the USA, Domenico and Windle (1993) found small but statistically significant differences on a number of measures including self-esteem, depression, and marital satisfaction. They also noted that, although daughters of problem drinkers did not report any greater alcohol consumption than others, they did report more drinking for reasons of 'coping'.

The data reported in Chapter 5 add substantially to this picture. The detailed interview method that we utilised did not lend itself to an examination of sickness records, so we are unable to compare our sample with others; but in terms of the other variables which previous research has highlighted, our data match some previous findings quite well, and call others into question. We did not find that our offspring participants were more likely to be depressed: although a specific depression inventory was not included, neither the sub-scale of our Adulthood Problems Checklist (which included depression), nor the Demoralisation factor from the adulthood adjustment factor analysis revealed significant differences between offspring and comparison groups. On the other hand, the finding that the offspring group were somewhat less gregarious, and in the case of women also less extraverted, than the comparisons, could be seen as supporting the Jones and Houts (1992) findings relating to verbal social expression.

Sons in our research did not prove to be more socially unstable in the ways other research had shown, although they were significantly less likely than comparison participants to improve on their socio-economic status in relation to that of their parents. They were more likely than comparisons to have had children. As with previous research, the daughters in our study were also more likely to have had children; and in addition, they were also more likely to be in a permanent relationship, to have had a longer relationship, and to have left home earlier. Although they were more likely to be relatively introverted, they were no more likely to be depressed, or to have eating disorders.

There was very little evidence that daughters were more likely to marry problem drinkers. Although more offspring daughters did report current partners who were problem, very heavy, or fairly heavy drinkers, the numbers were extremely small. There were quite substantial numbers in both the offspring and the comparison groups, and of both sexes, who reported having had a *previous* relationship with a problem drinker, and offspring women seemed substantially more likely to report this (36% *vs* 20–23% for the other groups). There were also six women in all (5 offspring, 1 comparison, out of the 132 women) who reported both a previous, and a current, relationship with a problem drinker; it is these women who most closely resemble the popular stereotype of women who seem repeatedly attracted to heavy drinking men. The fact that there were so few of them in our sample implies that this stereotype is not as commonly borne out in practice as some writers would have us believe; the fact that there were any at all implies that the 'co-dependency' hypothesis may be worthy of some future study. The notion of 'co-dependency' has been much criticised for its vagueness and lack of specificity to relationships involving excessive drinking (e.g. Sher, 1991), but there has been some experimental evidence which provides at least some validation of part of the idea. Lyon and Greenberg (1991) found support for their hypothesis that daughters of fathers with drinking problems would, when given the opportunity in an experimental situation, provide help to a man who was acting in an 'exploitative' fashion.

We made a number of specific predictions based on previous research and theory as to what differences we might expect to find between the two groups of participants. One of the most important findings was that so many of these differences were completely lacking in this sample. It was not the case that offspring had generally poorer mental health as young adults, nor that they reported greater anxiety, lower self-esteem, or a greater dissatisfaction with their lives. Nor were they leading lives which were less stable in terms of home, close relationships, friendships, work or education. And the differences which were to be found need, as we argued in Chapter 5, to be understood within a broad framework relating to the transition from adolescence to adulthood.

A great deal of research has shown that there is a large and negative early impact on children of having a parent with a drinking problem. This is the case whether the children are assessed whilst they are still children (West and Prinz, 1987), or whether they provide retrospective material after they have grown to adulthood (Velleman and Orford, 1993). Yet one of the most striking features of the results presented here is that the large differences between the two sub-groups of offspring and comparisons relating to their recollections of childhood, are not reflected in young adulthood in differences between the groups in self-reported adjustment—there were very few significant differences between offspring and comparison groups when respondents described present adulthood adjustment. The results demonstrate quite strongly that even in a sample which retrospectively reported substantial ill-effects of problem-drinking parenting during childhood, there are few reported effects which last into adulthood and very few that relate equally to sons and daughters.

We might begin to understand these findings by recourse to the theme of coping. In Chapter 4 we suggested that there might be a link between the most commonly reported coping mechanism which the offspring group used to deal with their problem-drinking parent—that of 'avoidance', mentioned by 54% of the sample—and other findings, particularly the fact that many of the offspring group deliberately separated off their friendships outside of the family from their internal family relationships. Leaving home earlier may be another method of pursuing the same end and, especially for women, getting married and/or having children early might serve the same function of legitimately removing the child from the parental sphere of influence. These ideas are supported by Quinton and Rutter's (1988) findings of earlier cohabitation and earlier childbirths in their sample of women brought up in local authority care, as well as by some of the findings reviewed by Browne and Finkelhor (1986) concerning the likely effects of child sexual abuse upon the transition of young women to adulthood relationships. It is clear of course that getting married early does not always turn out positively—indeed, some of the qualitative accounts from our respondents suggest that getting married early was a seriously negative experience.

One area where significant differences between the offspring and the comparison groups did emerge was with Adulthood Factor 4, where membership of the offspring group was significantly correlated with being at the negative pole: having left home relatively early, taking risks with tobacco and alcohol, becoming involved with minor delinquencies, having more children and not improving socio-economic status relative to parents. Individually some of the variables contributing to this factor represent risks for women whilst others are greater risks for men, but scores on the factor as a whole distinguished offspring of each sex from like-sex comparisons. Factor 4 draws together a number of the themes to do with the transition from family of origin to independent adulthood which have been remarked upon above. For a substantial number of offspring participants 'home' was not a pleasant place to be in, and many sought to escape or avoid it as much as possible. One way of doing this is by physically leaving home, and for many women a viable way of doing this is via entering into a cohabiting or marital relationship, and/or having children. A second, not necessarily opposing method of avoidance, is via becoming involved in a semi-deviant sub-culture involving early tobacco and alcohol use, and minor delinquency. Both of these methods of avoidance could quite easily lead to a reduction in opportunities to improve socio-economic status relative to parents.

Although there was a relationship between offspring status and Factor 4, on which alcohol and tobacco use, and minor delinquency, loaded quite heavily, there was no association between offspring group membership and Adulthood Factor 3, which combined excess and deviance with socialising and gregariousness. As we outlined in Chapter 5, the fact that risky or problematic substance use, and delinquency, splits between two factors in this way may be important: it may suggest why research has found it difficult to establish a clear correlation between having a parent with a drinking problems, and excessive drinking in adulthood. Drinking excessively, and being delinquent, may be parts of one pattern of transition from childhood to adulthood to which the children of problem drinking parents may be more than averagely prone; but they are parts of other patterns of young adulthood as well. It is perhaps in the nature of much risky adolescent and young adult behaviour, including alcohol and drug use and misuse, that it is linked both to adversity and to positive aspects of personality such as sociability and peer group affiliation. Findings of a study by Molina *et al.* (1994) are also consistent with this view. They found that early adolescent substance use and affiliation with drug-using friends were associated both with adolescent-father difficulties via negative adolescent feelings, and with the adolescent's sociability (which was associated with feeling good rather than bad).

MIGHT THE PRESENT RESULTS BE MISLEADING?

The present finding that the offspring of problem drinking parents, as a group, do not have much poorer adulthood outcomes than comparisons, and that in the case of many variables of interest differences are completely absent, is contrary to the expectations engendered by the strong ACOA

(Adult Children of Alcoholics) movement in the USA and elsewhere. Their writings suggest that large numbers of adult offspring of problem drinking parents (or even all of them) will have quite severe and long-lasting problems as adults. How might we account for this stark difference in conclusions? There are five hypotheses which might account for the discrepancy. First, our sample might have been biased in that the people interviewed might have been children of people who were not 'really' problem drinkers; second, that the present sample was biased due to recruitment problems, in that females were proportionately over-represented, and those from clinical sources proportionately under-represented, in the offspring group, and that as a whole the sample had something of a middle-class bias; third, that the sample was biased in that the interviewees were more representative of the survivors of such parenting than of those who experienced significant adulthood problems; fourth, that we simply did not ask the correct questions or ask them in the correct ways to discover the adulthood problems; or fifth, that in fact the ACOA movement, in common with some of the published literature reviewed above, has over-predicted the likelihood of negative adulthood outcomes on the basis of untested assumptions and research which is itself biased.

The results presented in Chapter 4, and in previous papers (Orford and Velleman, 1990; Velleman and Orford, 1993), go a long way towards discounting the first hypothesis: although we do not have measures that allow a direct comparison, these adults reported adverse parental drinking patterns and childhood experiences that seemed, from our experience, to equate with those reported by the children of currently or recently treated 'alcoholics' or severe problem drinkers (e.g. Wilson and Orford, 1978). These reports cover high quantities, frequencies and negative effects of parental drinking, and include descriptions of considerable levels of childhood family disharmony, domestic violence, and high levels of childhood psychological difficulties.

Given the fact that our research suggests that parental problem drinking may have only a limited effect on the offspring once they reach adulthood, many commentators are likely to argue that our sample was very different to the samples which previous research has investigated. It is important, therefore, that the present participants have revealed a retrospective picture of their upbringing and experiences which is remarkably similar to the picture given by the children of problem drinkers while they are still children. Even though these were now young adults—some as old as 35—who were having to recall events after sometimes as much as 30 years, what they told us matches very directly with the reports of children of serious problem drinkers given while these children were still young, and still living within the environments where these events were taking place.

The critieria for inclusion in the present sample were, as explained in Chapter 3, largely psychosocial rather than psychiatric. The interviewers were very careful to establish that parental drinking had constituted a real and significant problem for the participating interviewees, and whenever this was in doubt data were excluded from the analysis. It was not our policy to try and make a diagnosis of 'alcoholism' or 'alcohol dependence' according to one of the well-known psychiatric classification systems. Not only would this have been very difficult, since we had no direct access to the parents' accounts of their drinking, but also we remain unconvinced that the attempt to 'diagnose' is other than a forlorn attempt to make a discrete category out of a complex phenomenon that is best conceptualised as lying on a continuum. Both of us have experience, as clinical psychologists, of working in British National Health Service units providing services for people with alcohol problems, and one us (RV) currently directs such a service. We are in no doubt that, from the participants' accounts, all the parents whose problem drinking was described would have been considered suitable candidates for treatment in such services. Those who approach this field from a psychiatric perspective, however, may be concerned that the sample included an unknown number of offspring of parents whose drinking would not have qualified them for diagnosis according to, the fourth revision of the Diagnostic and Statistical Manual of the American Psychiatric Association or the 10th revision of the World Health Organisation's International Classification of Diseases. In fact the rules for diagnosing 'alcohol dependence', 'alcohol abuse' or 'harmful alcohol use' according to DSM-IV or ICD are very flexible, reflecting the varied ways in which significant alcohol problems manifest themselves, and we believe our participants' parents would all have qualified, with at most a handful of exceptions.

Also from a psychiatric perspective, a related problem with sampling is the unknown extent to which the parents' problems were representative of the variation to be found in clinical samples of 'alcoholics' (Sher, 1991). Although there is much controversy and little agreement about 'types' of 'alcoholism', a number of typologies are popular. Cloninger's (1987) distinction between Types I and II, and Zucker's (1987) four-fold typology, are amongst the best known. The inclusion of a good proportion of young adults with mothers with drinking problems ensured that types often excluded from research (Cloninger's Type I and Zucker's 'negative affect alcoholism'—both considered more common amongst women) were included in the present study. Many examples in the present sample corresponded more closely to Cloninger's Type II and Zucker's 'anti-social alcoholism' (likely to have a positive family history of drinking problems, to have an early onset, to be associated with criminality or anti-social behaviour, and to have a relatively poor prognosis), with the majority fitting most easily into Zucker's 'developmentally cumulative' type (developing as a cumulative extension of heavy drinking and problem behaviour). His fourth type ('developmentally limited') is less likely to be relevent since this type is thought to have a high probability of natural recovery as drinkers take on adult responsibilities with increasing age.

The second hypothesis is that our inability to meet perfectly our sampling aims might have biased the results. We failed to meet these aims in three ways. First, the offspring group came proportionately more often from clinical sources than did the comparison group—45% of the offspring group were recruited from clinical sources *vs* 22% of the comparisons. Second, the offspring group contained proportionately more females. If these mis-matches were to produce a distortion in the results, however, they should have been in the direction of the offspring group reporting more negative adult outcomes than the comparisons since they came disproportionately from clinical sources, and offspring scoring more highly on Factor 1 (where depression loads heavily and positively) since depression is more common amongst women. The final issue is of middle-class bias. Although broadly based in terms of socioeconomic status, it is the case that the sample was somewhat skewed in this way compared to the general population. The two groups shared this bias, however, so it is unlikely to have produced spurious results as far as group differences are concerned. Furthermore, although SES is a regular and powerful correlate of adulthood mental health (Dohrenwend and Dohrenwend, 1969), correlations between SES of parents and later offspring adulthood mental health are likely to be much less strong. Vaillant (1983), for example, has argued strongly on the basis of his very long term prospective studies that, "parental social class correlates only in the most minimal way with a variety of adult outcome variables... in other words, parental social class... may be more important in cross-sectional studies than they are in studies with a life-span perspective" (p. 56). It is arguable, nevertheless, that the present results might generalise more readily to middle to higher SES groups in the population that to lower SES groups.

Another point is that the present sample was still relatively young (16–35) and that the largest recruiting shortfall occurred in the male offspring who were in the oldest age-group (31–35), where we only achieved 70% of our target. If an outcome of interest is of a kind that does not show itself until later in adulthood, a study confined to young adults will miss it or under-estimate it (Sher, 1991). This may be a particular problem for drinking problems among daughters since women are known to develop drinking problems on average later than men (e.g. Orford and Keddie, 1985). It is less likely to be a problem in the case of sons' drinking problems or general deviancy, and is unlikely to be a major problem either in the case of general mental health outcomes since these were uncorrelated with age in the present sample. Other studies reaching similar conclusions to the present one (e.g. Drake and Vaillant, 1988) employed older aged samples.

The third hypothesis suggests that we over-recruited successful 'survivors'. In one sense this is clearly not the case. Many respondents told us a great deal about their problems with alcohol, drugs, and other areas of adult adjustment (Orford and Velleman, 1990, and Chapter 5). For example, 14%, 28%, 11% and 8% of the offspring group said they had considered their alcohol, tobacco, prescribed drug, and illicit drug use, respectively, to be a problem. Many respondents reported low self-esteem, and problems with depression and anxiety. This is clearly not a group made up solely of survivors! What makes these results interesting, however, is that the comparison group participants often reported similar problems and, in the case of many adulthood variables, were just as likely to report these negative outcomes.

On the other hand, there is some evidence which does support this 'survivors' hypothesis. Part of the interview focussed on the drinking and other adulthood problems which interviewees thought had occurred amongst their siblings. Sixteen per cent of the offspring group reported that a sibling had a drinking problem, and a further 9% were unsure; this contrasts with only one member of the comparison group who reported a sibling with a drinking problem, and one unsure. The difference between these two groups is highly statistically significant. In terms of siblings thought to have other adulthood problems, however, there was no such contrast. Twenty-six per cent of the offspring group reporting a sibling with some other adulthood problem, with a further 19% being unsure, compared with 23% and 14% in the comparison group: a statistically non-significant difference. Furthermore, in some cases (56 respondents from 25 families) 2 or even 3 siblings from the same family were interviewed, and it was not the case in these families that one sibling was the 'survivor' and another a 'casualty'. The idea that mainly survivors were interviewed, then, although it might partly explain the lack of many significant differences on alcohol-specific variables, is unlikely to provide a total explanation of the findings.

The 'over-representation of survivors' hypothesis, however, does have the merit of credibility. It is reasonable to suppose that offspring who have come to terms with having been brought up in a family where one or both parents had a serious problem might be more inclined to take part in a research project that involved a considerable commitment of time and a requirement to ponder and reflect upon childhood and adulthood events and adjustments. Those with serious difficulties might find it difficult to enter into such an engagement. On the other hand, it is also plausible to argue that those who had not come to terms with their pasts, or who were having adjustment difficulties, might be especially attracted to taking part in such research. It was for this reason that interviewers routinely asked participants at the end of interviews whether they wished to be put in touch with a source of help for any difficulties they might be experiencing. Fifteen (9.1 %) of the offspring group and 6 (7.5 %) of the comparisons took up this offer. The fact still remains, however, that the direction and extent of this bias is unknown, and it is conceivable that the present results under-represent the real chances of offspring of problem drinking parents developing alcohol-related or other difficulties themselves as adults.

The fourth hypothesis is that inadequate questions were asked or that questions were asked in the wrong way. In fact we know of no other recent study which has interviewed as carefully over such an extended period, using methods (including the coupling together of 'in-depth' and 'structured' interview techniques, and the careful reconstruction of biographies) which have previously been shown to yield the most useful results (Rutter *et al.*, 1981; Robins *et al.*, 1985). The training and quality control exercised over the interviewers has been described in Chapter 3. Although the interviewers were not clinically experienced, they were sufficiently expert to conduct interviews that extended for several hours and to engage respondents for that time period, to get 90% of the respondents to return to be interviewed 12 months later, and to get the respondents to divulge detailed information relating to often painful material in their past and current lives. Accordingly, we feel that this hypothesis has comparatively little force. It must be acknowledged, however, that even state-of-the-art interviewing can not hope to reveal certain findings if the right lines of questioning were not followed. It remains a possibility that some of the effects of parental problem drinking on offspring have been undetected by formal research methods because the techniques for uncovering them have not been used.

A good example might be that of interpersonal difficulties in childhood. West and Prinz (1987), in their review, found no evidence for such difficulties. They did not have access to the work of Matejcek (1981) in then-Czechoslovakia, who used a sociometric technique and found that children of problem drinking parents were less often nominated as 'best friends' by their school mates. And since their review, Corrao *et al.* (1993), in Italy, have reported that teachers gave lower ratings for general social functioning to children from homes where there were thought to be alcohol problems. Interpersonal difficulties later in life might also be difficult to detect by means of personal interview and might therefore have been missed in the present study. Specific areas of adulthood difficulty, such as unusual grief reactions to loss in adulthood (Brabant and Martof, 1993), may have been missed altogether.

The final explanation for the apparent discrepancy between the present conclusions and those of others who have stressed the many and severe risks that offspring of problem drinking parents face as adults, is that these risks have sometimes been over-estimated in the past. As outlined in Chapter 2, there has in fact been suprisingly little research into general adulthood outcomes for the offspring of problem-drinking parents, but that which has been performed with community samples (e.g. Benson, 1980; Clair and Genest, 1987; Hill *et al.*, 1992; Tweed and Ryff, 1991) and using prospective studies of children for whom there was no reason to think that they were at risk (e.g. Vaillant, 1983; Beardslee *et al.*, 1986; Knop *et al.*, 1985) comes to the conclusion that the risk of negative adulthood outcomes for the children of problem drinking parents has been exaggerated (Heller *et al.*, 1982). Hence, for example, Drake and Vaillant (1988) report that their 'adult children of alcoholics' were no more likely to suffer a 'personality disorder' than were their comparison group (25% *vs* 23%). Indeed in general the present findings reinforce those of a number of researchers and reviewers who have been impressed by the paucity of strong effects in this area and the large number of instances where no significant effects have been found, and who have been struck by the resilience shown by the children of parents with drinking problems. For example Drake and Vaillant (1988) conclude:

Although the COA's [children of alcoholics] were predictably stressed…during adolescence, the adult consequences…were somewhat surprising…poor adolescent adjustment…had little continuity with the chronic adult maladies of alcoholism and personality disorder. Most of the boys with adjustment problems in early adolescence were remarkably resilient and had somehow overcome their difficulties by midlife (p. 805).

In like vein, Tweed and Ryff (1991), discussing their results, write:

...the most notable aspect of the present findings was the general absence of differences between the self-reports of adult children of alcoholics and the comparison group. Despite extensive clinical descriptions that children of alcoholics suffer long-term psychological consequences, the present data indicate that these adult children of alcoholics did not feel less happy, have less purpose in life or lower self-esteem than their same-aged counterparts from nonalcoholic families (p. 139).

POSSIBLE MECHANISMS OF TRANSMISSION

Findings comparing the adulthood outcomes reported by offspring and comparison groups are important. Equally important, however, are questions about causation or mechanisms of inter-generational transmission. The fact that adulthood adjustment outcome is very varied for children of problem drinking parents is now widely accepted in the scientific literature at least (Sher, 1991; Seilhamer *et al.*, 1993) and the present results concur with this conclusion. Since there are some offspring who do develop problems especially drinking problems as adults, and others who appear not to, we want to know what set of variables allows us to best predict one sort of outcome or another.

As outlined in Chapter 2, three general mechanisms have been suggested to account for any transmission of problems that occurs between generations. The research reported within this book has not attempted to answer questions concerning the first of these—genetic or biological mechanisms. That the offspring group were somewhat more at risk for alcohol related problems, and were certainly more at risk for risky multiple drug use (albeit only experienced by a minority), does mean that such mechanisms cannot be discounted. Given the ideas expressed by Cloninger *et al.* (1981) and others that there may be different types of 'alcoholism', each with a different pattern of causation and only some of them related to genetic influences, it would not be surprising to find that the effects of genetics would be diluted in a 'mixed' sample, and hence any genetic-related influences would only be apparent in a minority of the sample. Recent studies have tended to support the conclusions that reviewers such as Sher (1991) have arrived at: that the extent of heritability depends upon the exact drinking/drinking problem criterion (e.g. Prescott *et al.*, 1994); that the evidence for some genetic inheritance is strongest in the case of male alcohol problems of relatively early onset and least consistent for women (e.g. McGue *et al.*, 1992); that the whole question is complicated by gene-environment interactions; and that when genetic inheritance does play a part, a complex form of poly-genetic inheritance is more likely to be operating than a simple genetic form. Although heritability estimates vary with the criterion and with the amount of both genetic and environmental variation to be found in a population, all investigators agree that a large proportion, probably the larger part, of adult variation in drinking and drinking-related problems needs to be explained in environmental terms. McGue *et al.*'s (1992) conclusion is not untypical:

...our findings suggest that in the headlong rush to identify molecular genetic processes, researchers may be ignoring the significant influence that the environment has in the origins of alcoholism (p. 15).

The two other major inter-generational theories discussed in Chapter 2 are environmental ones: alcohol-specific mechanisms on the one hand, and non-specific environmental mechanisms on the other. The most frequently suggested alcohol-specific mechanism is one of behavioural modelling, and data relating to this mechanism have been examined in Chapter 5, as well as in two papers previously published by ourselves (Orford and Velleman, 1990, 1991).

Evidence for modelling of problem drinking behaviour in the present results was mixed. On the one hand there was no evidence of a stronger same-gender (father-son, mother-daughter) rather than opposite-gender effect; nor has previous research unequivocally supported such a same-gender link although it has often been assumed to exist. Nor was there clear, overall evidence in the present findings relating problem drinking outcomes to the degree of perceived positive relationship with the problem drinking parent, although there was evidence of this kind for one sub-group (daughters of problem drinking fathers).

On the other hand it was shown that if the parent drank excessively or problematically at home as opposed to outside of the home, there was an increased alcohol and drug-related risk; and if both parents were problem drinkers, then there was a much increased risk for all three drinking and drug risk outcomes examined, for both sons and daughters. Both of these findings are at least consistent with the idea that it is the availability of the problem-drinking parent as a role model that is important. Jacob and his colleagues (e.g. Seilhamer *et al.*, 1993) have identified in-home *vs* out-of-home drinking as a variable in studying problem drinking but there is to date no evidence from other research to corroborate the present suggestion that it might be an important variable in the transmission of problems to the next generation. There is corroborative evidence, however, for the likely importance of having two parents who drink in a problematic way, although this is largely confined to studies of children and retrospective studies of adult patients (McKenna and Pickens, 1981; Reich *et al.*, 1993).

The evidence in support of an alcohol-specific modelling mechanism in the form of a link between risky drinking and a remembered positive relationship with the problem drinking parent, largely specific to daughters of problem drinking fathers, is interesting since other researchers have also come up with some positive findings specific to this group of offspring. Harburg *et al.* (1990), in their community survey in the USA, found that women were likely to be heavy drinkers if their fathers were also heavy drinkers but without signs of problem drinking. Where there was heavy paternal drinking with signs of problem drinking then abstinence or very light drinking were likely outcomes for the daughters. Donald *et al.* (1993) found that daughters who drank heavily like their heavy drinking fathers, did not have the worst mental health outcomes, and Lyon and Greenberg (1991), in their experimental study of co-dependency, found that the daughters of problem drinking fathers who took part were mostly quite positive about their fathers.

One suggestion would be that daughters may be prone to either of two ways of accomodating to having had a father who drank excessively: one by identifying with him and adopting his ways, the other by rejecting his example and adopting forms of behaviour that are contrary to his. The latter might be the more likely if problems related to drinking are severe or obvious, and this might be encouraged if a close alliance is possible with the young woman's mother who has also adopted a clear stance of rejection towards her husband. The former might be the more likely if heavy drinking has not so obviously been identified as the source of family problems or if heavy drinking is seen as part of the whole family's style of life. The absence of a non-heavy drinking parental model, and the pervasion of the family atmosphere with a norm of heavy drinking, might also explain the relationship between having had two parents with drinking problems and risky drinking and drug use in the next generation.

Others are also finding complex relationships of these kinds. For example a further analysis of the Cambridge-Somerville follow-up data, McCord (1988, cited by Sher, 1991) found that the link between father and son problem drinking was moderated by the esteem in which the father was held by the mother: transmission was more likely if the problem drinking father was held in relatively high esteem.

Although the evidence is largely indirect, here is some evidence, then, for alcohol-specific modelling mechanisms as being one way that effects of drinking problems might be transmitted from generation to generation. What becomes abundantly clear is that the mechanisms involved are complex, perhaps involving the interaction of a number of factors (number of heavy drinkers in the family, obviousness of problems linked to drinking, relationship with the problem drinking parent, and attitude of the other parent) and likely to be affecting sub-groups of offspring differently. Nor is it immediately apparent how modelling of problem drinking might work. Sher (1991), for example, has suggested that what is passed on from parent to offspring might be 'alcohol expectancies', in other words the positive expectation that drinking will enhance cognitive or emotional functioning. As others working in related fields have concluded, modelling mechanisms are themselves likely to be complicated (e.g. Kalmuss, 1984; Belsky and Pensky, 1988—see Chapter 2). The possibility that modelling might be role-specific, and therefore age-related, with the manifestation of intergenerational effects delayed until offspring are of similar age and life stage to their parents (Kalmuss, 1984) is especially intriguing.

The third type of mechanism that might explain transmission is also environmental but of a more general nature. Many previous writers have suggested that it may be via family dysfunction, parental arguing and quarrelling, inconsistency of parental discipline, an absence of enjoyable joint family activities, a tense family atmosphere, domestic violence, child abuse or neglect—that effects are passed on from one generation to another (Benson and Heller, 1987; Kandel *et al.*, 1994; Pardeck *et al.*, 1991) or at least that general family dysfunction mediates the process of intergenerational transmission (Moos *et al.*, 1990; Sher, 1991). Benson's finding (described in Chapter 2), for example, was that very little of the variance in outcome in her study was related to the existence of a parent with a drinking problem per se, finding instead that family climate and social support were the more important variables (Benson and Heller, 1987). This more general kind of hypothesis is strengthened by the wide support that such explanations have received in fields allied to the study of the intergenerational transmission of alcohol problems. Not only have the reviews of childhood problems referred to in Chapter 2 concluded that the presence or absence of parental conflict is probably a key to understanding the effects upon children of parental divorce and separation and parental psychological difficulties (Emery, 1982; Grych and Fincham, 1990), but studies of the longer-term effects upon offspring of such events and adversities as psychiatric disorder, family economic hardship, and even child physical and sexual abuse have also tended to conclude that the general quality of family life or of individual relationships within the family may be as important if not more important than the fact of the adverse events and circumstances themselves (Rutter and Madge, 1976; Nash *et al.*, 1993; Mullen *et al.*, 1993).

The trend of the present findings is strongly in support of this sort of general family functioning explanation. The results presented in Chapters 4 and 6 demonstrate that family disharmony, which includes such factors as violence, arguments, and lack of cohesiveness of parental and family relationships, is a stronger correlate of offspring problems (both when they are children, and in adulthood) than is the existence of a parental drinking problem. The statistical correlations and 'path analyses' showed that although having had a parent with a drinking problem was strongly correlated with reporting disharmony in the family of origin, any effects of having a parent with such a problem were largely mediated by family disharmony. Indeed in the case of childhood adjustment problems and adulthood mental health, all such effects appeared to be mediated in this way, leaving no negative effects of having had a problem drinking parent in the absence of family-of-origin disharmony. More than that, the net effect upon adult mental health appeared to be nil since, in the absence of family-of-origin disharmony, the effect of having a parent with a drinking problem appeared to be moderately positive for mental health in adulthood.

Family disharmony, identified as a key explanatory variable in the present research, was a composite variable embracing a number of aspects of family functioning which covaried in the present sample. It is possible that this covariation was a product of the self-report and retrospective nature of the data, with young adults presenting a rounded, over-simplified view of past family events. On the other hand, a general disharmony or dysfunction factor may be a true reflection of the reality, with a number of aspects of family life coming together to make for a relatively disharmonious and risky, or harmonious and protective, family environment. Our cautious conclusion is that 'disharmony' may be a useful concept subsuming a number of the specific suggestions concerning risk factors that have appeared in the literature, and which were reviewed in Chapter 2. These included parental conflict, unsatisfactory parent–child relationships, inconsistent or abusive parental discipline, poor parental monitoring of adolescent behaviour, poor communication especially regarding emotional expression, a high level of criticism, a low frequency of joint family activities, and a tense and non-cohesive atmosphere (e.g. Bennett *et al.*, 1987; Benson and Heller, 1987; Chassin *et al.*, 1993, 1996; Clair and Genest, 1987;

Hill *et al.*, 1992; Jarmas and Kazak, 1992; Moos *et al.*, 1990). Each of the foregoing represents, in our view, too specific a conceptualisation of the kind of family dysfunction that characterises many homes where a parent is drinking excessively, and which places the children at risk in the short term and, less certainly, in the longer term also. More attractive than single concept explanations, from this viewpoint, are the more complete, multi-component models of such as Clair and Genest (1987) in the alcohol field, and Grych and Fincham (1990) in the general area of marital conflict. The former see certain features of family atmosphere (low cohesion, expressiveness, and independence) in combination with parental modelling of ineffective coping skills and little informational and emotional social support, collectively putting offspring at risk. The latter's contexual-cognitive model pinpoints such factors as memory and expectations of parental conflict, child temperament and mood, attributions, blame and coping behaviours.

Also to be explained is the net adverse effect of having had a parent with a drinking problem on that aspect of young adulthood adjustment captured by the fourth factor identified in the factor analysis of adulthood outcome data. We described in Chapter 5 the variables which loaded most heavily on Factor 4—leaving the parental home at a relatively early age, being a heavy smoker, being a risky drinker now or having had some problem with drinking in the past, having relatively many psychological problems of the delinquency/deviance kind, having relatively more children, and having made relatively little improvement in socioeconomic status relative to parents. Our cautious interpretation of this factor was that it may represent, at its positive end, a relatively careful and unproblematic transition from childhood and the parental home to adulthood and independence. At the negative pole, towards which offspring are somewhat more likely to find themselves, is a relatively impulsive and problematic transition.

There are clear links here with the work of Bennett and her colleagues (e.g. Bennett *et al.*, 1987), and with that of Rutter and his colleagues (e.g. Rutter *et al.*, 1990), both reviewed in Chapter 2. Bennett's work has focussed on family rituals in the families of problem drinkers, and suggests that one protective factor in determining whether or not family patterns (including problem drinking) are carried through to the next generation is that of 'planfulness' or 'deliberateness' on the part of the offspring and spouse in choosing to follow the family rituals of one or another family of origin. Rutter's work has focussed on issues other than the transmission of alcohol problems across generations, but there are strong echoes of the present findings. His work examining adulthood outcomes for those who had been in care as children showed the impact (particularly for women) of a variable termed 'planning'—combining a definite job or career choice with planning for a long-term relationship (positive choice of a partner, not as a means of escape or because of external pressure, and only after knowing the person for at least six months). Planning was significantly related to marital support for both sexes. There are strong similarities here between these concepts of 'planfulness' or 'deliberateness', and 'planning', and our 'careful and unproblematic versus impulsive and problematic transition' to adulthood and independence which emerged as the only adulthood factor upon which there was an offspring/comparison difference. Each of these ideas concerns people making clear decisions and choices about their lives, in ways that enable them to step aside from the particular circumstances in which they have been raised. This does not mean that people forget their pasts or their upbringings—indeed, the evidence from Chapter 4 shows clearly that the children of problems drinkers are well able to recollect and describe the experiences, negative and positive, of their growing-up years. But it is also likely that many are able to then make decisions, either at the time of transition to adulthood, or somewhat later, to put their pasts behind them, and get on with the business of living more positive lives in the future, both for themselves, and for the next generation.

It may seem strange to suggest that the experience of having had a parent with a drinking problem might for some people turn out to be positive in certain ways once they reach adulthood. But in Chapter 2 some evidence was presented that might lead one tentatively to draw that conclusion. On reflection perhaps, knowing how varied is the picture presented by families with such problems, how different are the roles that children can adopt in the face of them, and how complex and uncertain is the path from childhood adversity to adulthood adjustment, it is not so surprising that some people who have had that experience might have been made somewhat more independent as a result (Berkowitz and Perkins, 1988) or might later turn up in Who's Who (Karlsson, 1985) or might make more than averagely sensitive mothers for their own infant children (Bensley *et al.*, 1994). In the present study, too, there was some evidence that offspring whose parents' drinking problems were associated with lower than average disharmony were more positive about themselves and their lives than most comparison young adults (e.g. offspring with harmonious family backgrounds had higher mean life satisfaction and self-esteem, and lower life dissatisfaction, than did the total group of comparisons). Many were of the opinion that having experienced such a problem in childhood, and having survived it, they had learnt important and helpful life lessons as a result or had gained strength in the process.

A general point that should be mentioned here concerns the very idea of attempting to make sense of young adults' lives by examining their childhood upbringing. Although many of the childhood-to-adulthood correlations reported here are highly statistically significant, their predictive power is relatively slight. For example, the highest such correlation is +0.39 (childhood difficulties with adult demoralisation). Similarly, the path analyses showed that the variables entered—childhood disharmony, parental problem drinking, childhood difficulties, SES of family-of-origin, current age-group, sex, and recruitment source—between them did not explain most of the variance in the outcome factors. Between 15% and 26% of the variances in the adulthood adjustment factors were accounted for by these variables, implying that why young adults are demoralised, behave excessively, or stay at home and do not take risks, is either inexplicable or, more probably, is due to variables other than the ones assessed in the present research.

These facts, however, have to be viewed from an inter-generational perspective. Other researchers in this and related fields, using longitudinal and prospective research designs (as opposed to our cross-sectional community design), report findings of similar magnitude. For example, the correlation of +0.39 mentioned above compares well with the correlation coefficient of greatest magnitude (+0.28) reported in the study by Beardslee *et al.* (1986), which also examined the relationships between exposure in childhood to problem drinking in the family environment, and such adult outcome measures as problem drinking and mood disturbance. Reviews of intergenerational continuity, as was pointed out in Chapter 2, suggest that levels of association between the generations in terms of such things as child maltreatment, spouse abuse, marital divorce and separation, and marital happiness, are quite low (Belsky and Pensky, 1988).

The present results, then, are not out of line with those reported by others who have examined inter-generational continuities. It might be argued, on the other hand, that it is surprising that there *are* so many links between childhood factors and adulthood adjustment. Although many theorists from Freud to Bowlby have argued that the links between childhood and adulthood are exceedingly strong, it would not in fact have proved surprising to discover that adulthood adjustment was almost totally under the control of current events rather than past ones. Yet this has not proved to be the case, and these findings (with two out of the four adulthood factors showing quite substantial associations with recalled childhood issues) do lend weight to those theories which stress the importance of developmental factors.

The strongest correlates of adulthood adjustment certainly were current life circumstances and satisfactions—particularly with having a satisfactory marriage and social life and having a job—but the influence of childhood remained in the form of significant paths from disharmony and childhood emotional problems to adult demoralisation for women. Elsewhere we have reported that we also found a significant path from childhood conduct problems to adult deviancy for men (Orford and Velleman, 1995). For women there was some evidence suggesting that part of the effect of having had childhood emotional problems was mediated by marital and social dissatisfaction as an adult.

Nevertheless it is a fact that the intercorrelations and path coefficients, although highly statistically significant, only provided weak predictive power. This finding lends support to Rutter and Madge's (1976) important conclusion that inter-generational discontinuities in psychological and psychiatric problems are numerous, and that children's resilience to upbringing-induced stress should not be ignored.

RESILIENCE FOLLOWING CHILDHOOD ADVERSITY

In Chapter 2 evidence was reviewed suggesting that the pathways from various forms of childhood adversity to adulthood outcomes was far from simple and straightforward, and that even when there were harmful 'initial' effects upon children longer-term resilience was very common and harmful adulthood consequences far from inevitable. This was the case, for example, with childhood physical abuse which had not been found to lead to offspring becoming abusive parents themselves later in life with anything like the inevitability that had at one time been assumed (Widom, 1989; Kaufman and Zigler, 1993). Even in the case of childhood sexual abuse, which has attracted a great deal of research in the last few years, the evidence is suggesting a complex picture. Evidence of harmful effects lasting into adulthood, including an increased risk of alcohol and drug abuse, has continued to accumulate (e.g. Mullen *et al.*, 1993; Roesler and Dafler, 1993). At the same time, however, some researchers are concluding that it is difficult to disentangle the specific effects of abuse from the general effects of family dysfunction with which it is often associated (Browne and Finkelhor, 1986; Mullen *et al.*, 1993; Nash *et al.*, 1993), and, furthermore, that many victims of abuse survive into adulthood with either moderate or no obvious problems (Browne and Finkelhor, 1986).

The same is turning out to be the case with the long-term lifetime effects of having had a parent with a drinking problem. Many previous theories in this field have stressed the importance of childhood-to-adulthood continuities, arguing that the children of problem drinkers, especially those raised by problem-drinking mothers, will show marked deficits in adulthood adjustment. Yet the findings presented in this book imply that many children may grow to be well functioning adults despite having experienced a very deleterious upbringing. Much previous research and commentary in this field has focussed almost entirely on the problems, and the concomitant need for interventions, which the adult offspring of problem drinkers were presumed to experience. This presumption was based on the research findings relating to children, and the rather biased sampling of ·adults who already had drinking problems.

The findings presented in this book, together with those from other research, imply that the outlook for adult offspring is not as bleak as had been supposed, and that many of these offspring go on to make as happy and successful lives as do those without such a background. This is not to say, of course, that all the offspring have unproblematic adulthoods; rather, the facts seem to imply that many young adults within the 16–35 year-old age range we examined, experience problems with their relationships, their mental health, and their substance use. Nevertheless, although there were a small number of areas where offspring did appear to fare worse, including a greater use of tobacco, more multiple drug risk, and more likelihood of an unplanned transition from the parental home, the offspring of problem drinkers as a group do not appear to be at much more risk than do others of this age range.

The work of Moos *et al.* (1990) has also shown how resilient children of parents being treated for drinking problems can be: those whose parents were successfully treated were subsequently found to be indistinguishable from community control children. This, and other similar findings (Chassin *et al.*, 1990, cited by Sher, 1991) raises the possibility that most of the effects of parental problem drinking might only last as long as the stress of living with a member of the family with such a problem lasts.

In order to understand this, the increasingly used term 'resilience' may be apposite. Werner (1986), for example, used the expression 'resilient children' to refer to children who had shown no signs of learning or behavioural problems by the age of 18, despite having had at least one parent with a serious alcohol problem while the child was aged 2–10 years.

Although some of her findings are in marked contrast to ours—for example, she found that children of problem-drinking mothers fared far worse than did those of fathers, and that boys fared worse than did girls—there were also some that match our own, most notably that more resilient children were less likely to grow up in homes where family conflict was apparent during infancy. It will be interesting to see what emerges when Werner's sample is followed up into adulthood.

Resilience may best be conceptualised as a process open to change, rather than a static attribute or skill. Children and adults appear to have different levels of resilience over time, and indeed traits or behaviours which are protective or adaptive at one time or in one context may not be so helpful in another. One obvious example from our own research is that of avoidance. It is clear that such behaviour as avoidance of the problem drinker, spending time with peers rather than family, were amongst the most common ways that offspring participants dealt with their situations. It is also clear that such a strategy is adaptive, as opposed, say, to adopting a strategy of open conflict with a problem drinking parent. Yet such a strategy may well cease to be so adaptive at a later stage of life, and may well have contributed to more offspring than comparisons avoiding further contact with parental problem drinking and its concomitant family disruption by their relatively unplanned transition into adulthood via leaving home early, earlier use of alcohol and drugs, and, for women, earlier marriages and child bearing.

There are many ways, then, whereby people may overcome adversity: resilience is a process, which changes as the child and adult develops, and as the environmental and personal context changes. It seems likely that people's ability to become resilient depends on a multitude of factors, including initial personality or disposition (Garmezy, 1985), the presence of a supportive family milieu (or a harmonious family environment, in the terms we have adopted in this book) (Werner, 1986), and an external support system—schools, career, church, other important adults, etc.—which aids the development of positive coping skills and gives the experience of success (Garmezy, 1985; Romans *et al.*, 1995; Valentine and Feinauer, 1993). There is beginning to emerge a consensus of opinion about 'lawful discontinuity'. A supportive adult relationship, particularly a partner relationship, emerges as the strongest contender for a place in the list of protective factors in adulthood (Belsky and Pensky, 1988; Kaufman and Zigler, 1993; Oliver, 1993), and the present findings, both statistical and qualitative, support this conclusion. 'Deliberateness', 'planfulness', or adopting a conscious resolution not to repeat the pattern as an adult, is another

(Bennett *et al.*, 1987; Kaufman and Zigler, 1993; Oliver, 1993). In the case of physical or sexual child abuse, an awareness of events in one's own history, and a capacity to face the past and the future in full knowledge of these events, has been identified as important also (Kaufman and Zigler, 1993; Oliver, 1993).

Although the present research and the discussion in this chapter have explored some of the complexities surrounding the question of the adulthood effects of parental drinking problems, many others have remained unexamined. Nothing has been said, for example, about ethnic or socio-cultural differences which are potentially so important (Sher, 1991), nor have we been able to take account of some of the undoubtedly important issues external to the immediate family such as parents' work, wealth or poverty, neighbourhood or community (Moos *et al.*, 1990; Belsky, 1993). The following is a summary of the main conclusions of the research described in this book, having considered the results in the light of what we judge to be some of the best supported research findings and ideas from elsewhere.

SUMMARY

General Conclusions

- The offspring of parents with drinking problems are at significant risk for a range of emotional, conduct, educational and learning, and friendship adjustment problems whilst they are children or adolescents living at home and in contact with a problem drinking parent. There is considerable variability in whether and to what extent such difficulties are experienced, however, and not all offspring of problem drinking parents will suffer childhood adjustment problems.

- Offspring of parents with drinking problems are significantly more likely to have experienced disharmony, often involving domestic violence, in their families of upbringing. Childhood family disharmony is an important mediator between having a parent with a drinking problem and experiencing childhood adjustment problems: when (and probably only when) a parental drinking problem is associated with family disharmony, children are at risk of experiencing adjustment problems. Family-of-origin disharmony may subsume, and be a more useful explanatory variable than, more specific concepts that have appeared in the literature.

- Offspring of parents with drinking problems are at increased risk of excessive alcohol and/or other drug use as young adults, but only a minority are affected in this way. The risk ratio in the present study was 1.8 to 1, with a higher ratio for daughters (3.5 to 1) than for sons (1.4 to 1). The overall risk is significantly higher for men. Measures of alcohol consumption alone, as opposed to measures of alcohol problems, show little difference between offspring and others. There is a tendency for more offspring than others to be abstainers or very light drinkers as adults. The majority do not take after their parents by developing drinking or drug problems themselves. Offspring of parents with drinking problems are more likely to be heavy smokers than other adults. In general they are as mentally healthy and as satisfied with themselves and their lives as young adults as are other people who have not had parents with drinking problems.

- Childhood family disharmony and childhood adjustment problems are mediators between having had a parent with a drinking problem and adjustment problems as young adults. When there have been family disharmony and adjustment problems in childhood, offspring are at greater risk of problems in the transition from adolescence to adulthood, including excessive alcohol and/or drug use, and of poorer mental health as young adults. In the absence of childhood family disharmony and adjustment problems, offspring have a somewhat increased risk of transition problems but have no increased risk of poor adulthood mental health. In fact they may be strengthened by the experience and may be particularly successful in various walks of life including parenting. In general the adulthood risks run by offspring of parents with drinking problems have been over-emphasised in the past, and the resilience of the majority of such offspring over-looked.

Other, More Specific, Conclusions

- The majority of offspring of parents with drinking problems are exposed to such problems at home, continuously, throughout most of the years of childhood and adolescence. Most of their parents' drinking problems remain untreated during this time. Concomitant mental health problems amongst problem-drinking parents, and amongst their non-problem drinking spouses, are commonly reported.
- Offspring of parents with drinking problems are more likely to experience, whilst living at home, a wide range of stressful events and circumstances. Amongst the commonest of these are: parental drunkenness, moodiness, unreliability and embarrassing behaviour; reduced family social life, joint family activities, and open family discussions; awareness

of rows, including violence between parents, and experiencing pressure to take sides or participate in parents' rows; a poor relationship, sometimes involving violence, with the problem-drinking parent; being required to adopt a caretaking or coping role more suitable to an older person.

- Although parental divorce or separation is more common amongst offspring, the difference was not significant in the present study, although others have found it to be so. Quality of family life much more clearly distinguishes offpring of parents with drinking problems from other people.

- When the parent with the drinking problem is the mother, problem drinking is more likely to occur at home and certain negative experiences for a child are greater (e.g. involvement in parental rows, and acting older). Relationships with problem-drinking mothers are less negative than are relationships with problem-drinking fathers, however, and the onset of mothers' drinking problems occurs on average later in childhood. Positive family experiences are on average better preserved when mothers rather than fathers have drinking problems.

- Offspring of parents with drinking problems are more likely than other people to experience a number of signs of childhood maladjustment. Boys are particularly likely to experience problems in the 'anti-social behaviour' group, which includes: destructive behaviour, aggression, stealing, self-injurious behaviour, and delinquency. Girls are particularly at risk of experiencing problems in the 'withdrawn, demoralised and problems at school' group, which includes: concentration difficulties at school, distractability, anxiety, frequent waking, inability to do homework at home, and depression. Adolescent offspring of parents with drinking problems are also more likely to be 'precocious' in their use of alcohol or other drugs. Sons are likely to be at least fairly heavy alcohol consumers by the age of 17. Daughters are more likely to have been prescribed psychoactive medication.

- Offspring of parents with drinking problems are more likely to report difficulties with friendships as children or adolescents. They are particularly likely to report feelings of embarrassment, concern about being shown up in front of friends, worry about bringing friends home, and trying to meet friends outside home as much as possible. They report a greater degree of division between their home and peer group than other children and adolescents. They leave home significantly earlier.

- As ways of reacting to living with a parent with drinking problems, offspring are particularly likely to report having tried to avoid the problem-drinking parent by refusing to talk to him/her, staying in their own bedroom, hiding, or going out. Such ways of coping combined with other signs of 'switching off' (building a shell around oneself, feeling lonely, daydreaming) and blaming oneself or feeling guilty, form a general 'detachment' coping factor. This factor correlates, for daughters, with emotional adjustment problems and a greater home-peer division in adolescence. Detached ways of coping with a parental drinking problem in childhood are related to both transitional problems and poorer adulthood mental health, for both sons and daughters.

- Another common way of responding, also equally likely for sons and daughters, is openly challenging the problem-drinking parent by rowing, threatening or hitting. Combined with emotional ways of attacking the parent (trying to show him or her up, or making him or her jealous) and actions directed against the self (threatening to kill oneself, refusing to eat, making oneself sick, or getting drunk), this forms a second coping factor—'confrontation and self-destructive action'. This factor is correlated with family violence and disharmony and, for sons, with anti-social adjustment problems and friendship problems.

- Daughters of parents with drinking problems are more likely than other women to be married or cohabiting as young adults, and sons and daughters of parents with drinking problems are more likely than other young adults to have children. Sons are less likely than other young men to have increased their occupational status compared with their parents. In general, sons of parents with drinking problems are less socially stable as young adults than other young men, but daughters of problem-drinking parents are more socially stable than other young women.

- There is no evidence that offspring of parents with drinking problems are at greater risk of excessive alcohol/or other drugs use as young adults if the parent with the drinking problem is of the same sex than if the parent with the drinking problem is of the opposite sex. There is some evidence, however, that daughters of fathers with drinking problems are more at risk if their relationships with their problem-drinking fathers were more positive. A greater length of exposure to a parental drinking problem in childhood does not confer greater risk, but having two parents with drinking problems does, particularly for daughters. If the problem-drinking parent drinks at home there is also an increased risk of excessive adulthood drinking or drug use.

- There is a tendency for daughters of parents with drinking problems to have adulthood relationships with heavy or problem drinkers more frequently than other young women, but the difference is not great, and only a small minority of daughters of parents with drinking problems go on to marry men with drinking problems.

- Although young adult offspring of parents with drinking problems were indistinguishable from other young adults on most measures of mental health and life satisfaction in the present study, they did score in a more introverted direction on a scale of introversion–extraversion (significant for women), and they reported fewer social activities in the last week (significant for men). It is possible that previous research may have failed to detect some real, interpersonal adulthood effects of having had a parent with a drinking problem.

- Excessive alcohol use as a young adult has a positive loading on two separate adult adjustment factors. One of these factors ('excess, delinquency and sociability') also subsumes regular cannabis use, risky other illicit drug use, more frequent social activities, minor delinquency, ability to form close relationships, and extraversion. This factor does not correlate with having had a parent with a drinking problem. The other factor ('problems in transition to adulthood') also subsumes heavy tobacco use, leaving home at an earlier age, having a greater number of children, minor delinquency, and lower occupational status improvement compared to the previous generation. It is on this factor that young adult offspring of parents with drinking problems have higher scores.

- Detailed analysis of individual cases suggest that there may be a number of mechanisms of intergenerational transmission. Very commonly described, however, are ways of escaping home situations. These 'escape attempts', although often beneficial, are sometimes costly in terms of an unplanned and problematic transition to adulthood, and an unsettled or unstable early adult life.

- Positive mental health as a young adult is best predicted by contemporaneously measured variables. In the present study adulthood mental health for women was best predicted by the quality of their social lives and of their marriages, and for men by the quality of their work lives (or alternative), the quality of their social lives, and marital quality. For women, but not for men, childhood family disharmony and childhood adjustment problems remained significant for adulthood mental health, via their indirect effects upon satisfaction with social life and marital quality.

CHAPTER **8**

IMPLICATIONS FOR INTERVENTION, SERVICE DEVELOPMENT AND PREVENTION

The research discussed within this book, both ours and that of others, has made it clear that the children of problem drinkers will often, as a consequence, develop problems of their own. Sometimes these problems will be severe. Such problems will be especially apparent while the offspring are still children, and sometimes they will continue into adulthood. The purpose of the present chapter is to raise for discussion some issues regarding the value of treatment and preventive interventions aimed at this group who are at high risk as children and at some risk as adults. We shall consider whether treatment interventions might usefully be specifically targeted at the pre-adult children of problem drinking parents, or whether the better approach might be a more general one. The likely importance of good inter-agency cooperation will also be discussed. Whether specific services should be offered to the adult offspring of problem drinking parents will then be considered. Finally the promise and pitfalls of attempting preventive interventions for this group will be examined.

WHAT HELP WOULD BENEFIT THE PRE-ADULT CHILDREN OF PROBLEM DRINKING PARENTS?

It is now well established, and the present research supports the conclusion, that children, living at home with a parent who has a serious alcohol problem, are often subject to high levels of stress and a quality of family climate and relationships with parents that is much less than ideal. More often than not this a chronic rather than temporary state of affairs for children. Whilst it is equally important to emphasise the variability that has been found in the present study as in others, it is the case that offspring, whilst living at home, are at considerably increased risk for a whole range of childhood problems—emotional, conduct, in their education, and in their relationships with friends and the links between the home and their peer group. The implications for intervention that this knowledge provides are that these children will often need specific help in those areas.

Yet, despite these obvious implications for intervention with the families of problem drinkers, the major issue that has arisen for these authors throughout many years work with such families in the UK is the lack of help that exists for them. This is especially the case for help which might be offered to the children in these families. Once these children are adults, access to appropriate services may be somewhat easier for them, and the evidence seems to suggest that by then the proportion of the group at risk is much reduced. The main issue is the need for help for these children while they are still most vulnerable and affected. What is available for them as children? The answer appears to be almost nothing.

As examples in the UK, *Al-Ateen*, a self-help group that exists to help the children of problem drinkers, is not very wide-spread, and will only help older children (usually mid-teens or older). *Childline* exists, and can offer a helpful telephone lifeline, but it requires someone both to be able to have access to a telephone which the child can use without fear of being interrupted, and to be old enough to be competent to use the telephone in the first place. Nevertheless, even given these difficulties, it is a measure of the needs to be met that in the four-month period from February to May, 1993, some 660 telephone calls were received by Childline from children aged 10–17, where alcohol, mostly their parents' excessive drinking, was part of the problem with which they wanted help. *Child and Family Counselling* services run by the Health Service exist in many areas, but legally they can only offer help ('treatment') if it is given with parental consent, which can make it very difficult and in some cases impossible to access help unless the child has the support of at least one parent. It may be impossible for a child who wants help because of the behaviour of one or both parents, to ask for that help if the agency then needs to tell the parents and ask them for consent to 'treat' the child. Other services do exist— *Youth Services, Voluntary Agencies* such as the Children's Society, and a limited amount of *In-School Counselling* services—but access to any of these by younger children is severely limited, and most have to follow statutory child protection procedures which would necessitate informing the parents of the fact that they have been approached by the child.

Developments in Other Countries

Although it is generally true to say that children of problem drinking parents have been almost totally neglected in the design of treatment and prevention in other countries as in Britain (Orford, 1990), there have been isolated reports of individual projects and programmes that are at least suggestive of some of the things that might be done. A number of the earliest reports came from Eastern European countries. For example, from then-Czechoslovakia came a report of an approach to 'families affected by alcoholism' which included holidays with children, monthly club meetings, intensive work with whole families, and a 14-day long rehabilitation camp (Ptacek, 1983). Former Yugoslavia was another country to have experimented with both family therapy for this group of families (Gacic, 1980) and family treatment including guidance to family members including children (Moser, 1980).

One of the earliest programmes to be reported from the USA was described by Homonoff and Stephen (1979). This began with a request from an Al-Anon mother, and participants were recruited largely by word of mouth and personal recommendation. Advertising and agency referrals were not very successful sources of recruits. The programme involved group meetings for children in the age groups 6 to 8 years old and 9 to 11 years old, and the aim was to educate children about 'alcoholism' and its effects on the family. Use was made of collage, plays and puppets, and the authors concluded, as others have done (e.g. Wilson and Orford, 1978) that service providers, "tend to ignore how much children of alcoholics see, hear and understand about alcoholism and how deeply they are affected by it" (p. 926). The advice they were given in the Homonoff and Stephen programme included: avoid confrontation, resist interferring in arguments, escape to your room or a friend's or relative's house, don't protect the drinking parent, assert your own needs for nurture and security, and take responsibility for tasks appropriate to your age.

Much of that advice is similar to that contained in self-help books aimed at families of problem drinkers (e.g. Meyer, 1982; Seixas, 1980). The message contained in many such books for family members (usually spouses) is roughly as follows: be realistic and look after your own needs, you are certainly not to blame; but try to understand that he (often the male pronoun is used alone and without comment in this context) is suffering from a kind of disease, try to find out as much about it as you can, show understanding, love, concern; but do not cover the problem up or protect the drinker from the consequences of his drinking; there are ways in which you can constructively confront him with the reality of the problem (e.g. Meyer, 1982).

The advice given specifically to children of problem drinking parents by Seixas (1980) in her book, *How to Cope with an Alcoholic Parent*, conforms closely in general outline to Meyer's advice but lays greater stress upon looking after the child's own needs. For example:

It may be that for now your task is to take responsibility for your own life. You can enrich it with many things including books, movies ... Be in charge of your own life and try not to concentrate on your parent's drinking. Build up your own world. How well do you know your district? What is there to do after school ...? (p. 60).

But Seixas recommends that children should adopt an understanding attitude towards both parents. For example:

A drinking parent is often unfair because he is confused or does not remember things. It is easier to accept unfairness if you know that your parent is not himself because of drinking (p. 24).

There is even a hint that children may be able to assist in confronting their drinking parents:

A person who is sick can be helped more and sooner if people do not join in hiding it. One way to help the person with alcoholism is to let him know the consequences of the drinking (p. 66).

And there are certainly positive things which according to Seixas children can do to help themselves and the rest of the family. For example:

Sit down with your parents and together write out some rules for the family, for example about defining household chores. At the end of the week have a family meeting to discuss it, so failures of assignments and resentments can be talked about promptly (p. 30).

Such advice is written from a position of close knowledge, often personal knowledge, of what living in a family where an adult has a serious drinking problem is actually like, and it undoubtedly contains a great deal of wisdom. Those without such knowledge can learn a lot from it. It has usually been written, however, from a position of confident certainty in the disease model of 'alcoholism' and the 12-Step AA and Al-Anon treatment philosophy associated with it. It sounds convincing but it may be unrealistically, and perhaps unreasonably, demanding for spouses let alone for children. Our position is less certain and our suggestions more tentative and general. We suggest, first, that counsellors need to encourage children to talk and think about the range of possible strategies which they might employ, both ones which they have already used, and ones which they have not yet tried; and second, to augment these ideas by providing the children with information about the different coping methods which we know have been employed by children of problem drinkers. As with any other counselling technique, the aim here is to enable the client to clarify the various advantages and disadvantages of one sort versus another sort of strategy, to empower the client to take action to implement one or more strategies, and to support the client while they are trying out this new method of coping. Counselling the children of problem drinkers is in this sense no different from counselling anyone else.

Specifically children need to *understand how best to cope with parental violence.* The study reported within this book is but the latest to record that whilst many of the children of problem drinkers experience no parental violence, many others suffer from parental anger, aggression, and violence, through large parts of their childhoods. Developing services need to plan out (using well respected tools such as anger management) interventions aimed at the children, and other family members, of problem drinkers, to enable them to better deal with this frightening phenomenon. Incidentally Seixas also gives a lot of what sounds like good advice on how to respond in emergencies, to avoid getting into rows with the drinker when he is drunk, getting help from outside the family, and not putting up with physical or sexual abuse.

Sher (1991) cites several specialised programmes that have been tried more recently in the USA. Davis *et al.* (1985), for example, described a programme for sixth grade children based on the CASPAR (Cambridge-Somerville Program for Alcoholism Rehabilitation) curriculum that has been used nationally in that country. Many of the children participating were referred from special education services or by teachers or parents, and the programme consisted of puppet shows, storybooks, arts and crafts and other activities. Children were taught that that they are not alone, that their parents' drinking is not their fault, that it is important to take care of their own needs and to have fun like other children.

Edwards and Zander (1985, cited by Sher, 1991) recommended the following for school counsellors working with children of problem drinking parents: establish a trusting relationship by demonstrating consistent care and interest; help the child overcome denial; explain and discuss alcoholism as a disease; help the child identify and express diverse feelings; help the child develop positive relationships; incorporate success into all excercises and activities; recognise the child's worth by providing praise; provide the child with a sense of control for facing family situations; and provide a realistic sense of hope. Sher (1991) also cites programmes spe-cially set up for high school student and higher education student offspring.

A number of workers in the USA have been attracted to the idea of screening for 'children of alcoholics'. For example Sheridan (1995) reported favourably on the 30-item Children of Alcoholics Screening Test (CAST). DiCicco *et al.* (1984) used the single question: Have you ever wished that either one or both of your parents would drink less? In one survey of junior and senior high school pupils in one town 30% answered this question in the affirmative. Those who did were more likely to opt for an after-school CAF ('children from alcoholic family') group which focussed on the effects of alcohol problems on the family, the child's rela-tionships with others, and means of surviving and coping with a parent with a drinking problem. Controversy surrounds the use of screening in this way. Hodgins and Shimp (1995), for example, conclude favourably about a short, six-item, version of CAST on the basis of their research. Roosa *et al.* (1993), however, have concluded that single-item or short screening instruments of this kind are insufficiently accurate for research or intervention applications, either lacking sensitivity or producing too many false positives.

A somewhat more sophisticated, three-stage recruitment strategy was tested by Gensheimer *et al.* (1990). At stage 1 all 4th, 5th and 6th grade pupils at 6 schools in the USA were shown a film (Lots of Kids Like Us) depicting the experiences of children of problem drinking parents. At the second stage a meeting was held at the end of the school day to discuss the film and hear about a programme for children with experiences similar to those depicted on the film. At stage 3 all children who attended the meet-ings were invited to take part in the programme that would teach children more about how children and families can be harmed by alcohol abuse, and parental permission letters were distributed. Of the 844 children who saw the film, 11% obtained parental permission to take part in the pro-gramme. Girls in the youngest age group predominated amongst those who obtained permission to take part, and a sizable proportion did not in fact express concern about their own parents' drinking. A further 26% attended the follow-up meeting but did not obtain parental consent.

Amongst the many problems in recruiting for intervention programmes, Gensheimer *et al.*, believe the issue of parental consent is crucial. As they say: "Since parents are the primary gatekeepers of the services chil-dren receive, a major issue is how to gain access to children whose par-ents may not be aware of, or who may deny, their children's problems" (1990, p. 708).

Although there have now been a number of interesting service developments such as these, designed specifically for children of problem drinking parents, especially in the USA, it is probably too early to be able to assess their effectiveness (Sher, 1991). Nor would all agree that this kind of specialised approach is the right one. One of the most important findings of the present research was that the link between a parental drinking problem and childhood difficulties was largely, and perhaps entirely, mediated by family disharmony. This is a finding in which we can have a great deal of confidence since it is in keeping with so many other findings both in the specialised research literature on children of problem drinking parents and in the wider literature on childhood adversities of various kinds. It is also the case that the kinds of difficulties for which children of problem drinking parents are most at risk are quite common childhood problems—fears and anxieties, difficult conduct, trouble at school—representing a range of presenting difficulties with which child clinical psychologists, for example, are very familiar. Hence, although the cause may be specific (i.e. the parental excessive drinking), both the immediate antecedents (family disharmony) and the problems for which the children are most at risk are not. There may, then, be a strong argument in favour of a non-specific response to these children's psychological needs. This may be even more the case in countries without the tradition of publicity and advocacy for 'alcoholism' and 'children of alcoholics' that there has been in the USA.

The Need for Good Inter-Agency Collaboration

Since the problems of childhood that we are concerned with here are both highly prevalent and liable to be disguised or invisible to service providers, we suggest that a broad strategy is called for, involving specialist agencies, non-specialist agencies, and good collaboration between the two. Part of what is needed may be more specialist services aimed at children of problem drinking parents, whether or not there is a supportive parent, which could escape the requirement to inform both parents of the child's attendance. These services could offer a listening ear—enabling the child to feel that at least someone was prepared to listen, and to hear; and they could also provide counselling, enabling the child to work through the various options open to him or her as to how best to cope with a problem-drinking parent, and to assess which option might be the best one to pursue in the situation.

As a minimum, then, agencies which deal with alcohol problems should, as a matter of course, widen their net and make their counselling services available to any family members affected by another's alcohol use. They should also designate one or more members of their team to specialise in work with children, and to set up cross referral systems, and joint working, with school counselling and child psychology and psychiatry services.

Similarly, generic services for children need to be aware that parental alcohol problems are extremely prevalent, and hence many difficulties presented by children may have this parental problem as an underlying causative factor. Often such parents will be very resistant to revealing their problems, and an important training need for staff within children's services may be the issue of how to raise these topics in an unthreatening manner (Velleman, 1992c).

The vital need for inter-agency collaboration has been stressed by both Blau *et al.* (1994) and by Tracy and Farkas (1990) writing from the USA. Tracy and Farkas are particularly direct in their call for coordinated, collaborative and comprehensive services in both child welfare and alcohol and drug treatment:

Alcohol and other drug (AOD) abuse treatment programs and child welfare services have tended to remain relatively separate from one another, ignoring the likelihood that they share a population of clients. Since child welfare workers have generally had limited training in AOD abuse treatment, they are often ill equipped to assess the level of risk and to develop appropriate case plans...Rarely do staff members at alcohol and other drug abuse treatment programs have any training in parenting skills, recognizing or treating child maltreatment, or child welfare...Changes in attitudes, knowledge, and skills are necessary for practitioners in both arenas (pp. 57–58).

They go on to outline a combined curriculum involving changes in attitudes and values (especially towards drug-abusing mothers), a knowledge base for practice, and skills training. In our view everyone who works with alcohol or drug users, whether or not they are paid or voluntary, requires some basic training in working with and understanding the families of these users. Currently, professional workers show scant regard for the needs and problems of relatives of alcohol or drug misusers. This was graphically demonstrated by the family members of drug users interviewed in one study (Velleman *et al.*, 1993). Although most had received some form of support, either from informal, self-help or formal agencies, many of these relatives were dissatisfied with this support, especially with that received from 'formal' agencies.

Building Family Harmony and Utilising the Whole Family

The research reported in this book has underlined the importance of family harmony. The most effective ways of helping children of problem drinking parents may be, therefore, to assist in rebuilding family harmony or preventing disharmony, involving one or both parents and possibly other family members. For example, the spouse of a problem drinker (increasingly being seen as a legitimate client in many alcohol-specific agencies) could be helped to not only cope better him/her-self, but also to enable any child to start to learn how to better deal with things. Spouses could be encouraged to talk with their children at home: problems could be discussed, different options as to how best to cope could be thought through, and action plans could be developed. Alternatively, the child could be enabled to access help in his or her own right, via the children's services, or via any school counselling that might exist.

A number of reports have now appeared, which show great promise, of interventions offered specifically to the spouses or partners of problem drinkers. Although these have as their principal aims the encouragement of the problem drinker to modify drinking and enter treatment, and the improvement of the partner's or spouse's quality of life, improvement of the lives of any children living in the family is likely to accompany these positive outcomes. Hence these partner-oriented programmes may be seen as amongst the most promising of approaches for children who stand to benefit at second hand (Barber and Crisp, 1994). They include a number from the USA (Sisson and Azrin, 1993; Thomas and Santa, 1982; Thomas and Ager, 1993) and Australia (Barber and Crisp, 1994, 1995) and two from the UK (Yates, 1988; Howells, 1997).

Many children will be greatly helped by their parents simply by their bringing the difficulties out into the open. Many problem drinkers hold onto the fiction that their children know nothing of their problems. Research shows that most children have a very definite idea of the existence of such a problem, and that the claims of successfully hiding it from the family are commonly wishful thinking. If counselling agencies were able to confront such statements, and enable problem-drinking parents to understand that their behaviour is being perceived by their children, then they might also be able to start to discuss the issues with their children. Such a move could well be beneficial to both child, and problem-drinking parent.

SERVICES FOR ADULT CHILDREN OF
PROBLEM DRINKING PARENTS

The discussion above has dealt solely with services for offspring while they are still children. But with the rise of the ACOA (Adult Children of Alcoholics) movement in the USA have come a number of attempts to provide services specifically for that group of *adults*. Seixas and Levitan (1984), for example, described the setting up of a counselling group. Members were recruited via newspaper advertisements and groups ran for eight sessions. At least one Al-Anon meeting was to be attended, and when basic information was needed, the disease model of 'alcoholism' was described, with an overview of Al-Anon, AA and Al-Ateen. Group members, nearly all of whom were women, were reported to have felt relieved to be able to talk about their common experiences, and to be able to face common issues such as trusting others, knowing whether their parents were really 'alcoholics', guilt, bad experiences at holiday times, their own drinking and drug-taking, and their own abilities as parents.

Sher (1991) reported that ACOAs had recently started to participate in Al-Anon family groups or to start groups of their own. He cited Cutter and Cutter (1987) who reported that the main problems discussed at 'adult children' groups were: depression and fear, alcoholism-related problems, feeling responsible for others, difficulty expressing feelings and being assertive, difficulty with intimacy and closeness, and problems working the programme. Although those authors noted that the greatest improvements were in lowered depression and greater self-acceptance, Sher (1991) concluded that there was to date little evidence of the effectiveness of any of the approaches to helping adult children of problem drinking parents that had been tried in the last few years.

One reason for the lack of clear-cut success of such programmes may be that many of the participants are not, in fact, at high risk. At the end of the present research the conclusion arrived at was that the *long-term* risks for adult offspring of problem drinking parents had been exaggerated in the past. The outlook is not so bleak as it has sometimes been painted. Offspring do not necessarily go on to develop further or continuing problems in adulthood. Yet there will be a minority who do develop such problems, and for them there may be a need to access services. Again this is a conclusion in which we have some confidence because of the added weight of other recent research findings with community groups and appropriate controls, plus a recently emerging consensus that intergenerational discontinuity and resilience in the face of childhood adversity are much more the norm than had at one time been supposed. This conclusion was tempered somewhat by the recognition that a possible 'survivors bias' in the selection of research participants could not entirely be dismissed. It should also be admitted that there may still be long-term, and more or less subtle, interpersonal effects of having had a parent with a drinking problem which research has so far failed to detect. Nevertheless the weight of the evidence suggests that most 'adult children' will not experience psychological difficulties as adults on account of their parents' excessive drinking, and that some will even have been psychologically strengthened by the experience.

There are undoubtedly, though, sub-groups who are at risk in the longer term, and arguably services should be targetted at those groups. One such group, the present results suggest, consists of maritally dissatisfied and demoralised women whose families of origin were disharmonious and who experienced emotional problems themselves as children or adolescents. Another is composed of men who adopted an acting-out role as youngsters in the face of parental problem drinking, who developed antisocial difficulties while living at home, and who have retained delinquent or deviant life-styles as adults.

Even then, the same question that was asked earlier about the specialist or general orientation of services for children, can be raised again here in relation to adult services. Again we lean towards the view that these services do not need to be designated ones for the adult offspring of problem drinkers. Many people who need help in adulthood do so due to problems and difficulties which stem at least in part from childhood; and these are issues which most mental health services are well equipped to handle. The concerns and difficulties of children of problem drinking parents as adults overlap with those of others who have experienced other kinds of serious problem as children, and generic services ought to be equipped to deal with them. Our overall view, as outlined earlier when speaking of services for children, is that services for the high risk groups with which we are concerned in this book should combine the best of generic intervention with a sensitivity to the special concerns and needs of these groups. A demoralised adult who experienced as a child some of the worst features of family life described in Chapter 4 may need both the benefits of a good general psychological or mental health service and the opportunity to talk about and come to terms with his or her childhood experiences. The person or people with whom he or she talks need to know something of the special circumstances that the children of problem drinking parents have faced.

CAN THE RISKS TO OFFSPRING OF PROBLEM DRINKING PARENTS BE PREVENTED?

Turning now to prevention issues, we wish to make a number of points. First, it is clear from the accumulated evidence that *offspring of problem drinkers, at least while they are children, are a particularly high risk group. They also run a somewhat increased risk of experiencing problems in the transition to adulthood and of suffering from substance abuse themselves as adults.* This knowledge has clear implications for prevention, besides the clear indications for intervention for those already experiencing difficulties, outlined above. Knowing as we do that the children of problem drinkers are at high risk of developing a wide range of serious psychological and physical problems during childhood, a strong argument could be made for a concerted preventive effort being aimed at all children of problem drinkers whether or not they are seeking help or treatment. At the very least, it might be argued, these at-risk sons and daughters should be warned about their risks of developing problems in childhood, and offered help in dealing with their difficulties in non-harmful ways. There might also be a strong case for these children being warned about their raised risk of developing substance abuse and certain other problems in the transition to adulthood.

Such a policy would undoubtedly raise ethical issues, however, with some arguing that it is unethical to warn offspring about future risks, in that this might lead to a self-fulfilling prophesy. Efforts at prevention are always attended by ethical problems particularly if they are of the high-risk, primary prevention kind that involves targeting people who have not yet shown signs of problems or difficulties but who are thought to be at particular risk, perhaps, as in this case, because their parents suffered from a particular problem or because they experienced certain conditions in childhood. The problem that arises is the danger of over-prediction, and of targetting preventive interventions at people who would not, in the absence of the intervention, have gone on to experience the difficulties for which they were thought to be at risk (Levine and Perkins, 1987; Orford, 1992). Preventive interventions for offspring of parents with drinking problems are a good case in point since the conclusion of our own and others' research is that the long-term risks, at least, may have been over-estimated in the past and that the large majority of such offspring may not be at risk of major diffulties of psychological adjustment as adults (see Chapter 7). The question has to be asked whether there is a danger that identifying young people as possibly at risk on the basis of their parents' drinking problems, and inviting them to participate in a preventive intervention, might not in some instances be actually harmful in certain ways (Sher, 1991). This might be the case, for example, if labelling as a 'child of an alcoholic' or equivalent, conferred some degree of stigma in the person's own eyes or those of others, and led to problems, rather than prevented them, by some process akin to a self-fulfilling prophecy.

Sher (1991) reports two experiments that do indeed seem to show that high school students, as well as mental health workers, have a bias towards assuming that a person said to have an alcoholic parent is more deviant or pathological than someone without such a parental problem (Burk and Sher, 1990). This, coupled with the possibility that typical descriptions of the ACOA personality contain traits that are very commonly found in the general population (Sher, 1991), could easily lead to identified and labelled offspring, and others who know this status of theirs, assuming deviancy and recognising as consequences of their parental problems characteristics and problems that should not be so attributed.

These are serious ethical dilemmas. It is our position, however, that it is the right of each individual to have access to information concerning him or herself, and that informing people about their risks, coupled with providing clear advice as to how to safeguard themselves from harm, is the most ethical course of action. Our conclusion is that a proper national and international policy for the maximisation of people's health should give much more serious attention, than has hitherto been the case, to the prevention of short- and long-term future psychological ill-health amongst the offspring of problem drinking parents. Many issues would need to be carefully considered. Whether preventive efforts should be targeted at this high risk group as a whole, or whether they would more effectively be targeted more selectively, for example at those where the parental problem is associated with family disharmony or where as a result of screening, girls and boys are found already to be experiencing emotional or conduct problems, is just one of those issues. Continuing to ignore the risks run by this large group of children, and allowing their problems to unfold without attempts at prevention should not be an option.

Nevertheless the fact of resilience touched upon above, and discussed in previous chapters will be a crucial issue for prevention. Any efforts at prevention targeted at the offspring of problem drinking parents as a high risk group must avoid over-estimating the risks, especially those relating to adulthood outcomes. The fact that most offspring are *not* in fact at risk as far as we can tell must be communicated along with a balanced statement of the risks that offspring do run and an assessment of the other factors such as childhood psychological problems and family disharmony that may moderate the risk relationship.

The research reported in this book has highlighted the fact that family disharmony is central in the development of both childhood difficulties and the transmission of problems across generations, and this raises further important issues for prevention. Indeed, there is growing evidence that a range of mental health problems affect families and children in similar ways, via the mediator of family dysfunction. This implies that a *general preventive strategy* is needed rather than a series of individual and highly specific ones, each focussed on a different and particular parental problem. Newton (1992), in the UK, and Bloom (1996), in the USA, have reviewed a wide range of such general strategies for prevention. Newton reviewed in detail preventive programmes for families with young children, including the highly successful Homestart programme which provides volunteer befriending support for mothers experiencing difficulties, as well as pro-grammes for young people during the transition from local authority child-care to independence as young adults. Bloom, on the basis of a comprehensive review, has provided an overall framework for primary pre-vention, covering programmes that aim to: increase individuals' strengths; increase social supports; increase environmental resources; decrease indi-viduals' limitations; decrease social stresses; or decrease pressures from the environment. Hawkins *et al.* (1992) have taken a general preventive approach such as this in their recommendations for the prevention of alco-hol and other drug problems in adolescence and early adulthood. They advocate interventions such as: early childhood and family support pro-grammes; parenting skills training; interpersonal competence skills training; academic achievement promotion; and the facilitation of youth involve-ment in alternative activities.

In relation to the prevention of future harm, as to interventions designed to help those already in need, we shall finish with a plea. The plea is that a child and family perspective be taken with respect to alcohol problems, and that, likewise, the importance of alcohol problems with respect to child and family problems be appreciated. There has undoubt-edly been much resistance to this in the past. Such resistance was touched upon in the first section of this chapter—and it is a resistance shared equally between researchers, practitioners, and policy makers. Over the years we have found it difficult to persuade specialist alcohol workers to acknowledge and deal with the problems other family members have, in coping with clients' difficulties; and equally difficult to persuade child and family services to acknowledge and deal with the alcohol-related problems which underlie, or coexist with, the family difficulties which lead to presentation at child and family services. We feel strongly that until this resistance is removed, we shall make little headway in dealing with the family casualties of alcohol problems.

REFERENCES

Achenbach, T. (1978) The Child Behaviour Profile I: Boys aged 6–11. *Journal of Consulting and Clinical Psychology*, **46**, 478–488.

Aitken, P. (1979) *Ten-to-Fourteen-Year-Olds and Alcohol*. HMSO; Edinburgh.

Alterman, A., Searles, J. and Hall, J. (1989) Failure to find differences in drinking behaviour as a function of familial risk for alcoholism: a replication. *Journal of Abnormal Psychology*, **98**, 1–4.

Baddeley, A. (1982) Domains of recollection. *Psychological Review*, **89**, 708–729.

Baekeland, F., Lundwall, L. and Kissin, B. (1975) Methods for the treatment of chronic alcoholism: a critical appraisal. In Gibbons, R., Israel, Y., Kalant, H. Popham, R., Schmidt, W. and Smart, R. (Eds.), *Research Advances in Alcohol and Drug Problems, Volume 2.* Wiley; New York.

Bahrick, H., Bahrick, P. and Wittlinger, R. (1975) Fifty years of memory for names and faces: a cross-sectional approach. *Journal of Experimental Psychology: General*, **104**, 54–75.

Baltes, P. (1968) Longitudinal and cross-sectional sequences in the study of age and generation effects. *Human Development*, **11**, 145–171.

Bandura, A. (Ed.) (1971) *Psychological Modelling: Conflicting Theories.* Chicago: Aldine-Atherton.

Barber, J.G. and Crisp, B.R. (1994) The effects of alcohol abuse on children and the partner's capacity to initiate change. *Drug and Alcohol Review*, **13**, 409–416.

Barber, J.G. and Crisp, B.R. (1995) The 'pressures to change' approach to working with the partners of heavy drinkers. *Addiction*, **90**, 268–276.

Barnes, G. (1990) Impact of the family on adolescent drinking patterns. In Collins, R., Leonard, K. and Searles, K. (Eds.), *Alcohol and the Family: Research and Clinical Perspectives.* New York; Guildford.

Barnes, J., Farrell, M.P. and Cairns, A. (1986) Parental Socialization Factors and Adolescent Drinking Behaviors. *Journal of Marriage and the Family*, **48**, 27–36.

Barnes, J., Benson, C. and Wilsnack, S. (1978) Psychosocial characteristics of women with alcoholic fathers. In Galanter, M. (Ed.), *Currents in Alcoholism, Vol. VI.* pp. 209–222.

Baron, R. and Kenny, D. (1986) The moderator-mediator variable distinction in social psychological research: conceptual, strategic and statistical considerations. *Journal of Personality and Social Psychology*, **51**, 1173–1182.

Barrerra, M.Jr, Li, S.A. and Chassin, L. (1993) Ethnic group differences in vulnerability to parental alcoholism and life stress: A study of hispanic and non-hispanic caucasian adolescents. *American Journal of Community Psychology*, **21**, 15–35.

Bartlett, F. (1932) *Remembering.* Cambridge University Press; Cambridge.

Bauman, K.E., Foshee, V.A., Linzer, M.A. and Koch, G.G. (1990) Effect of Parental Smoking Classification on the Association Between Parental and Adolescent Smoking. *Addictive Behaviours*, **15**, 413–422.

Beardslee, W., Son, L. and Vaillant, G. (1986) Exposure to parental alcoholism during childhood and outcome in adulthood: a prospective longitudinal study. *British Journal of Psychiatry*, **149**, 584–591.

Bebbington, P., Hurry, J., Tennant, C., Sturt, E. and Wing, J. (1981) Epidemiology of mental disorders in Camberwell. *Psychological Medicine*, **11**, 561–579.

Bell, R.Q. (1968) A Reinterpretation of the Direction of Effects in Studies of Socialisation, *Psychological Rev.*, **75**, 81–95.

Belsky, J. (1993) Etiology of child maltreatment: A developmental-ecological analysis. *Psychological Bulletin*, **114**, 413–434.

Belsky, J. and Pensky, E. (1988) Developmental history, personality and family relationships: toward an emergent family system. In: R. Hinde and J. Stevenson-Hinde (Eds.). *Relationships within families* (pp. 193–217). Oxford, England: Clarendon Press.

Bennett, L., Wolin, S., Reiss, D. and Teitelbaum, M. (1987) Couples at risk for alcoholism recurrence: protective influences. *Family Process*, **26**, 111–129.

Bennett, L., Wolin, S. and Reiss, D. (1988) Cognitive, behavioural and emotional problems among school-age children of alcoholic parents. *American Journal of Psychiatry*, **145**, 185–190.

Bennett, L. and Wolin, S. (1990) Family culture and alcoholism transmission. In Collins, R., Leonard, K. and Searles, J. (Eds.), *Alchohol and the family: research & clinical perspectives*. New York; Guilford Press. Chapter 7, 194–219.

Bensley, L.S., Spieker, S.J. and McMahon, R.J. (1994) Parenting behavior of adolescent children of alcoholics. *Addiction*, **89**, 1265–1276.

Benson, C. (1980) *Coping and Support among Daughters of Alcoholics*. Unpublished PhD thesis, Indiana University.

Benson, C. and Heller, K. (1987) Factors in the Current Adjustment of Young Adult Daughters of Alcoholic and Problem Drinking Fathers. *Journal of Abnormal Psychology*, **96**, 305–312.

Bergman, L.R. and Wingby, M. (1993) Adult adjustment problems of separated children: A longitudinal study from birth to the age of 23 years. *Scandinavian Journal Soc. Welfare*, **2**, 10–16.

Berkowitz, A. and Perkins, H. (1988) Personality characteristics of children of alcoholics. *Journal of Consulting and Clinical Psychology*, **56**, 206–209.

Black, C. (1979) Children of alcoholics. *Alcohol Health and Research World*, **4**, 23–27.

Black, C., Bucky, S.F. and Wilder-Padilla, S. (1986) The interpersonal and emotional consequences of being an adult child of an alcoholic. *International Journal of the Addictions*, **21**, 213–321.

Blau, G.M., Whewell, M.C., Gullotta, T.P. and Bloom, M. (1994) The prevention and treatment of child abuse in households of substance abusers: A research demonstration progress report. *Child Welfare League of America.*

Blechman, E. (1982) Conventional wisdom about familial contributions to substance abuse. *American Journal of Drug and Alcohol Abuse*, **9**, 35–53.

Block, J.H., Gjerde, P.F. and Block, J.H. (1991) Personality antecedents of depressive tendencies in 18 year olds—A prospective study. *Journal of Personality and Social Psychology* **60**, 726–738.

Bloom, M. (1996) *Primary Prevention Practices*. Thousand Oaks, California: Sage.

Bohman, M., Sigvardsson, S. and Cloninger, C. (1981) Maternal inheritance of alcohol abuse: cross fostering analysis of adopted women. *Archives of General Psychiatry*, **38**, 965–969.

Boyadjieva, M. undated, Alcoholism and the family: Review of the literature in some socialist countries. Prepared for WHO (Dept. of Alcoholism, Sofia).

Brabant, S. and Martof, M. (1993) Childhood experiences of complicated grief: A study of adult children of alcoholics. *The International Journal of the Addictions*, **28**, 1111–1125.

Bronfenbrenner, U. (1979) *The Ecology of Human Development*. Harvard University Press; London.

Brown, G. (1988) Casual paths, chains and strands. In Rutter, M. (Ed.), *Studies of Psychosocial Risk: the Power of Longitudinal Data*. Cambridge University Press; Cambridge.

Brown, G. and Harris, T. (1978) *The Social Origins of Depression*. London: Tavistock.

Brown, G., Bifulco, A. and Harris, T. (1987) Life events, vulnerability and onset of depression: some refinements. *British Journal of Psychiatry*, **150**, 30–42.

Brown, S.A., Creamer, V.A. and Stetson, B.A. (1987) Adolescent Alcohol Expectancies in Relation to Personal and Parental Drinking Patterns. *Journal of Abnormal Psychology*, **96**, 117–121.

Browne, A. and Finkelhor, D. (1986) Impact of child sexual abuse: a review of the research. *Psychological Bulletin*, **99**, 66–77.

Burk, J.P. (1985) Psychological correlates for children of alcoholics: Socialization as a moderator of adult alcoholism and symptoms of psychopathology. Master's thesis. University of Missouri, Columbia (cited by Sher, 1991).

Burk, J.P. and Sher, K.J. (1988) The 'forgotten children' revisited: neglected areas of COA research. *Clinical Psychology Review*, **8**, 285–302.

Burk, J.P. and Sher, K.J. (1990) Labelling the child of an alcoholic: Negative stereotyping by mental health professionals and peers. *Journal of Studies on Alcohol*, **51**, 156–163 (cited by Sher, 1991).

Burr, A. (1982) *Families and Alcoholics*. London: Constable.

Cadoret, R. (1990) Genetics of alcoholism. In Collins, R., Leonard, K. and Searles, J. (Eds.), *Alcohol and the family: research & clinical perspectives*. New York; Guilford Press. Chapter 2, 39–78.

Cahalan, D. (1970) *Problem Drinkers: A National Survey*. Jossey Bass; San Fransisco.

Callan, V. and Jackson, D. (1986) Children of alcoholic fathers and recovered alcoholic fathers: personal and family functioning. *Journal of Studies on Alcohol*, **47**, 180–182.

Caspi, A. and Elder, G. (1988) Emergent family patterns: The intergenerational construction of problem behavior and relations. In R. Hinde and J. Stevenson-Hinde (Eds.), *Relationships within families* (pp. 218–240). Oxford, England: Clarendon Press.

Caspi, A., Elder, G.H. and Herbener, E.S. (1990) Childhood personality and the prediction of life-course patterns. In L.N. Robins and M. Rutter (Eds.), *Straight and Devious Pathways from Childhood to Adulthood*. Cambrige: Cambridge University Press; 13–35.

Chandy, J.M., Harris, L., Blum, R.W. and Resnick, M.D. (1993) Children of alcohol misusers and school performance outcomes. *Children and Youth Services Review*, **15**, 507–519.

Chandy, J.M., Harris, L., Blum, R.W., and Resnick, M.D. (1995) Female adolescents of alcohol misusers: Disordered eating features. *International Journal of Eating Disorders*, **17**, 283–289.

Chassin, L., Mann, L. and Sher, K. (1988) Self-awareness theory, family history of alcoholism, and adolescent alcohol involvement. *Journal of Abnormal Psychology*, **97**, 206–217.

Chassin, L., Pillow, D.R., Curran, P.J., Brooke, S.G., Barrera, M., and Barrera, M., Jr. (1993) Relation of parental alcoholism to early adolescent substance use: A test of three mediating mechanisms. *Journal of Abnormal Psychology*, **102**, 3–19.

Chassin, L., Curran, P.J., Hussong, A.M. and Colder, C.R. (1996) The relation of parent alcoholism to adolescent substance use: A longitudinal follow-up study. *Journal of Abnormal Psychology*, **105**, 70–80.

Chassin, L., Rogosch, F. and Barrera, M. (1990) Substance use and symptomatology among adolescent children of alcoholics. Manuscript under review (cited by Sher, 1991).

Chassin, L., Pillow, D.R., Curran, P.J., Molina Brooke S.G. and Barrera, M., Jr. (1993) Relation of parental alcoholism to early adolescent substance use: A test of three mediating mechanisms. *Journal of Abnormal Psychology*, **102**, 3–19.

Chipperfield, B. and Vogel-Sprott, M. (1988) Family history of problem drinking among young male social drinkers: Modeling effects on alcohol consumption. *Journal of Abnormal Psychology*, **97**, 423–428.

Clair, D. and Genest, M. (1987) Variables associated with the adjustment of offspring of alcoholic fathers. *Journal of Studies in Alcohol*, **48**, 345–355.

Claydon, P. (1987) Self-reported alcohol, drug and eating-disorder problems among male and female collegiate children of alcoholics. *Journal of American College Health*, **36**, 111–115.

Cloninger, C. (1987) Recent advances in family studies of alcoholism. In Goedde, H. and Agarwal, D. (Eds.), *Genetics and Alcoholism*. Alan Liss; New York.

Cloninger, C., Bohman, M and Sigvardsson, S. (1981) Inheritance of alcohol abuse: cross fostering analysis of adopted men. *Archives of General Psychiatry*, **38**, 861–868.

Collins, G.B., Kotz, M., Janesz, J.W., Messina, M. and Ferguson, T. (1985) Alcoholism in the families of bulimic anorexics. *Cleveland Clinic Quarterly*, **52**, 65–67.

Coombs, R.H. and Landsverk, J. (1988) Parenting styles and substance use during childhood and adolescence. *Journal of Marriage and the Family*, **50**, 473–482.

Cork, M. (1969) *The Forgotten Children: a Study of Children with Alcoholic Parents*. Alcoholism and Drug Research Foundation of Ontario; Toronto.

Corrao, G., Busellu, G., Valenti, M., Lepore, A.R., Sconci, V., Casacchia, M. and Orio, F.di. (1993) Alcohol-related problems within the family and global functioning of the children: A population-based study. *Social Psychiatry and Psychiatric Epidemiology*, **28**, 304–308.

Cotton, N. (1979) The familial incidence of alcoholism: a review. *Journal of Studies on Alcohol*, **40**, 89–116.

Cowen, E. and Work, W. (1988) Resilient children, psychosocial wellness and primary prevention. *American Journal of Community Psychology*, **16**, 591–607.

Crockenberg, S. (1987) Predictors and correlates of anger toward and punitive control of toddlers by adolescent mothers. *Child Development*, **58**, 964–975.

Cummings, E.M., Zahn-Waxler, C. and Radke-Yarrow, M.(1981) Young children's responses to expressions of anger and affection by others in the family. *Child Development*, **52**, 1274–1281 (cited by Grych and Fincham, 1990).

Cummings, E.M., Zahn-Waxler, C. and Radke-Yarrow, M. (1984) Developmental changes in children's reactions to anger in the home. *Journal of Child Psychology and Psychiatry*, **25**, 63–74 (cited by Grych and Fincham, 1990).

Cummings, E.M., Zahn-Waxler, C. and Radke-Yarrow, M. (1985) Influence of conflict between adults on the emotions and agression of young children. *Development Psychology*, **21**, 495–507 (cited by Grych and Fincham, 1990).

Cutter C.G. and Cutter, H.S.G. (1987) Experience and change in Al-Anon family groups: Adult children of alcoholics. *Journal of Studies on Alcohol*, **48**, 29–32.

Dahlgren, L. (1979) The familial incidence of alcoholism: A review. *J. Stud. Alcohol*, **40**, 89–116.

Davies, J. and Stacey, B. (1972) *Teenagers and Alcohol*. HMSO; London.

Davis, R.B., Johnston, P.D., DiCiccio, L. and Orenstein, A. (1985) Helping children of alcoholic parents: An elementary school program. The School Counsellor. May, 357–363 (cited by Sher, 1991).

DiCicco, L., Davis, R., Travis, J. and Orenstein, A. (1984) Recruiting children from alcoholic families into a peer education program. *Alcohol Health and Research World*, **8**, 28–34.

Djukanobic, B., Fridman, V., Milosavljevic, V., Vasev, C. and Ljububratic, D. (1978) Les familles parentales de alcooliques et de leurs epouses. *Rev. Alcoolisme*, **24**, 245–250.

Dobash, R. and Dobash, R. (1987) Violence towards wives. In Orford, J. (Ed.), *Coping with Disorder in the Family*. Croom Helm; London.

Dohrenwend, B.P. and Dohrenwend, B. (1969) *Social Status and Psychological Disorder: a Causal Inquiry*. New York: Wiley (cited by Bebbington *et al.*, 1981).

Domenico, D. and Windle, M. (1993) Intrapersonal and interpersonal functioning among middle-aged female adult children of alcoholics. *Journal of Consulting and Clinical Psychology*, **61**, 659–666.

Donald, M., Dunne, M. and Raphael, B. (1993) Young women and alcohol: Psychosocial factors associated with their own drinking, their fathers' drinking and both. *International Journal of Addictions*, **28**, 959–972.

Drake, D. and Vaillant, G. (1988) Predicting alcoholism and personality disorder in a 33-year longitudinal study of children of alcoholics. *British Journal of Addiction*, **83**, 799–807.

Edwards, D.M. and Zander, T.A. (1985) Children of alcoholics: Background and strategies for the counselor. *Elementary School Guidance and Counseling*, **20**, 2 (cited by Sher, 1991).

Egeland, B., Jacobvitz, D. and Papatola, K. (1987) Intergenerational continuity of abuse. In R. Gelles and J. Lancaster (Eds.), *Child abuse and neglect: Biosocial dimensions*. (pp. 255–276). Chicago: Aldine.

El-Guebaly, N. and Offord, D. (1977) The offspring of alcoholics: a critical review. *American Journal of Psychiatry*, **134**, 357–365.

El-Guebaly, N. and Offord, D. (1979) On being the offspring of an alcoholic: an update. *Alcoholism: Clinical and Experimental Research*, **3**, 148–157.

El-Guebaly, N., Walker, J.R., Ross, C.A. and Currie, R.F. (1990) Adult children of problem drinkers in an urban community. *British Journal of Psychiatry*, **156**, 249–255.

Elder, G.H. Jr. and Caspi, A. (1988) Economic Stress in Lives: Developmental Perspectives. *Journal of Social Issues*, **44**, 25–45.

Ellickson, P. and Hayes, R. (1991) Antecedents of drinking among young adolescents with different alcohol use histories. *Journal of Studies on Alcohol*, **53**, 398–408.

Emery, R. (1982) Inter-parental conflict and the children of discord and divorce. *Psychological Bulletin*, **92**, 310–330.

Engs, R. (1990) Family background of alcohol abuse and its relationship to alcohol consumption among college students: an unexpected finding. *Journal of Studies on Alcohol*, **51**, 542–547.

Estaugh, V. and Power, C. (1991) Family disruption in early life and drinking in young adulthood. *Alcohol and Alcoholism*, **26**, 639–644.

Farrington, D. (1988) Studying changes within individuals: the causes of offending. In Rutter, M. (Ed.), *Studies of Psychosocial Risk: the Power of Longitudinal Data*. Cambridge University Press; Cambridge.

Fidler,W., Michell, L., Raab, G. and Charlton, A. (1992) Research Report: Smoking: a special need? *British Journal of Addiction*, **87**, 1583–1591.

Finkelhor, D. and Dziuba-Leatherman, J. (1994) Victimization of children. *American Psychologist*, **49**, 173–183.

Finn, P. and Pihl, R. (1987) Men at high risk for alcoholism: the effect of alcohol on cardiovascular response to unavoidable shock. *Journal of Abnormal Psychology*, **96**, 230–236.

Folkman, S. and Lazarus, R. (1980) An analysis of coping in a middle-aged community sample. *Journal of Health and Social Behaviour*, **21**, 219–239.

Foxcroft, D. and Lowe, G. (1991) Adolescent drinking behaviour and family socialization factors: a meta-analysis. *Journal of Adolescence*, **14**, 255–273.

Gacic, B. (1980) Experiences in evaluation of the family therapy of alcoholism: the Institute for Mental Health in Belgrade. Paper presented at 26th International Institute on the Prevention and Treatment of Alcoholism, Cardiff (Center for Family Therapy and Alcoholism. Institute for mental Health, Belgrade).

Garmezy, N. (1985) Stress-resistant children: the search for protective factors. In Stevenson, J. (Ed.), *Recent Research in Developmental Psychopathology*, a book supplement to the *Journal of Child Psychology and Psychiatry*, 4, Pergamon; Oxford.

Garmezy, N. (1988) Longitudinal strategies, causal reasoning and risk research: a commentary. In Rutter, M. (Ed.), *Studies of Psychosocial Risk: the Power of Longitudinal Data*. Cambridge University Press; Cambridge.

Gelles, R. (1976) *Family Violence*, Beverley Hills, CA: Sage (cited by Kalmuss, 1984).

Gensheimer, L.K., Roosa, M.W. and Ayers, T.S. (1990) Children's self-selection into prevention programs: Evaluation of an innovative recruitment strategy for children of alcoholics. *American Journal of Community Psychology*, **18**, 5.

Goodwin, D. (1979) Alcoholism and heredity. *Archives of General Psychiatry*, **36**, 57–61.

Goodwin, D., Schulsinger, F., Hermansen, L., Guze, S. and Winokur, G. (1973) Alcohol problems in adoptees raised apart from alcoholic biological parents. *Archives of General Psychiaty*, **28**, 238–243.

Goodwin, D., Schulsinger, F., Moller, N., Hermansen, L., Winokur, G. and Guze, S. (1974) Drinking problems in adopted and non-adopted sons of alcoholics. *Archives of General Psychiatry*, **31**, 164–169.

Goodwin, D., Schulsinger, F., Moller, N., Mednick, S. and Guze, S. (1977) Psychopathology in adopted and nonadopted daughters of alcoholics. *Archives of General Psychiaty*, **34**, 1005–1009.

Grych, J. and Fincham, F. (1990) Marital conflict and children's adjustment: a cognitive—contextual framework. *Psychological Bulletin*, **108**, 267–290.

Gurling, H., Oppenheim, B. and Murray, R. (1984) Depression, criminality and psychopathology associated with alcoholism: evidence from a twin study. *Acta Geneticae Medicae et Gemellologiae*, **33**, 333–339.

Haaken, J. (1990) A critical analysis of the co-dependence construct. *Psychiatry*, **53**, 396–406.

Harburg, E., Difranceisco, W., Webster, D.W., Gleiberman, L. and Schork, A. (1990) Familial transmission of alcohol use: imitation of and aversion to parental drinking (1960) by adult offspring (1977). *Journal of Studies on Alcohol*, **51**, 245–256.

Harter, S., Alexander, P.C. and Neimeyer, R. A. (1988) Long-term effects of incestuous child abuse in college women: social adjustment, social cognition, and family characteristics. *Journal of Counselling and Clinical Psychology*, **56**, 1, 5–8.

Hawker, A. (1978) *Adolescents and Alcohol*. London; Edsall.

Hawkins, J.D., Catalano, R.F. and Miller, J.Y. (1992) Risk and protective factors for alcohol and other drug problems in adolescence and early adulthood: Implications for substance abuse prevention. *Psychological Bulletin*, **112**, 64–105.

Helgason, T. and Asmundsson, G. (1975) Behaviour and social characteristics of young asocial alcohol abusers. *Neuropsychobiology*, **1/2**, 109–120.

Heller, K., Sher, K. and Benson, C. (1982) Problems associated with risk overprediction in studies of offspring of alcoholics: implications for prevention. *Clinical Psychology Review*, **2**, 183–200.

Helzer, J. and Pryzbeck, T. (1988) The co-occurrence of alcoholism with other psychiatric disorders in the general population and its impact on treatment. *Journal of Studies on Alcohol*, **49**, 219–224.

Hereenkohl, E., Herrenkohl, R. and Toedtler, L. (1983) Perspectives on the intergenerational transmission of abuse. In D. Finkelhor, R. Gelles, G. Hotaling and M Straus (Eds.), *The Dark Side of Families*. (pp. 305–316). Beverley Hills, CA: Sage.

Herman, J.L. (1981) *Father-daughter incest*. Cambridge, MA: Harvard University Press (cited by Browne and Finkelhor, 1986).

Hetherington, E.M. (1988) Parents, children and siblings six years after divorce. In R.A. Hinde and J. Stephenson-Hinde (Eds.), *Relationships within Families* (pp. 311–331). New York: Oxford University Press.

Hetherington, E., Cox, M. and Cox, R. (1982) Effects of divorce on parents and children. In Lamb, M. (Ed.), *Nontraditional Families: Parenting and Child Development*. Erlbaum; Hillsdale, NJ.

Hill, E.M., Nord, J.L. and Blow, F.C. (1992) Research Report: Young-adult children of alcoholic parents: protective effects of positive family functioning. *British Journal of Addiction*, **87**, 1677–1690.

Hinde, A. (1988) Continuities and discontinuities: conceptual issues and methodological considerations. In Rutter, M. (Ed.), *Studies of Psychosocial Risk: the Power of Longitudinal Data*. Cambridge University Press; Cambridge.

HMSO (1992) *Children Act Report—presented to Parliament by the Secretaries of State for Health and for Wales*. London; HMSO.

Hodgins, D.C. and Shimp, L. (1995) Identifying adult children of alcoholics: methodological review and a comparison of the CAST-6 with other methods. *Addiction*, **90**, 255–268.

Homonoff, E. and Stephen, A. (1979) Alcohol education for children of alcoholics in a Boston neighborhood. *J. Stud. Alcohol*, **40**, 923–926.

Howells, E. (1997) Coping with a problem drinker: the development and evaluation of a therapeutic intervention for the partners of problem drinkers, in their own right. Unpublished PhD thesis, University of Exeter U.K.

Hrubek, Z. and Omenn, G. (1981) Evidence of genetic predisposition to alcoholic cirrhosis and psychosis: twin concordances for alcoholism and its biological end points by zygosity among male veterans. *Alcoholism*, **5**, 207–215.

Huesmann, L.R., Eron, L.D., Lefkowitz, M.M. and Walder, L.O. (1984) Stability of aggression over time and generations. *Development Psychology*, **20**, 1120–1134.

Hughes, J., Stewart, M. and Barraclough, B. (1985) Why teetotallers abstain. *British Journal of Psychiatry*, **146**, 204–205.

Hunter, R.S. and Kilstrom, N. (1979) Breaking the cycle in abusive families. *American Journal of Orthopsychiatry*, **136**, 1320–1322.

Isohanni, M., Moilanen, I. and Rantakallio, P. (1991) Determinants of teenage smoking, with special reference to non-standard family background. *British Journal of Addiction*, **86**, 391–398.

Jacob, T. (1988) Alcoholism and family interaction: Clarifications resulting from subgroup analyses and multi-method assessments. In *Understanding Major Mental Disorder* by M.K. Hahlweg and M.J. Goldstein (Eds.) Family Press, New York.

James, J. and Goldman, M. (1971) Behaviour trends of wives of alcoholics. *Quarterly Journal of Studies on Alcohol*, **32**, 373–381.

Jarmas, A.L. and Kazak, A.E. (1992) Young adult children of alcoholic fathers: Depressive experiences, coping styles and family systems. *Journal of Consulting and Clinical Psychology*, **60**, 244–251.

Jessor, R. and Jessor, S. (1977) *Problem Behavior and Psycho-social Development. A longitudinal Study of Youth*. Academic Press, New York.

Jones, D.C. and Houts, R. (1992) Parental drinking, parent-child communication, and social skills in young adults. *Journal of Studies on Alcohol*, **53**, 48–56.

Kalmuss, D. (1984) The Intergenerational Transmission of Marital Aggression. *Journal of Marriage and the Family*, 11–19.

Kammeier, M. (1971) Adolescents from families with and without alcohol problems. *Quarterly Journal of Studies on Alcohol*, **32**, 364–372.

Kandel, D.B. (1978) Convergences in prospective longitudinal surveys of drug use in normal populations. In Kandel, D. (Ed.) *Longitudinal Research on Drug Use*. Hemisphere; Washington DC.

Kandel, D.B. and Andrews, K. (1987) Processes of adolescent socialisation by parents and peers. *International Journal of the Addictions*, **22**, 319–342.

Kandel, D.B., Davies, M. and Bayder, N. (1990) The creation of interpersonal contexts: Homophily in dyadic relationships in adolescence and young adulthood. In L. Robins and M. Rutter (Eds.) *Straight and Devious Pathways from Childhood to Adulthood*, Cambridge: Cambridge University Press, 221–241.

Kandel, D.B., Rosenbaum, E. and Chen, K. (1994) Impact of maternal drug use and life experiences on preadolescent children born to teenage mothers. *Journal of Marriage and the Family*, **56**, 325–340.

Karlsson, J. (1985) Mental characteristics of families with alcoholism in Iceland. *Hereditas*, **102**, 185–188.

Kattan, L. *et al.* (1973) Characteristics of alcoholism in women and evaluation of its treatment in Chile (Sp.) *Acta Psiquiatr. Psicol. Am. Lat.*, **19**, 194–204 [translated into English for the present authors].

Kaufman, J. and Zigler, E. (1993) The intergenerational transmission of abuse is overstated. In R. Gelles and D. Loseka (Eds.), *Current Controversies in Family Violence*. New York: Sage.

Kendler, K.S., Neale, M.C., Prescott, C.A., Kessler, R.C., Heath, A.C., Corey, L.A. and Eaves, L.J. (1996) Childhood parental loss and alcoholism in women: A causal analysis using a twin-family design. *Psychological Medicine*, **26**, 79–95.

Knop, J., Teasdale, T., Schulsinger, F. and Goodwin, D. (1985) A prospective study of young men at risk for alcoholism: school behaviour and achievment. *Journal of Studies on Alcohol*, **46**, 273–278.

Kolvin, I., Miller, F., Fleeting, M. and Kilvin, P. (1988) Risk/protective factors for offending with particular reference to deprivation. In Rutter, M. (Ed.) *Studies of Psychosocial Risk: the Power of Longitudinal Data*. Cambridge University Press; Cambridge.

Kritsberg, W. (1988) *The Adult Children of Alcoholics' Syndrome*. New York: Bantam.

Kruttschnitt, C., Ward, D. and Sheble, M.A. (1987) Abuse–resistant youth: Some factors that may inhibit violent criminal behavior. *Social Forces*, **66**, 501–516.

Kubie, L. (1956) Psychoanalysis and marriage: practical and theoretical issues. In Eisenstein, V. (Ed.) *Neurotic Interaction in Marriage*. Tavistock; London.

Laszlo, C. (1970) The internalisation of deviant behaviour patterns during socialisation in the family (Hu). *Demografia*, **13**, 386–393 [translated into English for the present authors].

Latcham, R. (1985) Familial alcoholism: evidence from 237 alcoholics. *British Journal of Psychiatry*, **147**, 54–57.

Levine, M. and Perkins, D.V. (1987) *Principles of Community Psychology, Perspectives and Applications*. New York, Oxford University Press.

Lewis, C., Rice, J. and Helzer, J. (1983) Diagnostic interactions: alcoholism and antisocial personality. *Journal of Nervous and Mental Disorders*, **171**, 105–113.

Liker, J. and Elder, G. (1983) Economic hardship and marital relations in the 1930's. *American Sociological Review*, **48**, 343–359.

Link, B. and Dohrenwend, B.P. (1980) Formulation of hypotheses about the true prevalence of demoralisation in the United States. In: B.P. Dohrenwend, B.S. Dohrenwend, M. Gould *et al.* (Eds.) *Mental Illness in the United States: Epidemiological Estimates*. New York: Praeger.

Lobdell, J. and Perlman, D. (1986) The intergenerational transmission of loneliness: A study of college females and their parents. *Journal of Marriage and the Family*, **48**, 589–595.

Loehlin, J. and Nichols, R. (1976) *Heredity, Environment, and Personality*. University of Texas Press; Austin.

Long, N., Slater, E., Forehand, R. and Fauber, R. (1988) Continued high or reduced interparental conflict following divorce: Relation to young adolescent adjustment. *Journal of Consulting and Clinical Psychology*, **56**, 467–469 (cited by Grych and Fincham, 1990).

Loranger, A.W. and Tulis, E.H. (1985) Family history of alcoholism in borderline personality disorder. *Arch. Gen. Psychiatry*, **42**, 153.

Lynskey, M.T., Fergusson, D.M. and Horwood, L.J. (1994) The effect of parental alcohol problems on rates of adolescent psychiatric disorders. *Addiction*, **89**, 1277–1286.

Lyon, D. and Greenberg, J. (1991) Evidence of codependency in women with an alcoholic parent: Helping out Mr Wrong. *Journal of Personality and Social Psychology*, **61**, 435–439.

MacDonald, D. (1956) Mental disorders in wives of alcoholics. *Quarterly Journal of Studies on Alcohol*, **17**, 282–287.

Martin, M.J., Schumm, W.R., Bugaighis, M.A., Jurich, A.P. and Bollman, S.R. (1987) Family violence and adolescents' perceptions of outcomes of family conflict. *Journal of Marriage and the Family*, **49**, 165–171.

Matejcek, Z. (1981) Children of families of alcoholics II: competency in school and peer group (Cz). *Psychologija i Patopsychologia Dietata*, **16**, 537–560 [translated into English for the present authors].

Maughan, B. and Pickles, A. (1990) Adopted and illegitimate children growing up. In Robins, L.N. and Rutter, M. (Eds.) *Straight and Devious Pathways from Childhood to Adulthood*, Cambridge University Press; Cambridge, 36–61.

Maughan, B. (1988) School experiences as risk/protective factors. In Rutter, M. (Ed.) *Studies of Psychosocial Risk: the Power of Longitudinal Data*. Cambridge University Press; Cambridge.

McCord, W. and McCord, J., with Gudeman, J. (1960) *The Origins of Alcoholism*. Stanford University Press; Stanford, California.

McCord, W. and McCord, J. (1962) A longitudinal study of the personality of alcoholics. In Pitman, D. and Snyder, C. (Eds.) *Society, Culture and Drinking Patterns*. Wiley; New York.

McCord, J. (1988) Identifying developmental paradigns leading to alcoholism. *Journal of Studies on Alcohol*, **49**, 357–362 (cited by Sher, 1991).

McGue, M., Pickens, R.W. and Svikis, D.C. (1992) Sex and age effects on the inheritance of alcohol problems: A Twin Study. *Journal of Abnormal Psychology*, **101**, 3–17.

McKeganey, N. (1995) Quantitative and qualitative research in the addictions: An unhelpful divide. *Addiction*, **90**, 749–751.

McKenna, T. and Pickens, R. (1981) Alcoholic children of alcoholics. *Journal of Studies on Alcohol*, **42**, 1021–1029.

Mechanic, D. and Hansell, S. (1989) Divorce, family conflict and adolescents' well-being. *Journal of Health and Social Behaviour*, **30**, 105–116.

Meiselman, K. (1978) *Incest*. San Francisco: Jossey-Bass (cited by Browne and Finkelhor, 1986).

Meltzer, H., Gill, B. and Petticrew, M. (1994) The prevalence of psychiatric morbidity among adults aged 16–64, living in private households in Great Britain. London: *OPCS Surveys of Psychiatric Morbidity in Great Britain*.

Merikanges, K.R., Risch, N.J. and Weissman, M.M. (1994) Comorbidity and co-transmission of alcoholism, anxiety and depression. *Psychological Medicine*, **24**, 69–80.

Meyer, M. (1982) *Drinking Problems Equal Family Problems: Practical Guidelines for the Problem Drinker, the Partner and all those Involved*. Lancaster: Momenta.

Midanik, L. (1983) Familial alcoholism and problem drinking in a national drinking practices survey. *Addictive Behaviors*, **8**, 133–141.

Miller, D. and Jang, M. (1977) Children of alcoholics: a 20-year longitudinal study. *Social Work Research and Abstracts*, **13**, 23–29.

Molina, B.S.G., Chassin, L. and Curran, P.J. (1994) A comparison of mechanisms underlying substance use for early adolescent children of alcoholics and controls. *Journal of Studies on Alcohol*, **55**, 269–275.

Moos, R. and Billings, A. (1982) Children of alcoholics during the recovery process: alcoholic and matched control families. *Addictive Behaviors*, **7**, 155–163.

Moos, R., Finney, J. and Cronkite, R. (1990) *Alcoholism Treatment: Context, Process and Outcome*. Oxford University Press; New York.

Moos, R. and Moos, B. (1981) *Family Environment Scale Manual*. Consulting Psychologists Press; Palo Alto, CA.

Moser, J. (1980) *Prevention of Alcohol-related Problems: An International Review of Preventive Measures, Policies and Programmes.* Alcoholism and Drug Addiction Research Foundation. Toronto.

Mullen, P.E., Martin, J.L., Anderson, J.C., Romans, S.E. and Herbison, G.P. (1993) Childhood sexual abuse and mental health in adult life. *British Journal of Psychiatry,* **163**, 721–732.

Murray, R. and Stabenau, J. (1982) Genetic factors in alcoholism predisposition. In Pattison, E. and Kaufman, E. (Eds.) *Encyclopedic Handbook of Alcoholism.* Gardner Press; New York.

Nash, M.R., Hulsey, T.L., Sexton, M.C., Harralson, T.L. and Lambert, W. (1993) Long term sequelae of childhood sexual abuse: Perceived family environment, psychopathology and dissociation. *Journal of Consulting and Clinical Psychology,* **61**, 276–283.

Newton, J. (1992) *Preventing Mental Illness in Practice.* London: Tavistock/Routledge.

Nici, J. (1979) Wives of alcoholics as 'repeaters'. *Journal of Studies on Alcohol,* **40**, 677–682.

Nylander, I. (1960) Children of alcoholic fathers. *Acta Paediatrica Scandinavica,* Supplement 121.

Nylander, I. (1979) A 20-year prospective follow-up study of 2164 cases at the child guidance clinics in Stockholm. *Acta Paediatrica Scandinavica,* Supplement 276.

Nylander, I. and Rydelius, P. (1982) A comparison between children of alcoholic fathers from excellent versus poor social conditions. *Acta Paedriatrica Scandinavica,* **71**, 809–813.

Oliver, J.E. (1993) Intergenerational transmission of child abuse: rates, research and clinical implications. *Americal Journal of Psychiatry,* **150**, 1315–1323.

Orford, J. (1975) Alcoholism and marriage: the argument against specialism. *Journal of Studies on Alcohol,* **36**, 1537–1563.

Orford, J. (1985) *Excessive Appetites: A Psychological View of Addiction.* Wiley, Chichester.

Orford, J. (1987) (Ed.) *Coping with Disorder in the Family.* Croom Helm; London.

Orford, J. (1990) Alcohol and the family: an international review of the literature with implications for research and practice. In Kozlowski, L., Annis, H., Cappell, H., *et al.* (Eds.) *Research Advances in Alcohol and Drug Problems, Vol. 10.* New York; Plenum.

Orford, J. (1992) *Community Psychology: Theory and Practice,* Chichester, UK: Wiley.

Orford, J. and Keddie, A. (1985) Gender differences in the functions and effects of moderate and excessive drinking. *British Journal of Clinical Psychology,* **24**, 265–279.

Orford, J. and Velleman, R. (1990) Offspring of parents with drinking problems: drinking and drugtaking as young adults. *British Journal of Addiction,* **85**, 779–794.

Orford, J. and Velleman, R. (1991) The environmental intergenerational transmission of alcohol problems: a comparison of two hypotheses. *British Journal of Medical Psychology,* **64**, 189–200.

Orford, J. and Velleman, R. (1995) Childhood and adulthood influences on the adjustment of young adults with and without parents with drinking problems. *Addiction Research,* **3**, 1–15.

Orford, J., Waller, S. and Peto, J. (1974) Drinking behaviour and attitudes and their correlates amongs English University students. *Quarterly Journal of Studies on Alcohol,* **35**, 1316–1374.

Orford, J., Rigby, K., Miller, A., Tod, A., Bennett, G. and Velleman, R. (1992) Ways of coping with excessive drug use in the family: a provisional typology. *Journal of Community and Applied Social Psychology,* **2**, 163–183.

Pagelow, M. (1981) Factors affecting women's decisions to leave violent relationships. *Journal of Family Issues,* **2**, 391–414 (cited by Kalmuss, 1984).

Pandina, R.J. and Johnson, V. (1990) Serious alcohol and drug problems among adolescents with a family history of alcoholism. *Journal of Studies on Alcohol,* **51**, 278–282.

Pardeck, J., Callahan, D., Allgier, P., Fernandez, N. *et al.* (1991) Family dysfunction and the potential for alcoholism in college students. *College Student Journal,* **25**, 556–559.

Parker, D. and Harford, T. (1987) Alcohol-related problems of children of heavy-drinking parents. *Journal of Studies on Alcohol,* **48**, 265–268.

Parker, D. and Harford, T. (1988) Alcohol-related problems, marital disruption and depressive symptoms among adult children of alcohol abusers in the United States. *Journal of Studies on Alcohol,* **49**, 306–313.

Paschenkov, S. (1976) Specificity of familial forms of alcoholism (Ru). *Sovetskaiya Meditsina,* **11**, 76–79 [translated into English for the present authors].

Patterson, G.R. and Dishion, T.J. (1988) In Hinde, R.A. and Stevenson-Hinde, J. (Eds.) *Relationships within Families*. New York: Oxford University Press.

Peele, S. (1986) The implications and limitations of genetic models of alcoholism and other addictions. *Journal of Studies on Alcohol*, **47**, 63–71.

Pilat, J. and Jones, J. (1982) A screening test and treatment program for children in alcoholic families. Paper presented at the 30th National Alcoholism Forum of the National Council on Alcoholism, Washington, DC. April 1982 (cited by Claydon, 1987).

Plomin, R., DeFries, J. and Loehlin, J. (1977) Genotype-environment interaction and correlation in the analysis of human behaviour. *Psychological Bulletin*, **84**, 309–322.

Prescott, C.A., Hewitt, J.K., Truett, K.R., Heath, A.C., Neale, M.C. and Eaves, L.J. (1994) Genetic and environmental influences on lifetime alcohol-related problems in a volunteer sample of older twins. *Journal of Studies on Alcohol*, **55**, 184–202.

Ptacek, P. (1983) Experience of the care of children from families affected by alcoholism (Cz). *Psychol. Patopsychol. Dietata*, **18**, 245–249.

Pulkkinen, L. (1983) Youthful smoking and drinking in a longitudinal perspective. *Journal of Youth and Adolescence*, **12**, 253–283.

Quinton, D. (1988) Longitudinal approaches to intergenerational studies: definition, design and use. In Rutter, M. (Ed.) *Studies of Psychosocial Risk: the Power of Longitudinal Data*. Cambridge University Press; Cambridge.

Quinton, D. and Rutter, M. (1988) *Parenting Breakdown: the Making and Breaking of Intergenerational Links*. Avebury; Aldershot.

Quinton, D., Rutter, M. and Gulliver, L. (1990) Continuities in psychiatric disorders from childhood to adulthood in the children of psychiatric patients. In Robins, L.N. and Rutter, M. (Eds.) *Straight and Devious Pathways from Childhood to Adulthood*. Cambridge University Press; Cambridge, 259–278.

Rearden, J.J. and Markwell, B.S. (1989) Brief Report: Self-concept and drinking problems of college students raised in alcohol-abused homes. *Addictive Behaviors*, **14**, 225–227.

Reich, T., Winokur, G. and Mullaney, J. (1975) The transmission of alcoholism. In Fieve, R., Rosenthal, D. and Brill, H. (Eds.) *Genetic Research in Psychiatry*. John Hopkins University Press; Baltimore, pp. 259–271.

Reich, W., Earls, E. and Powell, J. (1988) A comparison of the home and social environments of children of alcoholic parents. *British Journal of Addiction*, **83**, 831–839.

Reich, W., Earls, F., Frankel, O. and Shayka, J.J. (1993) Psychopathology in children of alcoholics. *Journal of the American Academy of Child and Adolescent Psychiatry*, **32**, 995–1002.

Rhodes, J. and Blackham, G.J. (1987) Differences in character roles between adolescents from alcoholic and non-alcoholic homes. *American Journal of Drug Alcohol Abuse*, **13**, 145–155.

Ricks, D. and Berry, J. (1970) Family and symptom patterns that precede scizophrenia. In Roff, M. and Ricks, D. (Eds.) *Life History Research in Psychopathology*. University of Minnesota Press; Minneapolis.

Robins, L. (1966) *Deviant Children Grown Up*. Williams and Wilkins; Baltimore.

Robins, L. (1972) Follow-up studies of behavioural disorders in children. In Quay, H. and Werry, J. (Eds.) *Psychopathological Disorders of Childhood*. Wiley; New York.

Robins, L. (1988) Data gathering and data analysis for prospective and retrospective longitudinal studies. In Rutter, M. (Ed.) *Studies of Psychosocial Risk: the Power of Longitudinal Data*. Cambridge University Press; Cambridge.

Robins, L., Bates, W. and O'Neil, P. (1962) Adult drinking patterns of former problem children. In Pitman, D. and Snyder, C. (Eds.) *Society, Culture, and Drinking Patterns*. Wiley; New York, pp. 395–412.

Robins, L., Murphy, C., Woodruff, R. and King, L. (1971) Adult psychiatric status of black schoolboys. *Archives of General Psychiatry*, **24**, 338–345.

Robins, L., Schoenberg, S., Holmes, S., Ratcliff, K. Benham, A. and Works, J. (1985) Early home environment and retrospective recall: a test for concordance between siblings with and without psychiatric disorder. *American Journal of Orthopsychiatry*, **55**, 27–41.

Robins, L., West, P., Ratcliff, K. and Herjanic, B. (1977) Father's alcoholism and children's outcomes. *Currents in Alcoholism*, **4**, 313–327.

Roesler, T.A. and Dafler, C.E. (1993) Chemical Dissociation in Adults sexually victimized as children: Alcohol and drug use in adult survivors. *Journal of Substance Abuse Treatment*, **10**, 537–543.

Romans, S.E., Martin, J.L., Anderson, J.C., O'Shea, M.L. and Mullen, P.E. (1995) Factors that mediate between child sexual abuse and adult psychological outcome. *Psychological Medicine*, **25**, 127–142.

Roosa, M.W., Sandler, I.N., Beals, J. and Short, J. (1988) Risk status of adolescent children of problem drinking parents. *American Journal of Community Psychology*, **16**, 225–229.

Roosa, M.W., Beals, J., Sandler, I.N. and Pillow, D.R. (1990) The role of risk and protective factors in predicting symptomatology in adolescent self-identified children of alcoholic parents. *American Journal of Community Psychology*, **18**, 725–741.

Roosa, M.W., Michaels, M., Groppenbacher, N. and Gersten, J. (1993) Validity of Children's Reports of parental alcohol abuse. *Journal of Studies on Alcohol*, **54**, 71–79.

Rosenbaum, A. and O'Leary, K.D. (1981) Children: The unintended victims of marital violence. *American Journal of Orthopsychiatry*, **51**, 692–699.

Rosenberg, M. (1965) *Society and the Adolescent Self Image*. Princeton University Press; Princeton.

Rowe, D.C. (1990) Behavior genetic models of alcohol abuse. In Collins, R.L., Leonard, K.E. and Searles, J.S. (1990) *Alcohol and the Family: Research and Clinical Perspectives*, 107–133. New York, The Guilford Press.

Russell, M. (1990) Prevalence of alcoholism among children of alcoholics. In Windle, M. and Searles, J. (Eds.) *Children of Alcoholics: Critical Perspectives*. New York; Guildford.

Russell, M., Henderson, C. and Blume, S. (1985) *Children of alcoholics: a review of the Literature*. Children of Alcoholics Foundation, Inc; New York.

Russell, M., Cooper, M.L. and Frone, M.R. (1990) The influence of sociodemographic characteristics on familial alcohol problems—data from a community sample. *Alcoholism—Clinical and Experimental Research*, **14**, 221–226 (cited by Russell, 1990).

Rutter, M. (1985) Resistance in the face of adversity: protective factors and resistance to psychiatric disorder. *British Journal of Psychiatry*, **147**, 598–611.

Rutter, M. (1988) Longitudinal data in the study of causal processes: some uses and some pitfalls. In Rutter, M. (Ed.) *Studies of Psychosocial Risk: the Power of Longitudinal Data*. Cambridge University Press; Cambridge.

Rutter, M., Cox, A., Egert, S., Holbrook D. and Everitt, B. (1981) Psychiatric interviewing techniques: IV. Experimental study: Four contrasting styles. *British Journal of Psychiatry*, **138**, 456–465.

Rutter, M. and Madge, N. (1976) *Cycles of Disadventage: a Review of Research*. Heinmann; London.

Rutter, M., Quinton, D. and Hill, J. (1990) Adult outcome of institution-reared children: males and females compared. In Robins, L. and Rutter, M. (Eds.) *Straight and Devious Pathways from Childhood to Adulthood*. Cambridge University Press; Cambridge.

Rydelius, P. (1981) Children of alcoholic fathers: their social adjustment and their health status over 20 years. *Acta Paediatrica Scandinavica*, Supplement 286.

Schuckit, M.A. (1987) Biological vulnerability to alcoholism. *Journal of Consulting and Clinical Psychology*, **55**, 301–309.

Schuckit, M.A. and Sweeney, S. (1987) Substance use and mental health problems among sons of alcoholics and controls. *Journal of Studies on Alcohol*, **48**, 528–534.

Schurygin, G. (1978) Concerning a psychogenic pathological personality formation in children and adolescents in families with fathers suffering from alcoholism (Ru). *Nevropatologii i Psikhiatrii Imeni s s Korsakova*, **10**, 1566–1569 [translated into English for the present authors].

Searles, J. (1988) The role of genetics in the pathogenisis of alcoholism. *Journal of Abnormal Psychology*, **97**, 153–167.

Seilhamer, R.A., Jacob, T. and Dunn, N.J. (1993) The impact of alcohol consumption on parent–child relationships in families of alcoholics. *Journal of Studies on Alcohol*, **54**, 189–198.

Seixas, J. (1980) *How to Cope with an Alcoholic Parent*. Edinburgh: Canongate.

Seixas, J. and Levitan, M. (1984) A supportive counseling group for adult children of alcoholics. *Alcoholism Treatment Questionnaire*, **1**, 123–132.

Sher, K.J. (1991) Children of Alcoholics: A critical appraisal of theory and research. *Clinical Psychology Reviews*, **14**, 87–90.

Sheridan, M.J. (1995) A psychometric assessment of the children of alcoholics screening test (CAST). *Journal of Studies on Alcohol*, **56**, 156–160.

Silbereisen, R. and Walper, S. (1988) A person-process-context approach. In Rutter, M. (Ed.) *Studies of Psychosocial Risk: the Power of Longitudinal Data*. Cambridge University Press; Cambridge.

Sisson, R.W. and Azrin, N.H. (1993) Community Reinforcement Training for families: A method to get alcoholics into treatment. In O'Farrell, (Ed.) *Treating Alcohol Problems: Marital and Family Interventions*. New York: Guilford Press, 34–53.

Sroufe, L.A., Jacobvitz, D., Mangelsdorf, S., DeAngelo, E. and Ward, M.J. (1985) Generational boundary dissolution between mothers and their preschool children: A relationship systems approach. *Child Development*, **56**, 317–325 (cited by Hinde, 1988).

Stiles, W.B. (1993) Quality control in qualitative research. *Clinical Psychology Review*, **13**, 593–618.

Swiecicki, A. (1969) Adult adjustment of children from alcoholic and non-alcoholic families: a 10-year follow-up study. (Polish) *Probl. Alkzmu, Warsaw*, **17**, 1–7 (CAAAL No. 14047).

Thomas, E.J. and Ager, R.D. (1993) Unilateral Family Therapy with spouses of uncooperative alcohol abusers. In O'Farrell, T.J. (Ed.) *Treating Alcohol Problems: Marital and Family Interventions*. New York: Guilford Press, 3–33.

Thomas, E.J. and Santa, C.A. (1982) Unilateral family therapy for alcohol abuse: A working conception. *American Journal of Family Therapy*, **10**, 49–58.

Thompson, W., Orvaschel, H., Prusoff, B. and Kidd, K. (1982) An evaluation of the family history method for ascertaining psychiatric disorders. *Archives of General Psychiatry*, **39**, 53–58.

Toteva, S. (1982) Neurotic symptoms in children with alcoholic parent. *Sofia Bull. NINPN*, **10**, 104–109 (cited in Boyadjieva, undated).

Toteva, S. (1984) Psychological disturbances and social desadaptation in children with alcoholic parent. Dissertation, Sofia (by Boyadjieva, undated).

Tracy, E.M. and Farkas, K.J. (1990) Preparing practitioners for child welfare practice with substance-abusing families. *Child Welfare League of America*.

Tweed, S.H. and Ryff, C.D. (1991) Adult children of alcoholics: Profiles of wellness amidst distress. *Journal of Studies on Alcohol*, **52**, 133–141.

Vaillant, G. (1983) *The Natural History of Alcoholism*. Harvard University Press; Cambridge, Mass.

Valentine, L. and Feinauer, L.L. (1993) Resilience factors associated with female survivors of childhood sexual abuse. *The American Journal of Family Therapy*, **21**, 216–224.

Velleman, R. (1992a) Intergenerational effects—a review of environmentally oriented studies concerning the relationship between parental alcohol problems and family disharmony in the genesis of alcohol and other problems. I: the alcohol literature. *International Journal of the Addictions*, **27**, 253–280.

Velleman, R. (1992b) Intergenerational effects—a review of environmentally oriented studies concerning the relationship between parental alcohol problems and family disharmony in the genesis of alcohol and other problems. II: the wider family disharmony literature. *International Journal of the Addictions*, **27**, 367–389.

Velleman, R. (1992c) *Counselling For Alcohol Problems*. London; Sage (Counselling in Practice Series).

Velleman, R. (1992d) The use of volunteer counsellors in helping problem drinkers: community work in action? *Journal of Mental Health*, **1**, 301–310.

Velleman, R. (1993) *Alcohol and the Family* Institute of Alcohol Studies Occasional Paper. London; Institute of Alcohol Studies.

Velleman, R. and Orford, J. (1984) Intergenerational transmission of alcohol problems—hypotheses to be tested. In Krasner, N., Madden, J. and Walker, R. (Eds.) *Alcohol Related Problems*. Wiley; London, pp. 97–113.

Velleman, R. and Orford, J. (1985) Methodological problems in social research: the reliability of the retrospective remembrances of 250 young adults aged 16–35. Paper presented at

Annual Conference of British Psychological Society, Social Psychology Section, Cambridge, UK.

Velleman, R. and Orford, J. (1990) Young adult offspring of parents with drinking problems: recollections of parents' drinking and its immediate effects. *British Journal of Clinical Psychology*, **29**, 297–317.

Velleman, R. and Orford, J. (1993) The importance of family discord in explaining childhood problems in the children of problem drinkers. *Addiction Research*, **1**, 39–57.

Velleman, R., Bennett, G., Miller, T., Orford, J., Rigby, K. and Tod, A. (1993) The families of problem drug users: the accounts of fifty close relatives. *Addiction*, **88**, 1275–1283.

Vitaro, F., Dobkin, P.L., Carbonneau, R. and Tremblay, R.E. (1996) Research Report: Personal and familial characteristics of resilient sons of male alcoholics. *Addiction*, **91**, 1161–1177.

Waldfogel, S. (1948) The frequency and effective character of childhood memories. *Psychological Monographs*, **64**, whole issue.

Wall, W. and Williams, H. (1970) *Longitudinal Studies and the Social Sciences*. Heinemann; London.

Werner, E. (1986) Resilient offspring of alcoholics: a longitudinal study from birth to age 18. *Journal of Studies on Alcohol*, **47**, 34–40.

Warner, R. and Rosett, H. (1975) The effects of drinking on offspring: an historical survey of the American and British literature. *Journal of Studies on Alcohol*, **36**, 1395–1420.

Werner, E. and Smith, R. (1982) *Vulnerable But Invincible—A Longitudinal Study of Resilient Children and Youth*. McGraw-Hill; New York.

West, M. and Prinz, R. (1987) Parental alcoholism and childhood psychopathology. *Psychological Bulletin*, **102**, 204–218.

Widom, C.S. (1989) Does violence beget violence? A critical examination of the literature. *Psychological Bulletin*, **106**, 3–28.

Wilson, C. (1980) The family. In Camberwell Council on Alcoholism (Eds.) *Women and Alcohol*. Tavistock Press; London, pp. 101–132.

Wilson, C. (1982) The impact on children. In Orford, J. and Harwin, J. (Eds.) *Alcohol and the Family*. Croom Helm; London, pp. 151–166.

Wilson, C. and Orford, J. (1978) Children of alcoholics: report of a preliminary study and comments on the literature. *Quarterly Journal of Studies on Alcohol*, **39**, 121–142.

Windle, M. (1990) The temperament and personality attributes of children of alcoholics. In Windle, M. and Searles, J. (Eds.) *Children of Alcoholics: Critical Perspectives*. Guilford; New York.

Winokur, G. (1972) Depressive spectrum disease: Description and family study. *Compr. Psychiatry*, **13**, 3–8.

Winokur, G., Reich, T., Rimmer, J. and Pitts, F. (1970) Alcoholism III: Diagnosis and familial psychiatric illness in 259 alcoholic probands. *Archives of General Psychiatry*, **23**, 104–111.

Wolin, S., Bennett, L., Noonan, D. and Teitelbaum, M. (1980) Disrupted family rituals: a factor in the intergenerational transmission of alcoholism. *Journal of Studies on Alcohol*, **41**, 199–214.

Wolkind, S. and Coleman, E. (1983) Adult psychiatric disorder and childhood experiences: the validity of retrospective data. *British Journal of Psychiatry*, **143**, 188–191.

Woodside, M. (1988) Research on children of alcoholics: past and future. *British Journal of Addiction*, **83**, 785–792.

Yarrow, L., Campbell, J. and Burton, R. (1970) *Recollection of Childhood: A Study of the Retrospective Method*. Monographs of the Society for Research in Child Development, 33, 5, Chicago.

Yates, F. (1988) The evaluation of a 'cooperative counselling' alcohol service which uses family and affected others to reach and influence problem drinkers. *British Journal of Addiction*, **83**, 1309–1319.

Zucker, R. (1987) The four alcoholisms: a developmental account of the etiologic process. In Rivers, P. (Ed.) *Alcohol and Addictive Behaviours: Nebraska Symposium on Motivation, 1986*. University of Nebraska press; Lincoln.

APPENDIX

Recalled childhood symptoms by offspring *vs* comparison and sex

Symptoms	Offspring		Comparisons	
	Sons (N=72) %	Daughters (N=92) %	Sons (N=40) %	Daughters (N=40) %
Foodfads	27	21	18	8
Overweight	10	25	10	26
Nailbiting	42	40	31	39
Reading Difficulties	15	7	23	8
Arithmetic Difficulties	19	24	23	36
Concentration Difficulties at School	39	32	15	13
Truancy	31	17	21	8
Inability to do Homework at Home	33	33	26	13
Distractability	45	24	26	26
Frequent Waking	15	22	8	5
Nightmares	30	25	18	—
Sleepwalking	9	14	10	—
Rocking Prior to Sleep	6	11	5	5
Bedwetting	21	11	10	8
Emotional Detachment	34	27	18	3
Prone to Crying	13	33	5	23
Anxious	34	48	26	36
Depressed	28	32	23	10
Allergies	10	20	18	31
Accident Proneness	10	12	15	18
Asthma	6	5	10	5
Ulcers	3	8	5	3
Temper Tantrums	25	17	21	13
Aggression	22	9	18	10
Destructive Behaviour	15	5	13	—
Stealing	28	13	21	5
Delinquency	13	8	5	—
Hyperactivity	16	10	10	8
Head Banging	3	3	3	—
Other Self-injurious Behaviour	6	7	5	—
Tics	6	2	3	—
Stammering	6	—	—	3
Wetting During the Day	2	1	—	5
Soiling During the Day	3	—	—	—

SUBJECT INDEX

AUTHOR INDEX